Where Was Jennifer Blagg?

A search warrant was obtained to search the Mesa County Landfill. Officials set off an area that was most likely to contain trash from November 2001. An excavator was brought in to remove refuse, and then investigators searched more closely through the excavated material using rakes and shovels. They also used global positioning system coordinates and detailed landfill records. It was a mammoth job. In a single day, they sorted through 130 tons of garbage using machines and hand tools.

The twenty-third day of the search, June 4, 2002, was hot, dusty, and the stench of the landfill filled the air. At 10:15 A.M., the excavator pulled a bucket of refuse from the area and was about to dump it when Investigator Stoffel suddenly yelled for the operator to stop. He had seen what he thought was a human leg and foot dangling out from the excavator's bucket.

All operations immediately ceased. A forensic team was called in to complete the search. Dr. Robert Kurtzman, of the Mesa County Coroner's Office, confirmed that what they were looking at was the right leg of an adult female.

The day after the leg was found, the decomposing body of an adult female was discovered, minus a left leg, in the same area of trash. Later, a left leg was found in a hole near where the bucket had first pulled the right leg out of the trash.

It was time to compare a vital young woman's dental X-rays to the teeth of a corpse.

Killer Dad

ROBERT SCOTT

PINNACLE BOOKS
Kensington Publishing Corp.
http://www.kensingtonbooks.com

Some names have been changed to protect the privacy of individuals connected to the story.

PINNACLE BOOKS are published by

Kensington Publishing Corp.
850 Third Avenue
New York, NY 10022

All Kensington Titles, Imprints, and Distributed Lines are available at special quantity discounts for bulk purchases for sales promotions, premiums, fund-raising, and educational or institutional use. Special book excerpts or customized printings can also be created to fit specific needs. For details, write or phone the office of the Kensington special sales manager: Kensington Publishing Corp., 850 Third Avenue, New York, NY 10022, attn: Special Sales Department, Phone: 1-800-221-2647.

Pinnacle and the P logo Reg. U.S. Pat. & TM Off.

ISBN-13: 978-0-7860-1818-5
ISBN-10: 0-7860-1818-6

First Printing: March 2007

10 9 8 7 6 5 4 3 2

Printed in the United States of America

This book is dedicated to Jennifer and Abby

Acknowledgments

I'd like to thank the staff at the Mesa County Courthouse in Grand Junction, Colorado, for their help on this book, and Sergeant Wayne Weyler and Investigator Steven King. I'd also like to thank Chris Darden, Don Wilson, and N and Y Chapman. Once again, thanks for all the help from my editor at Kensington Books, Michaela Hamilton, and my literary agent, Damaris Rowland.

Michael Blagg had an affair with Internet porn on his computer and used sex and the Bible to control his wife.

—District Attorney Frank Daniels

Chapter 1

911

Grand Junction, Colorado

It was a routine day for a 911 operator in Grand Junction until 4:20 P.M. on November 13, 2001, when a frantic phone call suddenly ripped apart the quiet afternoon.

911 OPERATOR: What's your emergency?

MIKE BLAGG: Oh, my God! It's in the house!

911 OPERATOR: Okay, what's going on?

BLAGG: I just got home from work and there's blood all over the bed and there's stuff all over the floor. My family's gone! My daughter and my wife aren't here!

911 OPERATOR: Okay. Calm down. You're at [address] Pine Terrace Court?

BLAGG: Yes.

911 OPERATOR: Okay. Hold on. And the blood's on the bed?

BLAGG: Yes, and the back door's open.

911 OPERATOR: Things are messed up in your house?

BLAGG: Um, just . . . just in the master bedroom. It looks like—

911 OPERATOR: How old is your wife?

BLAGG: Um, she's thirty . . . thirty-four. She'll be thirty-five this January.

911 OPERATOR: And how old is your child?

BLAGG: Six. Oh God!

911 OPERATOR: Okay. Calm down. Is your wife's car out front?

BLAGG: (Sob)

911 OPERATOR: Mike? [The 911 operator was guessing that the caller was Mike Blagg, based upon information from which residence the call was being made.]

BLAGG: Let me look in the garage.

911 OPERATOR: Okay.

BLAGG: Yeah. In the garage. (Cries)

911 OPERATOR: Okay. Hold on. Have you touched anything, Mike?

BLAGG: The front door. I came through the front door. And now I touched the garage door to look in the garage.

911 OPERATOR: Okay. And the phone? Correct?

BLAGG: Yeah, the phone.

911 OPERATOR: Okay. Don't touch anything else.

BLAGG: Okay.

911 OPERATOR: Can you tell me about the blood? What does it look like? Does it look like somebody laid there and bled? Does it look like it splattered?

BLAGG: Um, oh, her pillows are gone. Um . . .

911 OPERATOR: Her pillows?

BLAGG: Yeah. She sleeps with two pillows and they're gone and there's a big, big pool of blood, uh . . . about where they would be and there it's dripped all down the side of the bed onto the floor.

911 OPERATOR: Okay, hold on. So the blood's dripping off the bed onto the floor?

BLAGG: (Cries)

911 OPERATOR: Mike. Do you have a cordless phone?

BLAGG: Yes.

911 OPERATOR: Can I get you to go outside and talk to you, please?

BLAGG: Yes.

911 OPERATOR: Okay?

BLAGG: Okay.

911 OPERATOR: Let me know when you're outside.

BLAGG: Okay.

911 OPERATOR: Okay. You outside?

BLAGG: Yes.

911 OPERATOR: What I want you to do, Mike . . . can you sit on your stairs? Do you have a porch or something you can sit on?

BLAGG: I'm on the back porch.

911 OPERATOR: Okay. I want you to sit down. And I want you to breathe real deep and real slow for just a minute.

BLAGG: (Cries)

911 OPERATOR: Mike. How old are you?

BLAGG: Thirty-eight.

911 OPERATOR: Have you and your wife been having problems?

BLAGG: No.

911 OPERATOR: No?

BLAGG: No.

911 OPERATOR: And when was the last time you talked to your wife?

BLAGG: Last night before we went to bed. (Cries)

911 OPERATOR: And everything was okay?

BLAGG: Yes. (Cries)

911 OPERATOR: Does your daughter go to school?

BLAGG: Yes. She goes to Bookcliff Christian School.

911 OPERATOR: Did she go to school today?

BLAGG: Nobody's called. I don't know.

911 OPERATOR: When did you leave this morning?

BLAGG: I always leave at six o'clock in the morning. I'm going back inside. I'm gonna go look in my daughter's room.

911 OPERATOR: You're going to go look in your daughter's room?

BLAGG: Yes.

911 OPERATOR: Okay. You need to tell me what you're doing. You need to tell me what you're seeing.

BLAGG: I pushed open the door without touching anything.

911 OPERATOR: Okay.

BLAGG: Turned on the light switch.

911 OPERATOR: Uh-huh.

BLAGG: Her school clothes are still waiting for her. Her bed is messed up.

911 OPERATOR: Her bed is messed up as if she slept in it?

BLAGG: Um, the covers are pulled back and there's no blood.

911 OPERATOR: And her school clothes are still laid out, so she never put them on?

BLAGG: No, she never put them on. Her fan is still on, too. So she didn't turn off her fan this morning.

911 OPERATOR: So she never got dressed?

BLAGG: No.

911 OPERATOR: Okay, Mike, I need you to go back outside.

BLAGG: Okay.

911 OPERATOR: Let me know when you're back outside.

BLAGG: (Cries) Okay. I'm back outside. And sitting on my porch again.

911 OPERATOR: Take some deep breaths and let them out real slow. I don't want you to go into shock or anything.

BLAGG: (Barely audible) Okay.

911 OPERATOR: Mike, do you want me to send an ambulance to check you out?

BLAGG: I don't know. I don't know what to do.

911 OPERATOR: We have officers en route. And I'm gonna keep you on the phone 'til they get there.

BLAGG: (Cries)

911 OPERATOR: Okay, Mike. Let's take some deep breaths and let 'em out real slow.

BLAGG: Okay.

911 OPERATOR: Just continue to breathe for me, okay?

BLAGG: Okay.

911 OPERATOR: As soon as we get some deputies out there, hopefully we can piece this all together.

BLAGG: I can't see the front yard from where I am.

911 OPERATOR: That's okay. They know you're sitting in the back. Can they walk around the side of the house to where you're at?

BLAGG: Yeah.

911 OPERATOR: Okay. Keep breathing. You're doing good, Mike.

BLAGG: (Cries)

911 OPERATOR: I know it's really hard. And not knowing is really hard, but you're really doing a good job.

BLAGG: (Cries) Where can they be?

911 OPERATOR: I don't know, Mike. And you said you and your wife were getting along?

BLAGG: (Cries) Yes.

911 OPERATOR: And everything was okay?

BLAGG: (Cries) Yes.

911 OPERATOR: When you left this morning, was she up?

BLAGG: (Cries) No. She stays asleep until six-thirty. Both Abby and Jennifer get up at six-thirty.

911 OPERATOR: Where do you work?

BLAGG: AMETEK Dixson in Orchard Mesa.

911 OPERATOR: Your wife's a stay-at-home mom?

BLAGG: Yes. She usually helps at school.

911 OPERATOR: She works at the school?

BLAGG: She doesn't work. She volunteers.

911 OPERATOR: She volunteers? Okay. So you don't know if she went? Is there anybody that can be called to see if your daughter or your wife went to work or showed up at school?

BLAGG: (Cries) Yes. Diana Shirley. Jennifer and Diana are best friends and they usually work together at school.

911 OPERATOR: Okay. We'll call her. You're doing real good, Mike. Let's keep breathing. Just breathe long and breathe slow.

BLAGG: (Cries) Okay.

911 OPERATOR: When you were looking around the house, did you notice anything else missing?

BLAGG: I only went into the master bedroom and upstairs.

911 OPERATOR: You have an upstairs home, then?

BLAGG: Yes. It's a two-story.

911 OPERATOR: And you said you were in the garage and the car's still there?

BLAGG: Yes.

911 OPERATOR: So you didn't look in any of the other rooms?

BLAGG: No.

911 OPERATOR: Okay. That's fine. We'll let the deputies do that.

BLAGG: Okay.

911 OPERATOR: Do you have any weapons in the house?

BLAGG: Yeah, a pistol in our closet.

911 OPERATOR: In the master bedroom?

BLAGG: Yes.

911 OPERATOR: Does your wife know where it is?

BLAGG: Yes, she did. (Cries)

911 OPERATOR: All right.

BLAGG: We didn't keep it loaded, though.

911 OPERATOR: You didn't?

BLAGG: No.

911 OPERATOR: Okay. We'll just let the officers know that, that are en route.

BLAGG: Yes.

911 OPERATOR: Let's breathe again. Just breathe deep and slow. We want to maintain control here. You're doing good. Now, Mike, just to confirm your last name is Blagg?

BLAGG: Yes.

911 OPERATOR: Have you had any problems with your neighbors or anybody?

BLAGG: No. We're here in a very calm neighborhood. Mostly older couples live here. . . . What's your name?

911 OPERATOR: Pardon?

BLAGG: What's your name?

911 OPERATOR: My name is Vickie.

BLAGG: (Cries) Thank you, Vickie.

911 OPERATOR: You're welcome. That's what I'm here for, is to help you.

BLAGG: Okay.

911 OPERATOR: I'll let you know when the deputies get there, so you won't be startled.

BLAGG: Okay.

911 OPERATOR: Ray and Diana on [street name deleted]?

BLAGG: They live in Orchard Mesa. I'm not sure what the name of their road is.

911 OPERATOR: Okay. Looks like I found them. I'm gonna have somebody also call them and see.

BLAGG: Okay. I've got their phone number in our book if you want me to look it up.

911 OPERATOR: What's your wife's first name?

BLAGG: Jennifer.

911 OPERATOR: And what's your daughter's name?

BLAGG: Abby.

911 OPERATOR: And Abby's in what grade?

BLAGG: The first grade.

911 OPERATOR: The other dispatchers are gonna call. So we can find out about school.

BLAGG: She's in Ms. Fasnacht's class.

911 OPERATOR: Ms. Basnacht?

BLAGG: Fasnacht.

911 OPERATOR: Okay. He's calling for me. That way we can keep you on the phone.

BLAGG: Okay. (Cries)

911 OPERATOR: Come on. You're doin' fine. I know it's really hard. Let's just keep breathing 'til they get there. You didn't call and talk to your wife anytime during the day?

BLAGG: I tried about four times and never got through.

911 OPERATOR: So the phone just rang?

BLAGG: Well, we've got an answering machine.

911 OPERATOR: Oh, so did you leave a message?

BLAGG: Yes, I tried her cell phone and I tried her at home.

911 OPERATOR: She does have a cell phone?

BLAGG: Yes.

911 OPERATOR: Did you notice if it was missing?

BLAGG: No. Do you want me to go back and look?

911 OPERATOR: No. Let's just stay outside until they get there.

BLAGG: Okay.

911 OPERATOR: We don't want to—

BLAGG: It would be in the master bedroom and I don't want to go back in there.

911 OPERATOR: Okay, Mike. Take your phone and walk out to the front yard.

BLAGG: Okay.

911 OPERATOR: Let me know when you are out front.

BLAGG: Okay. I'm going through the side yard now.

911 OPERATOR: Do you have any dogs or anything?

BLAGG: No . . . okay, I'm in the front yard.

911 OPERATOR: And you're sitting on the front porch?

BLAGG: No, I'm still walking through the grass.

911 OPERATOR: Okay. Sit down. Does your wife have a medical problem?

BLAGG: Um, she's got a . . . she's got a multiple valve prolapse.

911 OPERATOR: What does that mean?

BLAGG: Uh, it's similar to a heart murmur.

911 OPERATOR: Oh, okay.

BLAGG: She's got a vulvar vestibulitis, which is a chronic problem with the vestibular glands in her genitals. She had her gallbladder removed. She had so many problems. (Cries)

911 OPERATOR: So she does have problems. Come on, Mike, let's take some deep breaths.

BLAGG: (Cries, unintelligible remark)

911 OPERATOR: Huh? I couldn't understand you?

BLAGG: Friday is our tenth anniversary.

911 OPERATOR: Have you lived in Grand Junction the entire time?

BLAGG: No. We moved around. I've been in the navy. I've been in Allied Signal. And now I'm with AMETEK.

911 OPERATOR: Okay. Let me know who that is that's showing up. I think it might be the ambulance.

BLAGG: Okay.

End of report.

In actuality, the person arriving was a Mesa County Sheriff's Office (MCSO) deputy, and when he pulled up, he spied a distraught man sitting on the front porch. The man was Michael Blagg, who claimed there was blood on the master bedroom bed, and his wife and daughter were missing. The man on the porch appeared as if the weight of the world had just come crashing down upon his head.

Chapter 2

Missing

Sheriff's patrol deputy Tim Moore was fifteen miles away from Pine Terrace Court when he received a call from the dispatcher about a possible crime scene at that area. The dispatcher clued him in that a thirty-four-year-old woman and a six-year-old girl were missing and that there was blood on the master bedroom bed, items scattered in the house, and the back door was open. The dispatcher then told Moore that the reporting person was identified as Michael Blagg, and that he was the woman's husband. Moore was also notified that blood was "dripping from the bed" onto the floor. Blagg had checked his daughter's room and found the bed unmade and her school clothes still laid out as if she had not dressed for school.

Moore had been a deputy with the Mesa County Sheriff's Office (MCSO) for five years by 2001. In Mesa County, sheriff's deputies most often traveled alone in a patrol car, and that was the case with Deputy Moore on November 13. He arrived at Pine Terrace Court, around 4:37 P.M., to find Michael Blagg sitting on his front porch, seemingly distraught at the events that had transpired there. At almost the same instant, Deputy Jeff Doty, who had been in Clifton, arrived at Pine Terrace Court as well.

Deputy Moore asked Mike Blagg how he was doing, and he answered, "Not so well." After making sure that Mike didn't need immediate medical attention, Deputy Moore took a key from Mike and opened the front door and entered into a foyer. Later, Deputy Moore said, "We immediately put on latex gloves." Neither one of the deputies wanted to contaminate the residence if it was a crime scene.

The first rooms the deputies observed were the living room, followed by the kitchen. It was in the kitchen that they noticed that the back door was open. Whether it had been left open by Mike or someone else, they couldn't say at this point. They walked down the hallway and entered the master bedroom to find a bed with the bedcovers pulled down. There was a large puddle of what they termed "red liquid" on the bed, which they believed to be blood. The red liquid had run off the top of the bed, down the side, and puddled on the floor. It was congealed at this point and no longer dripping.

On the bedroom floor lay a jewelry box with items scattered in disarray, and some money was also in the bedroom. The ceiling fan was turned on and running, which was odd, considering how cool a day it was. Other than the jewelry box and scattered items on the floor, nothing else seemed to be out of order in the room. In fact, none of the rooms downstairs in the house had items scattered about, except in the master bedroom.

Moving upstairs to the daughter's bedroom, they discovered a floor fan that was also running, which once again caught their attention, because it had been a cool day all day long. Unlike the master bedroom, everything in the girl's room seemed to be in order, with nothing scattered about or in disarray. Deputies Doty and Moore went through the whole house making sure that there were no bodies, or someone hiding within the house. As they checked each room, they didn't discover any bodies or signs of blood elsewhere in the house.

Yet something was bothering Deputy Moore—he had been to numerous burglary scenes during his law enforcement career, and something just didn't seem right about what he saw now at the residence on Pine Terrace Court. He later admitted, "This didn't have the same feel to it as other burglary scenes I'd been to." He couldn't quite place his finger on it, but something was just not right as far as he was concerned.

The next officer to arrive at Pine Terrace Court was MCSO sergeant John Coleman. Sergeant Coleman was an eleven-year veteran of the force and had been to many crime scenes over the years. When he arrived, there was an ambulance crew just arriving on the scene, and he asked them to check out Mike Blagg. Coleman also made a mental note that "Blagg looked nervous, excited, and shaking. He wasn't steady with his speech." This was not an atypical reaction for someone who had suddenly been traumatized, especially when the source of the trauma concerned a missing wife and daughter, and there were many unanswered questions.

Deputies Moore and Doty showed Sergeant Coleman the master bedroom and pointed out the apparent blood and scattered items on the floor. Making another mental note, Sergeant Coleman thought, *This blood looks to be about three or four hours old. Definitely less than twenty-four hours old.*

Coleman noted the blood pattern ran off the bed to the right onto the floor, and it was not dripping by 4:50 P.M. He briefly checked the garage and noticed a maroon/beige-colored Ford Windstar minivan parked inside. He then told the deputies to secure the house with yellow crime-scene tape, and they all awaited the arrival of investigators.

Because of the suspicious nature of the scene, MCSO deputy Albert Johnson, when he arrived, was instructed to canvass the neighborhood and ask about any suspicious activity in the area. A search warrant was asked for by Investigator Scott Ehlers, which stated that the MCSO was seeking "human bodies or body parts, photographs, measurements, latent prints, blood, hair, fibers, bodily fluids, indication of occupancy to establish ownership or control of said premises, any weapons or items that may cause death or injury, believed to be situated at Pine Terrace Court, Grand Junction, Mesa County, Colorado."

Investigator Ehlers noted that it was a single-family dwelling—a two-story white-colored residence with light-colored gray trim and attached garage. The house numbers were located on the right side of the garage as someone faced the residence, and an American flag was attached to the porch area. The search warrant was to include any outer building storage sheds, and/or other garages or vehicles located on the premises. Also it was to include a white-colored Dodge Stratus bearing Colorado license plate number 356BCM, which was currently parked in front of the residence on the street. This last item was the car that Michael Blagg drove. At 8:15 P.M., on November 13, 2001, Judge Massaro in Grand Junction signed the search warrant.

Soon thereafter, Investigators Glade Johnson and Jim Hebenstreit, who had arrived on the scene, suited up in protective clothing, so as not to contaminate the area, and entered the house. While going through the front door in the foyer, they observed clear liquid droplets on the floor, but didn't determine what the droplets were at the time or who may have deposited them there.

An investigator videotaped the scene with a JVC 8mm camera. One thing he noticed was that there was no broken glass anywhere, which suggested that no one had broken a window to gain entry. Investigator Hebenstreit recorded several messages that had been left on an answering machine, none of which contained a ransom request or mention of a kidnapping. These messages, in fact, had been left by Mike Blagg for his wife, Jennifer, throughout the day, asking why she wasn't home. Mike's messages seemed to show more and more concern as the day progressed.

Upstairs, investigators collected several samples from the red stains on the top right corner of the master bedroom bed and from the adjoining carpet. There weren't any significant blood spatter high-velocity patterns, or even medium-velocity patterns, on the sheets of the bed, which tended to rule out blunt-force trauma. All of the considerable amount of blood seemed to have pooled in one area, and there were no large cast-off spatters on the wall or other areas. Whatever had happened here, had happened in a very specific location, which seemed to show that a victim did not fight back against an attacker, or try to flee the room while being attacked.

The Ford Windstar minivan in the garage was checked and found to contain small droplets of red stains on the exterior and interior of the vehicle, which the investigators thought was odd. If bodies had been taken to the van, why were there no trails or droplets of bloodstains leading from the master bedroom to the minivan? Luminol was used in the house, but it did not detect any bloodstains or droplets leading from the master bedroom to the garage, except for perhaps one small stain near the steps to the garage. Once again, with so much blood on and near the master bedroom bed, it seemed odd that there would not be a trail of blood to the minivan, if the bloodstains in the minivan had a connection to those in the bedroom.

When he arrived, Sergeant Wayne Weyler, of MCSO, noted that the bloodstain on and near the bed "was unusual." He stated later, "The stain is generally in a circular pattern and unusual in that coagulated blood was along the perimeter or border of the circular pattern, roughly between a one o'clock and seven o'clock position. The top two-thirds of the stains are more watery than expected." Although blood will separate into a more watery substance, there appeared to be more clear fluid than would be expected, and other investigators who found the blood pattern to be unusual were CBI (Colorado Bureau of Investigation) agent Wayne Bryant and Jerry Hill, of the Grand Junction Police Department (GJPD).

Bryant had thirty years' experience in processing crime scenes and Hill had twenty years' experience. Both Sergeant Weyler and Hill conjectured that the clear liquid was added to the sheet when the bloodstain was present, but just why someone would do that was not readily apparent at the time. Was it to dilute the blood and try and get rid of it, or for some other reason? There was no easy explanation about this at the present time.

All these investigators noted that a bloodstained blanket and comforter were at the foot of the bed, and the blood that was on the carpet appeared to have run down the side of the bed and pooled. There was no clear void on the sheet on top of the bed, suggesting that a head might have been lying there, but there was a void on the side of the mattress and on the sheet, which appeared to be from a dripping motion. [In forensic terms, a void is an area where a body or object would hinder the accumulation of blood spatter.] And there were transfer patterns of blood on the sheet near the circular bloodstaining.

As a matter of fact, the patterning of blood could tell an awful lot about the potential crime scene. As Anne Wingate, Ph.D., pointed out in her book *Scene of the*

Crime, "No other type of investigation of blood will yield so much useful information as an analysis of the blood distribution patterns." It could tell the relative positions of persons and objects in the area at the time of the attack, as well as distances the blood flew and at what speed. This could give an estimated number of impacts and the elapsed time between the impacts. It could also give an estimate of movements of the person and objects after the attack, and if there were any attempts at cleanup by the perpetrator.

The minivan was found to contain trace amounts of blood on the front driver's side and on the steering wheel brake pedal, as well as the driver's-side front-door handle, and blood droplets on the driver's-side door frame. There were no large amounts of blood anywhere in the minivan, which would have indicated that bodies had been placed there. The investigators did determine, however, that a body or bodies could have been tightly wound in a protective covering, and placed in the minivan without leaving large bloodstains. Just why someone would want to do that was another mystery. If bodies had been placed into the minivan—what had then happened to them? Had they been driven away somewhere, dumped, and then the minivan returned to the garage? Or had bodies been placed in the minivan, removed before it was driven away, and the bodies taken away from the house by some other means? In fact—were there any bodies at all—or were Jennifer and Abby Blagg still alive and victims of a kidnapping? There were a lot of still unanswered questions about what had happened at the Blagg residence on Pine Terrace Court.

Back in the master bedroom, it was discovered that one pillow was still on the bed, whereas Mike Blagg had said that Jennifer usually used two pillows when she slept. A second pillow was not found. The jewelry box was inspected more closely and appeared to have been ransacked. The contents of the jewelry box were gone and the contents of a purse had been dumped on the floor next to the jewelry box. Nearby lay a pair of sweatpants with two sets of underwear inside. A set of keys for the minivan lay atop a dresser, but there was also a set of keys to the minivan in Jennifer's purse.

In Abby's room, the bed was unmade and a doll lay partially on one pillow. The bed was in a condition that suggested that Abby had never awakened and gotten ready for school. According to Mike, before she went to school, she always made her bed—but now the covers were turned down and it was unmade. Despite a search of the bed, no blood was found to be present or other evidence of some kind of struggle. Abby's pink Barbie backpack, with a note from Jennifer that Abby's homework was done, still sat in the entryway of the home.

Nothing else seemed to have been tampered with in the house—no drawers had been opened, no objects rifled, no closets torn apart, no furniture overturned. There were still valuable items everywhere, including portable safes, a bag of money, and a gun in the master bedroom closet. There was no evidence of a struggle between the killer/abductor and the occupants of the house at all. It led Sergeant Weyler to think briefly, *This crime scene has been staged!*

Dr. Robert Kurtzman, forensic pathologist and coroner for Mesa County, came to the scene and viewed the blood on the bed and floor. In his opinion, there was enough blood present to cause the death of a six-year-old child or an adult, if the person's wounds were not taken care of in a timely manner. The whole scene at the Pine Terrace Court residence appeared more and more as if someone had died at the home, or at least been seriously injured.

Matt Saluto, of the CBI, also arrived at the house at Pine

Terrace for a thorough crime scene investigation (CSI) and documentation of the premises. He was CSI II-certified and had years of college courses in that field. Saluto was there, along with Wayne Bryant and Janel Smith, out of the Montrose CBI Office. Saluto was assigned to photograph the house and to take latent fingerprints. His first impression of the scene: "It was relatively clean and freshly vacuumed, except for the master bedroom. The rest of the house was clean and orderly."

In the master bedroom, Saluto reported on what the others had seen, and noted as they had that there didn't seem to be any castoff from the bloodstains. The blood appeared to have pooled in one general area—on the right side of the bed, and then down onto the floor. There were no drag marks, no blood droplets leading elsewhere, no smeared bloodstains or apparent wipe marks. Later, he would remark on the lack of blood spatter—which would have been caused by a blunt-force blow, such as coming from a hammer or other heavy object. There was nothing to sustain a theory that something like that had been used as the murder weapon, if there had been a murder. In fact, with so much blood, a weapon of a different type, either a gun or a knife, might have been used.

Saluto started off by taking general photos of the exterior of the house, and then slowly worked his way inside through the front entrance way. Evidence was collected in each room and tagged, and the photos were numbered as well. As they went along, Wayne Bryant dusted for prints, and took several of what appeared to be important latent fingerprints. A couple of prints were lifted at the garage door handle and banister. Later, the nightstand in the master bedroom was dusted for prints as well.

Saluto discovered some empty boxes in the crawl space, and even went into the attic, but found nothing of interest there. A firearm storage box was taken from the master bedroom closet, as well as a .22 rifle, a shotgun, and a .22 handgun. None of these were loaded. The house was divided up in the search, and MCSO investigators mainly stayed in the garage area with the minivan, while CBI agents covered Abby's room and Mike Blagg's computer room, which was adjacent to Abby's room. A stain was found under the computer and checked if semen was present, but none was found there at the time. However, there was an unusual patterning of some kind of spots under the computer on the rug.

The backyard and fence were examined, and it was noted that there were some scuff marks on a few boards of the back fence. These were photographed and given an identifying number. Even more interesting, there had been a vehicle parked near the fence on the street side at one time, and it had knocked down some vegetation and disturbed the gravel. Whether it had parked there at the time of the disappearance was not known.

The search began to focus more and more on the minivan in the garage. Luminol in the van picked up small indications of blood on the rear driver's-side seat, and on the inside of the passenger door. Very small amounts of blood were also found on the left portion of the steering wheel and the armrest of the passenger side. Saluto later said of the process in the use of luminol, "We looked for an intense glow in the darkness. Certain areas where blood is present will have a fluorescent glow." A small amount of blood was also found on the brake pedal. The entire floor of the garage was luminoled, but no traces of blood were evident, nor were any found in the laundry room.

Saluto noted in the minivan that the captain chairs in front were in an upright position, but the middle seats lay flat. This indicated that at some point an object or objects were probably placed in the rear of the front seats, onto the flat surface. He asked himself, "was the area large enough to hold bodies?" The answer was yes, he surmised.

Police officer Geraldine Earthman, of the GJPD, was called to Pine Terrace Court; she had worked for ten years with the canine unit and specialized with tracking dogs. The dogs were trained to sniff certain items, and these smells were called "agitators." Her dog in 2001 was named Zara, and when Earthman and Zara reached the Blagg residence, she had Zara sniff two items that belonged to Jennifer and Abby.

Officer Earthman noted that the temperature outside at the time was 50 degrees and the humidity was 10 percent. Zara sniffed the ground around the porch and went to the garage area as well. While sniffing there, Zara gave telltale signs of recognition, which officers had dubbed "Hoover vacuums." These signs included a faster respiratory response and certain wagging of the tail. When Zara moved away from the house and garage, however, there were no more "alerts." It appeared that Jennifer had been in the house and garage recently, but had not walked away from the residence. Officer Earthman took Zara all the way around the house, and to the backyard, but the only alerts came at the front porch and garage area. Jennifer and Abby had not walked away from the house, but it couldn't be ruled out that they had been driven away. Whether dead or alive was also a mystery.

While all of this was going on, Michael Blagg was taken down to the Mesa County Sheriff's Office by his pastor for an interview with Investigator Steven King and, later, Sergeant Wayne Weyler. Mike told them that he had last seen his wife at approximately 6:00 A.M., before leaving for work. Mike said that he had called Jennifer several times during the day, but always got the answering ma-

chine. He thought that he'd called around 7:00, 7:05, 10:00
A.M., and 3:00 P.M., He added that by noon he was starting to get worried because his wife didn't answer the home
phone or her cell phone. Mike said that was not like her,
but he did admit that he never called Abby's school, Bookcliff Christian School, where Jennifer sometimes volunteered. This seemed somewhat odd to Weyler and King.

The interview went on, hour after hour—seven in all—
into the wee hours of the morning. Mike said that when he
returned home from work, he looked in the bedroom and
that two pillows were missing, but a third one was still
there. This seemed to contradict his original statement that
Jennifer used two pillows for sleeping, not three. Mike reiterated that the back door was open and that this door had
a small portable battery-operated alarm on the handle. The
alarm was still on the door handle when he got home, but
not sounding when he looked at it. He couldn't say for sure
if the batteries had been dead for a while in the alarm.

Mike pointed out which items had been tampered with
in the house, and since everyone was now a suspect, he
denied that he had anything to do with Jennifer or Abby's
disappearance or the reason that there was blood in the
house. He described himself and his wife as devout born-
again Christians. Then he added he had no idea who would
want to harm or kidnap his family.

Investigator King began to ask Mike questions about
how November 13 had begun. Mike told him that he had
put the American flag out on the porch at 6:00 A.M. and
closed the door behind him. He locked it and walked out
to where his white Dodge Stratus was parked at the curb
in front of the house. He went to work on his normal route
and said that he had a normal day at work. Mike said that
he generally phoned Jennifer every day at around 7:00
A.M. to make sure that she and Abby were awake, and that
everything was okay.

KING: So did you do that today? You called Jennifer?

BLAGG: No answer. I got the answering machine. Which happens sometimes, not often. But sometimes if Jennifer's in the bathroom or something, she'll let the answering machine get it.

KING: Did you leave a message?

BLAGG: I always leave a message.

KING: Do you remember what the message was that you left?

BLAGG: "Good morning. Hope you guys had a great night. I hope your day goes well at school." Because sometimes Abby will be listening on the extension. I called right back about five minutes later, because at AMETEK we're in the process of the open enrollment for health care for next year. I forgot to ask Jennifer last night if she wanted the same coverage as we had for this year. And I told her that unless I heard from her, I'm just gonna sign us up for the same stuff.

KING: So you called at seven-oh-five.

BLAGG: I got the answering machine again.

KING: And did you leave a message that time?

BLAGG: Um-hmm. I told her unless she called back, I was just gonna sign us up for the same stuff. She didn't [call back]. Then, just normal work stuff. Uh, I'm the director of operations and I gotta make sure manufacturing goes like it's supposed to right now. Our general manager's out of town, so basically, I'm in charge of the plant right now. Sometime later in the morning, I don't know what time, I think it was tenish . . . I called back. She's usually finished with whatever volunteering she would have done by that point. I just said, "Hey, when you get a chance, give me a call." Then I called again around lunchtime. And this time, I said, "I'm getting a little concerned. Haven't heard from you." I called her on her cell phone about that time. She doesn't like for me to leave messages on her cell phone. Then things started getting busy at work again, so I didn't get a chance to call her again until sometime around three or something. At this point, having not heard from her, I was pretty concerned. We never go all day without talking on the phone. I told her I was gonna be at a normal time coming home, because she's always interested in that. It helps her with planning dinner.

KING: I take it, you didn't talk to her. Again you were talking to the answering machine. So then what happened?

BLAGG: I left work a little bit after four. I came home on the normal drive and parked the car. I got the mail, and I had some Christmas presents that I was gonna try and hide in a closet before Abby got a chance to see me. I came in, saw the back door open . . . which was a little bit alarming. Usually when I come in, I close the door and say, "I'm home!" and Abby usually comes running and says, "Daddy!" Nothing this time.

Investigator King wanted to know if Mike had seen the back door open when he first arrived home at his residence. Mike said, "Yeah. From the time you open the front door, you've got a straight shot looking through to where the back door is. And the back door was open, which was real unusual. We never leave any doors or windows or any kind of stuff open. So a little twinge of panic went through me at that point. I dropped my packages down right away, right there in the entryway. I looked around real quickly and then off to the right-hand side where the master bedroom is, I got a view of stuff on the floor. That was not like Jennifer to leave anything on the floor.

"So I ran back into our bedroom and I could see blood on the bed and clothes. And her jewelry box and her purse contents were on the floor. I started to freak out a little bit. I called nine-one-one and ran into the kitchen. I didn't know who it was on the line, some girl, and she was really calm and good and managed to calm me down. She asked if the car (minivan) was still there. So I went to the garage and sure enough, the van was still there. Then she said, 'Why don't you go out of the house,' because she could tell every time I looked in the master bedroom, it was freaking me out."

King asked Mike what he had seen in the master bedroom when he was in there.

Mike answered, "I had gone in there to look around and saw all the blood and stuff on the floor. She (the dispatcher) told me to leave and sit down on the step of the back porch. Which I did. And I just took deep, long breaths. At that point, to try and calm me down, she said she had called the sheriff's office, and there would be someone coming in the near term, and that she would tell me when they got there so that it wouldn't scare me when they came around the side. But then she had me go around the front of the house anyway, before they showed up."

King said that he had not been in Mike's house, and he asked if Mike had gone upstairs at all. Mike answered, "Yeah, I was sitting on the back porch and she was asking me questions and I was talking about Abby. I forget now exactly how that went, but somehow we started talking about Abby, my daughter, and I said, 'I gotta go upstairs and check out her room.' So she said, 'You talk me through everything that you're doing.' So I went upstairs and I pushed open Abby's door like this (demonstrating), so I wouldn't mess up anything. I didn't touch her doorknob or anything. I did turn on the light switch.

"Abby's fan was on, which is an indication that she never got up. Her clothes were still sitting out on the table, where we set them the night before. The sheets had been pulled down about halfway, maybe two-thirds of the way, and they were crumpled. But there was no blood that I could see anywhere in there, so [the dispatcher] told me to go back out of the house."

King wanted to know how many bedrooms were upstairs, and Mike told him that there were two. When asked if he had checked any other rooms besides the ones mentioned, Mike said that he hadn't, except for the garage, and by doing that he had to pass through the laundry room. Mike said that he hadn't seen anything out of the ordinary in there.

King asked Mike what vehicle Jennifer drove, and Mike answered that she drove a minivan, and that it was still parked in the garage when he got home. After that, King wanted to know about Jennifer.

KING: So tell me about your wife, Jennifer.

BLAGG: She's the most energetic, enthusiastic, wonderful woman you could ever want to meet. She's a good Christian, warm, loving woman. She's about five foot four, blond hair, and she's letting it grow out. It was short, but now it's probably just a bit over shoulder length. Uh, she's got brown eyes, and she's just as cute as can be. I've never seen her not make friends with people. Everybody that she talks to is instantly a friend of hers. She could talk to anybody. She could talk to a wall, and have the wall laughing in ten minutes after she started talking to it.

KING: You said Christian woman. She actively involved in her church?

BLAGG: We have two things going on right now, one with the pastor we have out here at Monument Baptist Church. That's our home church. The Lord led us to this area to do prayer. And so we were led to a church in Clifton as well, called the New Hope Fellowship Church. And we initiated a prayer ministry there. So we've got a prayer team built at New Hope and we're working with Ray and Diana at Monument for the Christian (inaudible).

KING: So I take it that she knows quite a few people between the churches you were talking about, the home church and the one you're going to in Clifton. Is she actively involved in the prayer teams?

BLAGG: Yeah. The two of us initiated the prayer teams and there's about seven people on the core team and there are twelve or fourteen on the whole—

KING: Okay, what time did the two of you go to bed last night?

BLAGG: Ten. Around ten.

KING: Do you remember what time Abby went to bed?

BLAGG: She goes to bed at seven o'clock every night. Usually she falls asleep within half an hour.

KING: Before you guys went to bed . . . a fairly normal night, last night?

BLAGG: We watched the football game and—

KING: Did you watch the football game at home or someplace else?

BLAGG: At home.

KING: Okay. Was there anybody else in the house?

BLAGG: No. Just the three of us.

* * *

King asked Mike where his own car had been parked when he got up to go to work. Mike told him that his car was parked on the street right next to the curb. Asked if he'd seen anyone outside when he went to work, Mike said that he hadn't. King wanted to know if Mike had a newspaper delivered to his door, and Mike answered that he didn't. When asked about his neighborhood in general, Mike said, "I haven't heard of any break-ins or any kind of issues out there. It's an older community [that] lives in the neighborhood. A lot of retirees in that little area. Couple of younger couples, but not many. It's mostly retired older couples."

King asked about any kind of vandalism or problems with anything missing in the neighborhood. Mike said that he didn't know of any, and added that they rented the home from a man named Chris Durham. Mike and his family had only lived in the house for less than a year, and in that time there had been no kinds of theft or trouble in the neighborhood.

King wanted to know where Mike and his family had moved from, and Mike answered they had moved from Simpsonville, a suburb of Greenville, South Carolina, to Grand Junction, in April 2000. They had rented a place on 28½ Road for a while, and then moved into the home on Pine Terrace Court. The family had moved to Grand Junction, not because of family ties to the place, but because Mike had changed jobs and got a position in Grand Junction at AMETEK Dixson.

King asked if he or Jennifer had experienced any problems with salespeople coming by the house, or any kind of phone calls. Mike said that they hadn't. King wanted to know if Jennifer had any problems with someone around town, or anyone at the church they attended. Mike said that she hadn't. In fact, he said, he couldn't think of anyone who had a problem with either Jennifer or Abby. Then he added, "I mean, we're as plain as melba toast as you can get."

Once again, King asked about any annoying sales calls via the telephone, and Mike said that in the evening they generally let those types of calls go on the answering machine. He and Jennifer liked to have their own time together then, and not be bothered by salespeople.

At that point, Investigator King wanted to know how Mike viewed his marriage with Jennifer. He asked Mike how he would categorize his marriage at the present time, and Mike said, "Very strong. We've got a wonderful marriage."

King questioned what Mike saw as the biggest plus in his marriage, and Mike said that it was their love for the Lord, followed by their love for each other and Abby. Mike related that religion was a big part of their lives.

King asked, "What would you say would be the biggest hurdle or biggest challenge that the two of you are facing right now?"

Mike responded, "We both have pride issues that we . . . well, we love each other so much that sometimes we let that get in the way of prayer time or social events. More often than not, we're homebodies because we prefer to stay together. I'm an introvert. She's an extrovert. I mean, there's several things there, I guess, and there are differences or things that could cause outside types of issues. But nothing . . . well, we've got a strong marriage. It's wonderful." Mike related that the pluses in the marriage far outweighed any minuses.

King wanted to know who Jennifer's best friend was in the area, and Mike told him that it was Diana Shirley, his pastor Ray's wife.

King asked when Jennifer had last spoken with Diana Shirley, and Mike said that it had been the day before at school.

King said, "Did the pastor say anything to you about whether your wife had called his house at all today at any time?"

Mike replied, "I didn't ask him."

King wanted to know what Jennifer's parents' names were, and Mike told him Marilyn Conway, who had remarried, after her divorce, to a man named Harold Conway. Marilyn had originally been married to Roy Loman, who was Jennifer's father. Mike said that Harold and Marilyn now lived in Haltom City, a suburb of Dallas, Texas.

King asked about Mike's parents, and Mike said that his dad had passed away five years previously, and that his mother lived in Warner Robins, Georgia, not far from Atlanta. Her name was Elizabeth "Betsy" Blagg.

Asked about where Jennifer might go if she was in trouble, Mike answered, "To her mom, without a doubt."

Getting back to the house on Pine Terrace Court, King wondered if Mike had touched anything in the master bedroom. Mike said that he didn't think so. Then King had Mike tell about the events of the day in reverse order, starting with being in the master bedroom and working his way backward in time to when he had left the house that morning.

After this recitation by Mike was finished, King asked Mike about what he was currently doing at AMETEK Dixson, where he worked.

BLAGG: We're (AMETEK Dixson) moving to Mexico. Today and tomorrow are the pack-up days to put things on the truck, so I've been monitoring and managing that whole packing-up process. And the last part of the day, I was dealing with the Mexican brokers. We've got Mexican brokers that are signing off on the goods in the truck and then they seal the truck. They seal it with that seal so it can go just straight across the border. In the past, we had problems with

them having to stop at the border and it takes a week
or so to clear customs and get across. So anyway, the
last half-day was working on making sure that the
workbenches got shrink-wrapped and that all the fix-
tures and everything were properly packaged and that
the raw material was getting staged for tomorrow's inspection and then shrink-wrapped for tomorrow. The
other thing we have going is our computer system. It's
called MAX. It's a materials management system. In
Mexico, we have a system called GAIN. And as we're
trying to integrate the two facilities, we're now conducting some GAIN training here, so we had some
people in who were helping us to learn GAIN. And
most of the people that were being trained were
people that work for me, so I was in and out of that
training throughout the day.

KING: So, okay, does Jennifer work in Abby's class?

BLAGG: Yeah. She typically would be there grading
papers and picking up workbooks. And Ms. Fasnacht,
the teacher, will sometimes have Diana and Jennifer
work pretty closely together. They're best friends.
They'd pull out the next day's assignments for twenty
kids. That's a little bit of work to do that. On Mon-
days, Wednesdays, and Fridays, Jennifer goes to
Jazzercise with Diana in the morning.

King wanted to know where Jennifer went to Jazzercise,
and Mike told him that it was at Lincoln Park. He also told
King that Jennifer worked at the Bookcliff Christian
School on Tuesdays and Thursdays. She went to chapel on
Tuesday mornings, where a prayer group met in a room
and prayed during the morning hours. Jennifer was normally done with this at around 10:00 A.M., and she would

often be home a short time later. Mike said he had a habit of phoning her sometime after 10:00 A.M. at home, to see how she was doing. He had done that on November 13, but only left a message on the answering machine.

King wondered why the school hadn't called Mike if Abby hadn't gone to school that day. He wanted to know if the school would call him at work. Mike said he didn't know, but it was a question he thought himself, and he intended to find out if that was the case.

King said that of course the school wouldn't have called him or his home if Abby had been at school, but Mike assured him that Diana Shirley, who was at school during the day, never saw Abby there. Diana's husband, Ray, had told Mike this in his Jeep Cherokee as they were on the way to the interview at the sheriff's office.

Investigator King asked a few more questions, and then he introduced Sergeant Wayne Weyler to Mike Blagg. Weyler had been at the Blaggs' home that evening, and now wanted to talk to Mike about some of the things he had seen there.

WEYLER: I apologize, we're probably gonna go over a lot of things you just talked about. Like I said, I just came in and I'm trying to get caught up on things. Sometimes when another person asks you the same things, you might remember something else. You doing okay?

BLAGG: Yeah, like I've been hit by a truck, but—

WEYLER: What are you feeling?

BLAGG: Depressed. And sad. And scared. Honestly, if we can't find Jennifer and bring her back home, I don't know what I would do without her. We have been such a part of each other for so long. I feel a bit lost. Where do I go from here? What do I do? Uh, you

can do all things through Him, who gives you
strength. And I just keep repeating that to myself. The
Lord is gonna strengthen me and give me sustenance
to be able to make it through. I know that. That's
where I am right now.

WEYLER: What do you think happened? I mean, what
is your gut feeling?

Mike told him that he didn't know, but that he had been
running a lot of scenarios through his head. He couldn't
think of anyone who would want to hurt his family or had
any animosity toward them. Then he added, "I saw a lot of
blood. A lot of blood!"

Weyler wanted to know where he had seen the blood,
and Mike told him on Jennifer's side of the bed. "It was a
big pool of blood, and running down the side of the bed
was a good wide swath of blood that had dripped down
into a pool right at the base of the bed. I've never seen that
much blood before in my life. One of the deputies told
me you would have that much blood if you cut yourself
pretty good."

Weyler asked if he had seen blood anywhere else in the
house. Mike answered no, and then added that he had gone
into Abby's room and looked around in there. He said he
hadn't seen any blood in her room, and he took that to be
a good sign. And yet the very lack of blood in Abby's room
was disturbing in its own way. Why was she missing, if
there was no blood?

Weyler said, "Mike, some of these questions are really
tough, but we gotta ask 'em. You know?"

Mike said that he did know, and he was ready to answer
all of them.

Weyler asked, "How do you explain a whole bunch of
blood where you saw it on the ground and your wife's not
there?"

Mike answered, "I haven't a clue how it wouldn't trail someplace." He said it seemed strange that there was a lot of blood in the master bedroom—but not in other parts of the house—if Jennifer had been taken against her will from the residence.

Weyler asked him if he'd seen anything out of the ordinary in the rest of the house. Mike replied, "There was debris on the floor of the master bedroom. There were some clothes down. The jewelry box was there and her purse had been—"

Weyler interrupted him, "The purse next to the jewelry box?"

Mike continued, "Yes, it appeared to have been rummaged through."

Weyler wanted to know what had been in the jewelry box, and Mike answered, "All of her jewelry. She had quite a bit of jewelry."

Weyler asked if Mike had gone around the house to see if anything else was missing, and Mike said that he hadn't. "I came into the room and saw the blood and I really started freaking out. I had to get out of there and I went and called nine-one-one, and fortunately I got somebody who was very calm and talked me through it. She told me not to touch anything in the house, so I—"

Weyler interrupted him again. "Yeah, but sometimes, when you're in shock, you do funny things. That's why we gotta make sure. That will help in the search of the house. What you did touch and what you didn't. Which fingerprints would be there if you were picking up the box or whatever."

Mike replied, "No, I didn't do any of that. I did go to the back door and the garage door, because she wanted me to check to see if the van was still there."

Weyler asked where Mike had picked up the phone to

call 911. He answered that he'd picked up the handset in the kitchen.

Weyler said, "You left that out front, if I remember correctly." Mike said that he did.

Weyler wanted to know if they had a phone upstairs, and Mike said that they didn't, although they had one in the master bedroom. Mike then quickly added, "I couldn't stomach picking up the phone there. It's not a mobile phone. And I just couldn't call from there."

Weyler asked Mike which church he went to in the area, and Mike said that they actually attended two churches. He said the Monument Baptist Church was their home church, but that they had also been volunteering at the New Hope Fellowship Church in Clifton. Mike declared that the Lord had called Jennifer and him to start an Intercessory Prayer Ministry there for adults. The pastor was glad for their help, and Mike said that the prayer group had begun to thrive. This was something they had done before in a similar situation in South Carolina, where they had lived before moving to Colorado.

Weyler asked how long Mike and Jennifer had been married, and Mike answered, "Ten years on Friday. We have one child, Abby, and she's six years old." As far as any nicknames for her, he sometimes called her "Peanut" or "Sweetie." Just "standard six-year-old stuff," as Mike put it.

Asked how he felt about Abby, Mike answered, "She's the light of my life. I just love her to pieces. She is just a ball of energy. She's wonderful. When I come home through the door, even though she's six years old, she still says 'Daddy!' and comes running to me."

Asked if they had any pets, Mike said no, but that Abby wanted a dog very badly.

Weyler wanted to know where the Blaggs had moved from, and Mike told him Simpsonville, South Carolina, near the Greenville area. Weyler pointed out that that was a long way away, to which Mike answered that they'd come to Grand Junction because AMETEK Dixson had offered him a job. He had been working at Allied Signal/Honeywell during a transition period, but he was worried that they were going to close the plant, and he needed to look for work elsewhere for job security.

WEYLER: We have to ask standard questions. We have to ask them. I apologize. I know it's hard, but we have to just go through the whole gamut of things. Any problems between you and your wife? I mean physically?

BLAGG: She had a full hysterectomy.

WEYLER: How long ago was that?

BLAGG: October fourth of last year.

WEYLER: What brought that on?

BLAGG: She was having heavy menstrual cycles. So we went in and talked to her gynecologist, Dr. King, and he said that in addition to that, she also had some cysts in her ovaries. If we chose to go forward with the hysterectomy, it would be worthwhile to go ahead and do the whole shootin' match out.

WEYLER: Menstrual cycles . . . when she would bleed a lot . . . the "kind of blood you would see today" kind of bleeding?

BLAGG: No. Not like that.

WEYLER: Was she pretty devastated on not having more kids?

BLAGG: Uh, actually, no. We had made a decision right after Abby. She . . . we had some complications with delivering Abby. And, uh, about six months after Abby was born, well, leading up to that, we had been praying about it, seeing where the Lord was gonna go, but, um, I had a vasectomy about six months after Abby. So we knew that we weren't gonna be having any more children anyway, so that wasn't a problem.

WEYLER: Why did you have a vasectomy?

BLAGG: Because we didn't want to risk another pregnancy that would have some complications for Jennifer, that could possibly be life-threatening.

WEYLER: Have you been married before?

BLAGG: Uh . . . yeah, I've been married once before. Right after college.

WEYLER: How long did that marriage go for?

BLAGG: A year.

WEYLER: What brought about the end of that marriage?

BLAGG: I was in the navy, doing a lot of travel, and she was a professional woman that didn't want to be doing all that traveling. So we did a summary dissolution.

WEYLER: Have any children?

BLAGG: No.

WEYLER: You hesitated when you said you had been married once. I mean, were there other relationships? Other women?

BLAGG: Oh yeah. Yeah.

KING: How about Jennifer? Has she been married before?

BLAGG: (Inaudible, but the answer was that she had not been married before)

KING: And where did you meet her?

BLAGG: Jennifer?

KING: Yeah.

BLAGG: In San Diego. She was going to school at National University in San Diego and I was in the navy.

KING: What's National University? Sorry, I've never heard of that.

BLAGG: It's a nationwide chain of universities. It can also be a correspondence school.

KING: Oh, so you could learn from the computer?

BLAGG: Yeah, and her mom had at that point . . . her mom had just married Harold and moved out there. He was working for General Dynamics and moved out to San Diego. Jennifer was going to OSU prior to that, and wanted to be close to her mom, so she moved out to San Diego and went to National there.

KING: What was she studying?

BLAGG: Business administration.

WEYLER: So did she have relationships prior to you? Live-in relationships or anything?

BLAGG: Not live-in relationships. She had boyfriends, but no live-in ones. She was living with her mom in San Diego. I probably never would have met her—

WEYLER: How much younger is she than you?

BLAGG: Four years.

WEYLER: After you were married the first time, how long after that did you meet Jennifer?

BLAGG: A year, a year and a half, something like that.

WEYLER: Weren't forced to get married because of pregnancy, or anything like that?

BLAGG: No. No. We had Abby three years after we got married, or something like that.

WEYLER: No other pregnancies or miscarriages?

BLAGG: Oh no. No, no, no.

Weyler asked how long Mike had considered himself to be a Christian, and he answered since 1987. Mike added that Jennifer had been a Christian since the age of fourteen.

Weyler wanted to know if Mike had had a wild past, to which Mike replied that he'd had a "standard navy time."

"You know. I had a good time when we were on cruises, and a lot of stupid drinking and stuff like that. Doing dumb things that fortunately I was able to get away from."

Weyler said that he understood, and added, "We have a pretty wild early past and God delivers us from different areas."

Mike agreed with that.

Weyler wanted to know if Mike had lots of problems when he was younger.

Mike replied, "Yeah, I had lots of girlfriends. I had lots of drinking. No drugs."

Weyler asked, "Anger?"

Mike said that he didn't have problems with anger. In fact, he said he was a pretty mellow guy, and he and Jennifer addressed problems as they arose.

Weyler wanted to know if Mike had been arrested for anything, to which Mike said that he had never been arrested.

WEYLER: In trouble for anything?

BLAGG: No.

WEYLER: As a kid in juvy?

BLAGG: No.

WEYLER: Any mental-health problems at all?

BLAGG: No.

WEYLER: Difficult questions, but you understand that I have to ask them.

BLAGG: I understand.

WEYLER: Okay. How about Jennifer? Any mental-health problems?

BLAGG: No. Occasionally she'll battle depression, but no medication. Sometimes she'll be unhappy. When we first moved out here, we had a bunch of good friends in South Carolina. So probably the first four or five months we were out here, she was battling depression. She was having a hard time the first few months we were here. But she made new friends and found some good churches. We realized the Lord brought us here for a reason.

WEYLER: You talked about a fight two weeks ago. (This had come up earlier.) Any other fights recently?

BLAGG: No.

Weyler asked if he and Jennifer had financial problems or fights over finances. Weyler said that all couples occasionally had arguments over finances. Mike replied that their only financial problem was that they were renting. Both he and Jennifer wanted a large house in the area, but the houses they liked were out of their price range. He added, "The house we had in South Carolina was beautiful. A wonderful house. But it was in a close-out neighborhood when we had to leave. There were like ten spec homes that the builder was really discounting, so for us to compete with that, we had to really take a bath on our house. We basically lost our deposit is what it boils down to, so we were here, trying to build a deposit up and be able to put down a payment on a house."

Weyler asked how much they had lost on their deposit in South Carolina, and Mike told him eight thousand dollars. Weyler's reply to that was "Oooo!" Then he asked how much Mike made at AMETEK Dixson. When Mike told him $110,000 a year, Weyler said, "Geez! How much do you take home monthly?"

Mike said that after all the deductions he took home about $2,500 per paycheck. He said they were putting savings away and trying to build it up for a deposit on a new house in the area.

Weyler was still stunned about how much Mike made per year. Compared to the salary of a member in law enforcement, it seemed like an awful lot of money. Weyler asked, "You couldn't afford to buy a house with that?"

Mike answered, "We could, but we had to build up. . . . Our deal is that we want to put twenty percent on the house so we could get out of the P and I. And we don't have . . . If we're looking at a two-hundred-and-twenty-thousand-dollar house, that's forty grand. We don't have that kind of money socked away."

Weyler wanted to know if Jennifer made any money by working at Bookcliff school.

Mike replied that her work was strictly voluntary and she didn't make any money in that regard.

Weyler asked if she had any desire to go back to work at all. Mike answered that Jennifer didn't want to go back to work, and she treasured the time she had to spend with Abby.

Weyler said, "You're Abby's natural father, right?" Mike said that he was. Asked if Jennifer was Abby's natural mother, Mike said that was correct. Weyler then asked if he and Jennifer had any relatives close to Colorado. Mike replied that Jennifer's brother lived in Oklahoma, and Jennifer's mom lived in the Dallas/Fort Worth area of Texas.

He said that Jennifer was close to both of them, especially her mom, and that she phoned her mom quite often.

Weyler asked if Mike had given Investigator King all the phone numbers and addresses of Jennifer's family members, and Mike said that he had. Then Weyler said, "Jennifer wasn't pregnant—you've had a vasectomy. Were there any medical problems she had recently?"

Mike replied that she'd recently been seeing Dr. Reichs for blood tests concerning the medication Centhroid and the estrogen that she was taking. Weyler wanted to know if the estrogen was for the hysterectomy situation, and Mike answered that it was, since Jennifer had to go through hormone replacement therapy.

Weyler said, "So there were probably some tempermental issues due to lack of estrogen, like menopause?"

Mike answered, "Actually, when she came home, Dr. King put her on estrogen right away. And the hysterectomy was the best thing that ever happened to her as far as leveling out moods and smoothing the rough spots. She was in pain for the first six months, as you can imagine after a surgery like that. But after that, she's been saying all along that this was the best thing that ever happened to her."

Weyler wondered if before the hysterectomy Jennifer had a lot of mood swings. Mike answered that it was the normal PMS kind of things. "You know—anger during periods. Then smooth as silk for the weeks in between."

Weyler wanted to know how Mike handled these issues, and Mike answered that he was pretty flexible about the situation and handled things fairly well. He said, "I'm a pretty even-keeled kind of person. We would just work through it. I mean, it was no big deal. At least I didn't think it was a big deal."

At this point, King jumped back in and asked about Jennifer's mom, Marilyn Conway, and when the last time was that Jennifer had actually seen her mom in person. Mike answered that the whole family had visited Jennifer's mom in Texas on October 25 through October 28, less than a month previously.

King wanted to know if it was because of Marilyn Conway's health problems, and Mike said, "Yeah. We try and get down there a couple of times a year, 'cause Jennifer and her mom are really close. It's good to get a chance to get back there." [Investigator King had been informed by other investigators that Jennifer's mother did have medical problems associated with cancer treatments.]

Weyler asked, "So Jennifer would talk to her mom a lot? Tell her all her woes and stuff?"

Mike answered, "Almost every day they would talk by telephone."

King wondered if Mike had a cell phone, and Mike said that he did. Asked if he had called her on his cell phone during the day on the November 13, he answered that he thought he had.

Weyler had obviously been checking up on this angle and said, "Okay, you made two other calls before that."

Mike answered, "Well, it's just that it logs . . . um, one of them was a missed call which rang and there were those messasges."

Weyler wanted to know who Carmike was.

Mike said that referred to a movie at a theater, which pertained to *Monsters, Inc.* He'd called to find out when the movie was playing.

Weyler asked, "Who is Linda?"

Mike answered, "Linda is my production supervisor."

Weyler said, "Are you having an affair with anyone?"

Mike, point-blank, said, "No."

Weyler wanted to know if he'd had one recently, and Mike said that he hadn't. Weyler then asked why he had a phone number listed for a woman named Marilyn. Mike replied that Marilyn was the name of Jennifer's mother, and that's why he had her phone number.

Weyler got back into finances and wondered if Mike and Jennifer had credit card debt. Mike said that they didn't, and they paid off any credit cards each month as the bills came due.

Weyler then asked if they shared a checking account, and Mike said that they did. "Does she have a credit card, herself?" Weyler asked, and Mike answered that she did.

Weyler's questioning turned to Mike's place of work, and he asked, "Where are you as far as ranking within your business? How high up are you in the organization?"

Mike answered that there was a general manager who was over everyone, and there was a chief financial officer, and then he was next in line. He was essentially the third highest in the hierarchy at AMETEK Dixson.

Weyler wanted to know if Mike had a company vehicle, and Mike said that he didn't. Weyler added, "Do you drive a company vehicle?" to which Mike answered that he sometimes did. Asked if he had driven one on the day when Jennifer and Abby disappeared, Mike said that he had not.

The line of questioning once again shifted from Mike at work to the marriage between himself and Jennifer.

WEYLER: So what problems were you and Jennifer having?

BLAGG: Well, we have a very good marriage.

WEYLER: Tell me about it.

BLAGG: Well, we're very loving. We're very open with each other. We talk about everything. I mean, we talk about what happens at work, even mundane little nothing things. We're very touch . . . I mean, open with our affection for each other. We genuinely care about what goes on in each other's lives. We do whatever we can to help the other person through any kind of issues that are going on. If I have a bad day at work, she is there for me to help talk me through it, or, "Hey, let's go get some ice cream." Just little things that add up to show what an incredible love we have for each other. We hold hands all the time whenever we go anyplace. Abby picks up on it because she tries to get between us all the time and hold hands with us. We're just a very loving, affectionate family.

WEYLER: Sexual issues involving you and your wife sexually. How often a week, a month?

BLAGG: Once a week, probably.

WEYLER: Mental problems in that area?

BLAGG: No.

WEYLER: Describe Jennifer for me, physically.

BLAGG: She's about five foot four. She's kind of got sandy blond hair, down to about her shoulders. Brown eyes, just cute . . . as beautiful as she can be. About a hundred twenty-eight pounds, something like that.

WEYLER: Okay, and what about Abby?

BLAGG: Abby is a stick. She's about forty-eight inches tall and just about forty pounds. She's skinny and lanky, has blond hair, and [is] a blue-eyed beautiful little girl.

WEYLER: Michael, would you do anything to harm your daughter or wife?

BLAGG: No. I would never do anything like that.

WEYLER: Did you take 'em somewhere?

BLAGG: No, I did not. I would never do that.

* * *

Weyler wanted to know what Mike thought had happened in his house, and Mike replied that he didn't know what had happened, but whatever it was, it had probably occurred between the time he left the house at six o'clock, and before Jennifer got out of bed at 6:30 A.M.

Weyler asked if Mike had noticed anyone watching the house, and Mike replied that he hadn't seen anybody doing that.

Weyler said, "Any thoughts, and ideas? Anybody at work? Anybody trying to pick up on your wife that you've heard about?"

Mike responded, "No, she would have told me about that."

Weyler agreed and said, "Yeah, a woman's intuition is incredible. Did she ever talk about, 'I feel like somebody's watching me,' or anything like that?"

"No, I can't remember her ever talking about anything like that."

"Any old boyfriends of hers from in the past, way back, that she had concerns about. Were there any stalkers in her life?"

Mike answered, "No."

Sergeant Weyler mentioned the fact that the investigators knew that Mike and Jennifer had some visitors on Sunday, November 11, a man and a young woman. These people had originally gone to the wrong house on the block and then went to the Blagg home. Mike said, "Yeah, that's right. We were trying to find a babysitter, because we're kinda in between babysitters right now. Jennifer and I like to spend a little bit of time together on dates and things. The person who we were going to interview—her name is Jessica, and I forget her last name. But I've got it written down at home. We were gonna interview them on

Sunday at one o'clock. And they came to an address across the street. And the dad called a couple of hours later and said, 'Hey, I thought you were in Aspen and I didn't know where you went.' But we worked it out so that tomorrow we were supposed to interview her."

Weyler asked, "So they never made it to your house on Sunday?"

Mike said that they hadn't.

Weyler wanted to know how Mike had found out about those people, and Mike answered, "Through one of the youths at Monument Baptist Church. Ray's church. We've been trying to put out feelers for babysitters for quite some time now. And one of the youths that we wanted to be a babysitter was too busy, so she recommended this girl. Before we would use her as a babysitter, we wanted to interview her, talk to her and see how she and Abby interacted. But it just didn't work out on Sunday."

Weyler wanted to know if Mike had ever met these people before, and he said no.

Weyler asked if he knew anything about them, other than what the youth had mentioned. Mike said that he didn't.

Asked if there had been any strange vehicles in the neighborhood lately, or any noise on Greenbelt Drive that had concerned him, Mike said, "Well, the back of our house is on Greenbelt Drive, and cars go by there all the time. But nothing that would trigger any suspicion in my mind."

Investigator King broke in and said, "When you went out to the garage and you saw the van there, did you get in the van?"

Mike said that he hadn't. Asked if he had even looked in the van, Mike said that he hadn't done that as well.

King asked, "If Jennifer was gonna leave you, where would she go?"

Mike answered, "To her mom's. She'd probably fly. What I would anticipate is that she would take a flight out of Walker Field to Dallas. I don't see that as a real option, but you could call Jennifer's mom. I mean, I haven't gotten a chance to talk to her since all this happened."

King replied, "Oh, we probably will call Jennifer's mom. One, it saves you having to do it. And it makes her aware there's a problem. And I think the best way to do it would be to get ahold of the people in that city and have them go and be with them, you know. Because, obviously we don't want to make her health any worse. We don't want to stress her out. But if I were Jennifer's mom, I would definitely want to know there's a problem."

Mike agreed that that was probably the best way to handle things.

King told Mike that at that point they were looking at all the possibilities of what might have happened, and that they had to hit on every possibility, no matter what. He said that he wasn't doing this to stress Mike out, but rather to impart the idea that "knowledge is important here, and any alternative has to be looked at."

Mike answered, "I've tried to be really good about answering every question that you guys have asked me."

King replied, "Oh, and I totally appreciate the time and effort, and I realize this is not easy."

At that point, Mike said, "Can I ask you some questions?"

King answered, "Sure, absolutely."

Mike wanted to know what chance there was that Jennifer was still alive. "Please be honest," he said.

King replied, "I think there's always that possibility. My question in return would be 'Why would you think she's dead?'"

Mike said, "Because of the blood. I saw lots of blood.

I've never seen that much blood before in my life! And that scared me."

To this, King replied, "What about your daughter?"

Mike's answer to that was, "Well, the scenario that's going on in my head right now with my daughter is not a pretty one. Because she's such a . . . Well, I don't have any pictures of her [with me], but if you could come with me to work, you could see. I've got a Plexiglas top on my desk and it's just full of pictures of my family. And one or two looks at my daughter and you would fall in love with her. I mean, that's how pretty she is. She's just wonderful. She's just the most . . . Well, just as equal to her cuteness is her beauty. Her attitude and enthusiasm is every bit as contagious. I gotta tell you, the scenarios that are going on in my head right now are not real pretty about the fact that there's no blood in her room and she's gone. I mean, that scares me. From a father's standpoint. I can see that you're married. . . . Did you tell me you have children?"

King said that he had three.

Mike continued, "As you can imagine, a missing child is a nightmare that you wouldn't want to go through."

King replied, "No, absolutely right! And that's why, believe me, I'm just one person in a team of probably twenty-five or thirty people right now looking at every possibility. And I mean, just because I'm spending the time to speak with you, it's with the idea that I might come up with something that I can pass on to them that might help in this situation. And there are other people out there doing things, working on your behalf, trying to figure out what's going on here."

Mike said, "I know you guys have a full-court press going on with this, and I appreciate that. From a father to a father, I can tell you, I appreciate that."

King replied, "You asked me outright whether your wife

was still alive. My feelings are . . . a couple of things. One is that any type of blood, well, a lot of blood—"

Mike interrupted King and asked if he was just being paranoid about the blood. King answered, "Well, I don't know. All I know is that I tend to look at these types of things with an attitude of not going to the dark side unless there's a reason to. And I think that there are many things over the next twelve hours that we'll find out. And I think that you're a key to that."

Mike responded that he knew all the investigators were working hard and that it was probably horrible for them out there in the dark, looking for clues. He said, "Jennifer, on earth, is my life. I love my daughter to pieces, but there's a biblical backing to your spouse [that] comes first. And she does. And I'm having a hard time about what I'm gonna do if the dark side of things are what happened. I mean, I guess what I'm saying is, what can I do? Where can I go? Is there anything I can do to help?"

King said that what they were doing in the interview room was helping. He said there was no point in Mike going out and driving around, trying to look for Jennifer and Abby. King declared, "Give me a place in this valley, and we'll go look. Anyplace in Colorado and we'll go look. Anyplace in Colorado/Utah and we'll go look. Those are the options. But when you say is there anything I can do . . . we're doing it. We're coming up with different scenarios, different options, different ideas."

Mike wanted to give King a little background on himself, and King said go ahead. Mike told him, "From when I started working in the corporate world, about six or seven years ago, my jobs have always been in quality engineering. Continuous improvement and problem-solving scenarios. And the idea of not being able to do anything now has just kind of ripped my guts out. I mean, I do problem solving. That's what I like to do, and it's gonna be hard on me to . . . Well, I mean, this is good, being able to talk through everything that's in my head. Every detail that the Lord is allowing me to come out with right now is helpful because I feel like I'm able to be of help. But when this is done, whenever you guys have asked the last question of me, I can see a dark period for me when I don't really have the ability to help, and that's gonna be very frustrating for me. I may need someone to talk to.

"I have through my company . . . we have a company agency that . . . well, I could go that route. But I'm open to suggestions. I guess that's what I'm saying."

King said that he would work on that, and then Mike added, "There is a Biblical saying that 'tomorrow has its own worries.'"

"And its own hope," King replied. King added, "I think we'll focus on the leads that we get, the people that we talk to, and the help that we're getting from you. Like I said, over the next twelve hours, many things will be revealed. I think we'll deal with this one step at a time."

Then he asked if Mike was hungry and needed any dinner.

Mike answered that his stomach was turning inside out. All he wanted was a glass of water.

Weyler chimed in and said, "The good news about something like this is where we talk to everybody and get all the questions that we ask you . . . Well, I know you're tired, but the more information we get, the better it helps us. That make sense?"

Mike agreed that it did.

Weyler continued, "We're gonna ask you a few strong questions. We're gonna ask questions about (inaudible), because we gotta look at everything. Okay. So hopefully you can bear with us, and not get pissed and just help us in every way you can." Obviously, some of the questions were going to get into very personal matters. Other questions were going to be about some of Mike's previous answers, to see if there were any inconsistencies. Weyler, in particular, had some concerns about statements Mike had said that just didn't seem to add up.

Weyler said, "So, when you called nine-one-one, you didn't know if your daughter had gone to school, or did you?"

BLAGG: I didn't . . . I don't think I had any idea at that point. Don't really remember saying anything about that, but I do remember saying, when we started talking about Abby, I had to go upstairs and check her room to see if she was there.

WEYLER: It concerns me, Mike, a little bit . . . why you come home and you're very concerned about your wife—why wouldn't your daughter enter into your mind?

BLAGG: Because my first concern was for my spouse.

WEYLER: Okay. Give me the reasoning there. I mean, everybody thinks differently, so tell me why that is with you?

BLAGG: I love . . . I love my daughter, and I love my wife both. But my wife is the light of my life here on earth. That's . . . that's . . . that's the way it is with me. And when I saw that blood initially, that's where the fear was pulling me, 'cause I saw stuff that I wasn't expecting to see there.

WEYLER: Why did you think your daughter was at school? I mean, my first thought was—"Oh God, my wife! Something's gone on." But then that minute I'd catch myself and I'd run upstairs and think, "Where's my daughter?"

BLAGG: No. My only concern was at that point, once I started kinda freaking out . . . the nine-one-one operator was really good about calming me down. And I don't think I was thinking really well at that point until I was calmed down. And we started talking about Abby . . . I said, "I gotta go check on Abby." And so that's what I did.

WEYLER: I wanna go back to when you're first entering the house. Okay? Coming into the house, just from the time you get to the mailbox, walk me inch by inch through what happens.

BLAGG: Okay. I go to the mailbox, open it up. It's full. Letters and a package. Take it out and I've already got my hands kind of full, 'cause I got my Christmas-present stuff. So I'm walking into the house. Get to the front door and there's a long—

WEYLER: The front door's unlocked?

BLAGG: Locked.

WEYLER: Locked. Do you use your house key to get in? And is the house key the same as you have on the car keys?

BLAGG: Yes. Same key chain. But, before I open the door, I notice there's a FedEx or UPS package there.

WEYLER: How big was it?

BLAGG: It was longer than wide. Kinda square. So I scoop all that stuff up, open the door, go in, expecting to do the same thing I always do . . . "I'm home!" Close the door and right in front of me is the open door.

WEYLER: Did you say, "I'm home"?

BLAGG: I may . . . yeah.

WEYLER: Why would you say, "I'm home" if you gotta hide the Christmas present?

BLAGG: Just 'cause that's my standard greeting by now
. . . and the closet's right there. It's real easy to just pop
open . . . I'm gonna slide it in and be off with my jackets
and stuff like that. But then I got concerned. 'Cause I saw
the back door was open. And it's never open. So I obviously took a step or something or did something at that
point to get to the point where I could see around to the
bedroom. And that's when I saw the stuff on the floor.

WEYLER: Mike, why did you leave the keys in the
door?

BLAGG: I didn't leave my keys in the door.

WEYLER: How did your keys that are still in the door
get there?

BLAGG: I gave 'em to one of the sheriff's officers to
go into the house. When the sheriff showed up, uh, I
was gonna go in with him and he said, "Stop, you
stay out here." And I said, "The door's locked, here's
the keys." And he went in.

WEYLER: Why did you lock the door?

BLAGG: I always lock the door when I come in.

WEYLER: Dead bolt or knob lock?

BLAGG: I think I do both.

WEYLER: When you come in, you always lock those
two? So, when you went out before the sheriff's
deputies . . . did you go back in front, or—

BLAGG: No. I went out the back door. Then she (the
dispatcher) said that the sheriff's getting close. So I
went through the back gate around the side and she
said, "Tell me when you're getting closer to the
front." I told her I was getting closer to the front.

* * *

King asked, "Were these the clothes that you ended up wearing all day? You didn't change when you got home or anything?"

Mike said that he hadn't, and King wanted to know if Mike had a locker at work, where he would change clothes.

Mike replied that he didn't have a locker there, and never changed clothing at work.

Weyler jumped in and said, "What did you wear last night? Tell me about every bit of clothing you had on last night."

Mike replied, "I had on a T-shirt, and I wore a pair of shorts to bed."

Weyler asked, "What color T-shirt did you wear last night?"

Mike answered, "Orange."

Weyler questioned if the T-shirt would be in the dirty-clothes hamper or in the bedroom. Mike replied that it should be in the front bathroom, because that's where he had changed clothing before going to work.

"What kind of shorts?" Weyler asked.

Mike responded, "Blue. Tommy Hilfiger, I think."

"What did you have on before that?"

"Um, what did I wear yesterday? I wore khaki pants and a red shirt. I think I hung 'em up."

Weyler said, "But they'd be soiled. Are there any people at work that would know what you had on yesterday?"

Mike replied that he thought there would be.

Weyler asked, "When you got home that night, did you change from anything before you got into your pajamas?"

"No, I usually go into whatever T-shirt I'm gonna wear. I may put on a different pair of shorts or sweats if it's cold."

"What'd you do last night?"

"I think I just went straight to my shorts last night."

Weyler asked Mike to describe the red shirt that he had

been wearing on the previous day with the khaki pants. Mike said that it was red with maybe some black and khaki colors in it.

Weyler wanted to know when the last time was that Jennifer had done any laundry, and Mike replied that she had done a load the day before.

Weyler said, "I guess what I'm saying is, if you had blood on your clothes, that blood will be there."

Mike replied, "Yes."

King wanted to know what the relationship between Jennifer and Abby was like. Mike said that they were very close and had a loving relationship.

King asked if there were any problems, disciplinewise, between them. Mike answered that both he and Jennifer were decent disciplinarians, and that they tried Dr. Dobson's methods. If Abby did something she wasn't supposed to do, they would take away one of her privileges, like ice cream. If she did something with forethought, like looking around to see if anyone was watching, and then disobeyed, she would get a spanking. Mike said that he did the spanking, but that both he and Jennifer would take away privileges like the denial of ice cream.

King wanted to know what Jennifer's temperament was like. Had Mike ever seen her mad?

He said that yes, she got mad sometimes, but never mad enough to throw anything at him, except for one time that she threw a pillow at him. This had been in South Carolina, when they disagreed about buying a certain house. He wanted one house, and she wanted another one. When he went on and on about the house that he liked, Jennifer got mad and threw the pillow.

King said, "No frying pans? No rolling pins?"

Mike replied, "No, no, no!"

"No dishes?"

Mike answered, "No, more often than not, if we had an

argument, it was typically a good-natured argument, and we could end up talking our way through whatever it was. You know the Golden Rule, don't go to bed angry. So we would talk it out, sometimes late into the night, but we'd talk it out."

King said, "She never pushed you or shoved you?" And Mike replied, "No. I mean she wasn't a saint, like none of us are. She would get angry sometimes, just like all of us get angry. But she was able to contain it and it was never something that got out of control. She was never verbally abusive."

King wanted to know if Jennifer had postpartum depression after giving birth to Abby, and Mike said that she had: "From that standpoint with the pregnancy, Jennifer and I decided to have a baby right before one of my cruises in the navy. So we worked real hard and were successful before a cruise. And it was about a two-month period of time before I had to leave on the cruise. So, for six months, she was at home and I was gone, but she had Marilyn, her mom, and Harold there to help her through pretty much the whole time. She had some months, though, where she had some difficulties with the pregnancy. She wasn't gaining weight as the physician had hoped that she would.

"When she went in for one of those amniocentesis things, they couldn't draw fluid because there wasn't enough fluid in there. Abby kept shifting around every time they put the needle in there. The first time they put the needle in there . . . it came back as a potential Down syndrome baby. So, of course, there were follow-up tests that had to be done. And Abby didn't have any of that.

"But she (Jennifer) still wasn't gaining weight like her pediatrician wanted her to. So the doctor prescribed a vitamin supplement called Ensure. It's just kind of a liquid vitamin Jennifer could buy in a grocery store. It's got a high fat content. It was the only kind of vitamins Jennifer could take that she wouldn't throw up or have complications with. And she took it for about four months during the pregnancy and she gained seventy-something pounds. And Abby was an eight-pound child. You figure double that weight for the placenta and everything—twenty pounds there, and fifty pounds of excess weight, and Jennifer had never been big her whole life. It was devastating for her. We talked a bit about the depression. I forget who we were talking to about that, but she's had a battle with depression, off and on, since then."

King wanted to know if Jennifer had been medicated at any point, fighting the depression, and Mike answered no. Asked if Jennifer had sought psychiatric help in battling the depression, Mike answered no as well, but said that she had seen people about trying to lose weight.

King asked, "Could you tell when she was depressed?"

Mike answered, "Yes, because . . . well, normally she could talk to a wall and make the wall laugh. She's that kind of outgoing person. But when she's depressed, she's quiet and doesn't like to discuss things. She may ask you how your day was, but she doesn't want you to know how her day was. When those things are going on, well, you know when that's going on. We would work to try and work our way out of that depression. Sometimes it was a couple of days . . . sometimes four or five or six days that she would be feeling like that. But it was never . . . never to the point—"

King said, "Ever to the point of talking about suicide?"

"No, no!" Mike replied. "She had a strong enough belief that she knew when it was time for her to go. The Lord was gonna take her and it wasn't gonna be her doing. She never discussed any of those feelings with me. I know you guys are gonna call Marilyn and talk to her about all this kind of stuff, too, but I would bet you almost anything you wanna bet that she never talked to Marilyn about suicide. I would be very surprised if she did."

King wanted to know if Mike ever had suicidal thoughts, and Mike said, "No, too much to live for. I told you, Jennifer is the light of my life here on this earth. And for the past ten years that we've been married, and seeing each other for years before that . . . I have plenty of reason to stick around."

Weyler wanted to know when Mike was in the U.S. Navy. Mike answered that he'd been in from 1985 to 1995. "I was a helicopter pilot," he told him.

Weyler said, "The reason we keep on running out and checking people, trying to get information and things of that sort, is to make sure everything is copacetic. 'Cause there's a lot of other detectives out there working. Can we get you a sandwich or something?"

Mike answered, "My stomach is just turning round and round. I couldn't put anything in it right now."

Weyler asked, "So what year did you meet Jennifer?"

Mike had trouble with this one. He said, "I wanna say '91. No, it was '89 or '90."

Weyler said, "So you married her in what year?"

"1991. November sixteenth."

"And she got pregnant with Abby—"

"Well," Mike said, "we had Abby in '91. No, yeah, no. March 1995. So nine months prior to that Jennifer got pregnant."

Weyler asked, "Was it a surprise pregnancy?"

Mike replied, "Oh no. We planned it."

Weyler was surprised at that. "Planned it? That was kind of bad timing, you know. You going away on your tour and she gets pregnant."

Mike said, "Well, there were a couple of things going on right then. One of the physical problems that Jennifer had is called vulvar vestibulitis. I'm not sure if you're familiar with that. It's sort of an infection of the vestibular glands in the genital area. One way of fixing that problem completely is with a hormone boost beyond hormone boosts. Which happens when you get pregnant. And so we'd been talking about having children for a while before that. So after talking to this doctor that said that's one of the cures, we said okay, this is the time. So we started working on it."

Weyler still was skeptical about the timing. He said, "You were going on a tour for six months, if I remember correctly. You go out to sea for six months—I mean, most people don't plan to get pregnant and then plan on leaving. 'See ya six months later.' I mean, any hardships or difficulties with you guys?"

Mike responded, "No, actually we thought it would work out pretty well. Because I was there for the first couple of months, and then the middle part, I was gonna be away, but I knew that Harold and Marilyn were living only a quarter mile away from us in San Diego. I knew that Jennifer was gonna be well taken care of and I knew this was something that would solve her problem. The problem with the vestibulitis was so bad, she couldn't sit still for any length of time. It was burning and she described it as sitting on hot coals all the time."

Weyler said, "Back then, sex wasn't good, but I assumed she had it, though?"

"Yeah. There was a six-month period she was in a lot of pain."

Weyler asked, "Couldn't have sex at that point?"

Mike answered, "No, but we were creative. We'd do things and—"

Weyler quickly replied, "Well, I'm not gonna get personal." Then he shifted gears and asked, "So you had some concerns about Abby at the time. Was gonna be deformed or might have Down syndrome? Things of that sort?"

Mike began to answer, but then Weyler said, "Let me ask you, does Abby have any mental problems?"

Mike said, "Oh no. She came out perfect. But I was either in Korea or Hong Kong, and I was talking to Jennifer about this, and she just broke down on the phone and started crying and crying and crying. We finally worked around to that was the first amnio that came back with the potential Down's, and she said, 'What am I gonna do?' We talked for a long time about that. I know it's not right to terminate, and there were some other tests that we could do. 'Let's do the other tests and see what happens,' I said. And sure enough, Abby was fine."

Weyler said, "Describe Abby's personality. Strong-willed, compliant child?"

"Oh, strong-willed," Mike immediately replied.

To that, Weyler said, "Oh boy! I've got one of those, too."

Weyler asked Mike to describe this strong-willed aspect. He wanted to know the details of how Abby reacted to situations.

Mike said, "She definitely likes to have things her way. And being an only child, well, we never talked baby talk to her. We talked to her like a person all along. So she's considered herself an adult for quite some time. I mean, she would walk right up to a person in a room and say, 'Hi, my name's Abby, how are you doing?' And we'd say, 'Abby, you can't really do that.' And the next person would come along, and she'd say, 'Hi, my name is Abby, how are you doing?' She would do those kinds of things. She was very active in school. We had her in preschool, starting when she was three. And we had her tested for hyperactivity. There were some signs she might have ADHD.

"She's had inattention for short periods of time, but we're first-time parents, and all the things you would look for in ADHD, we looked for. We said, 'Let's take her in and get her tested.' And we took her to a doctor and the doctor said absolutely no to ADHD. 'She's just a three-year-old.' Well, sure enough, over the next year or so, she settled down quite a bit. Her attention span grew tremendously as she got older. She's making straight As right now in Bookcliff Christian School. She's one of the better students in class. Nevertheless, she likes having things her own way. When you say she can't have ice cream, then she's depressed for the whole rest of the day."

Weyler asked if she was depressed, or throwing a fit. He said a strong-willed child usually would throw a fit.

Mike replied that he and Jennifer never let Abby throw a fit. In fact, when Abby saw some other kid throwing a fit, she would tug on Mike's shirtsleeve and say, "Look at that!"

Weyler wanted to know how they had trained Abby in this regard. Weyler said, "I have a strong-willed child, and I could beat her and not get anywhere. Because strong-willed children, you could tell them a hundred times and they're still going to do things their own way, 'cause they gotta find out for themselves."

Mike said, "Abby's one really big bargaining chip is ice cream. She loves it and you can get her to do almost anything by taking away or giving her ice cream. And that's how we could control Abby's fits and do discipline."

"You don't have to do time-outs? You don't have to do spankings?"

Mike replied, "We did that when she was young before we realized the ice cream trick. Abby will earn herself a spanking about once a quarter, when like I was telling you, we tell her she's not allowed to do something and she'll do those kinds of things anyway. She doesn't see anybody looking and she'll do it and you catch her doing it."

Weyler asked, "How about lying? A strong-willed kid—you'll find their hand in the cookie jar, and they'll be lying, 'No, no, no, I didn't do it.'"

Mike replied, "Yeah, but when we'd do that, we knew the answer, and then we gave her several chances. We'd say, 'Abby, we want the truth. And it's better for you if you'll tell us what the truth is.' And nine times out of ten, that's what it takes, and she'll say, 'Yeah, I had my hand in the cookie jar.'"

Weyler said, "I've experienced this, normally the child will push for the attention of mom or dad, and pick one or the other. And try to interfere, 'cause they want the attention. Did you see that?"

Mike said, "Oh yeah. She would always try and get between us. That was her favorite place. Like when we were walking holding hands, Jennifer and I, well, Abby wouldn't have it holding one hand on the other side, she had to finagle her way in between the two of us. And you know, it got to be kind of cute, really. It was kind of fun to watch her do those kind of things, because we knew that was what she was trying to do. She was just trying to get as much attention as she could."

"Would she get involved and try to play one against the other?" Weyler wanted to know.

"She tried that," Mike answered, "But Jennifer and I have always been really good at not letting that happen. After one or two times, she wouldn't do it anymore."

"Who is the stronger disciplinarian?" Weyler asked. "You or your wife?"

Mike said, "I was the only one that spanked her, but the rest of the discipline was split pretty evenly between us."

"Did you yell a lot? I had to learn a hard lesson as far as figuring that out. It doesn't do any good."

Mike replied, "I think we raised our voices a lot of times early on. But again, you realize that that's not an effective method of doing it."

"Did she exasperate you?"

Mike said, "No, not really exasperate. She certainly

challenged us on many occasions, but never to the point of just throwing our hands up and saying, 'I'm sick of this!'"

Weyler wanted to know if he saw bad times ahead when Abby became a teenager.

Mike answered, "Oh, I had lots of nightmares about what it would be like to be a parent of a teenager, especially a strong-willed teenager. And honestly, I gotta tell ya, I wasn't a stellar teen. And Jennifer has told me she wasn't a stellar teen. So we had those things in the back of our minds, thinking, 'Oh man, what if she's like us?' And I think any parent is going to go through those kinds of fears—"

At that point, King interrupted and said, "I'd like permission to go into your house."

Mike said that was okay, and King added, "What I'd like you to do is have you, from a processing standpoint, be able to look at your clothing with a black light, which shows fibers and those types of things. Do you have any problem with that?"

Mike answered, "No."

To help in setting straight the times at which things had occurred, Mike gave the investigators a written timeline of his activities over the past two days, starting at 5:30 A.M., Monday, November 12.

5:30 to 6:00 A.M. on November 12—He woke up, got dressed, and walked up to Abby's room to close the door. Then he went downstairs and got dressed in the guest bathroom. He took his meds, Celebrex, and vitamins, and left through the front door, placing the American flag in its holder on the front porch.

6:00 to 6:20 A.M.—He drove to work, Broadway to First to Pitkin, then Fifth to Unaweep to 27 Road and AMETEK Dixson.

6:20 to 8:00 A.M.—He prepared for a weekly operations staff meeting.

8:00 to 9:15 A.M.—Operations staff meeting chaired by him.

9:15 to 10:00 A.M.—He prepared for the weekly senior staff meeting.

10:00 A.M. to 12:30 P.M.—He attended a senior staff meeting chaired by Wes Hardin.

12:30 to 1:30 P.M.—He phoned Jennifer and went to lunch at a Burger King.

1:30 to 2:00 P.M.—Hardin talked to him about the need for a "lean manufacturing" course.

2:00 to 3:00 P.M.—He went through his lean manufacturing material training manual.

3:00 to 3:15 P.M.—He phoned home.

3:15 to 4:00 P.M.—He went over a plan to consolidate the North AMETEK plant with a southern facility.

4:00 to 4:30 P.M.—He wrapped up his paperwork and checked his e-mails.

4:30 to 4:50 P.M.—He drove home, reversing his direction of the morning drive.

4:30 to 6:00 P.M.—He played with Abby, helped prepare dinner, ate dinner, talked to Abby about her day at school, and checked on how Jennifer was feeling and how her day went. He finished dinner and cleaned up the plates and silverware.

6:00 to 6:45 P.M.—He helped Abby with her bath and spent time with her reading her schoolbook.

6:45 to 7:00 P.M.—He got Abby ready for bed, read to her a nightly devotional, brushed her teeth, washed her face, and put her to bed.

7:00 to 8:00 P.M.—He talked to Jennifer and asked her how she was feeling. She said a little better than on Sunday. Then he talked about the lean manufacturing meeting at work.

8:00 to 8:15 P.M.—A neighbor from across the street, Helen West, called and talked to Jennifer about setting a lunch date.

8:15 to 9:30 P.M.—While watching the football game, he and Jennifer talked some more about his opportunity at work. He said that she was excited about it, because it would be a teaching opportunity, which he enjoyed.

9:30 to 10:00 P.M.—He took a shower, got ready for bed, put out his clothes for tomorrow's work in the guest bathroom. Took some clonazepam and noted, "It takes about an hour to work on me."

10:00 to 11:00 P.M.—Falling asleep.

Monday/Tuesday—Into November 13

11:00 P.M to 5:30 A.M.—Sleeping.

5:30 to 6:00 A.M.—He woke up, closed the bedroom door, went upstairs, closed Abby's door, came back downstairs, and got dressed in the guest bathroom. Went through his normal routine and put the flag out at 6:00 A.M.

6:00 to 6:20 A.M.—Drove the regular route to work.

6:20 to 7:00 A.M.—He went through e-mails and voice mails. Noted, "nothing unusual."

7:00 A.M.—He called home, but only got the answering machine. "Not unusual," he wrote on the list, "she could have been in the bathroom or eating breakfast."

7:00 to 7:05 A.M.—Finished e-mails and voice mails.

7:30 to 8:00 A.M.—Gave welcome and opening to the GAIN training that was starting that day. There were associates from Florida, Pennsylvania, and Mexico in for training. GAIN was a major computer system that tracked raw materials..

8:00 to 9:00 A.M.—He discussed with Brian McConnell the opportunity for him to become a lean manufacturing engineer after the plant consolidated.

9:00 to 10:00 A.M.—He talked with Linda Gardiner, his manufacturing manager, and Rita Mayhew, his CAT supervisor, about how production in the T2000 pack-up was going on. T2000 was a product line that had been moved to Mexico.

"10 AM ish"—Called Jennifer again, but got the answering machine. (Side notation: "Still not unusual. She may not have been back from helping at school.")

10:30 to 11:30 A.M.—Talked with Brian McConnell and George Mayrose, North plant manager, about the preparations for the North to South move.

11:30 A.M. to 12:15 P.M.—He put together some of the lean manufacturing material, including the books that would be reading prerequisites. He laid out all this material on the table in his office.

"Noon ish"—He called Jennifer again. This time he called on both the home and cell phone. (Side notation: "Now it is starting to get unusual. However, she could have been running errands or Christmas shopping and left her phone in the van. That happened sometimes.")

12:15 to 1:00 P.M.—He had lunch that had been catered for the GAIN training and ate it in the large conference room.

1:00 to 2:30 P.M.—He worked with the team that was packing the T2000 line for shipment to Mexico, including shrink-wrapping some of the workbenches.

2:30 to 3:30 P.M.—He talked with Marty Carroll and Wayne Allen about the transitions and moves that were going on.

3:30 P.M.—He called Jennifer again and got the answering machine. (Side note in margin: "Now I'm worried. Jennifer and I almost never go a whole day without talking.")

3:30 to 4:00 P.M.—He wrapped up at work and went home early.

4:00 to 4:20 P.M.—He drove home.

4:20 to 4:25 P.M.—He got home, checked the mail, and went inside the house, where he saw the back door was open. He called for Jennifer and Abby and got no response. He walked to the master bedroom and saw the bed unmade and blood on the sheets. He also saw debris on the floor—Jennifer's jewelry box and some clothes. He walked around the side of the bed to see if Jennifer was lying on the floor and saw an even bigger pool of blood. He said he got panicky and called 911 from the kitchen phone. The operator calmed him down and they talked about Jennifer and Abby. The dispatcher told him to sit on the back porch, but he said he realized he had not checked Abby's room, so he went back inside and went into her room, where he saw her school clothes were still on the bed. He went to the backyard and said he saw that the gate to the backyard was not latched. It was hard to latch it, he said.

"4:25 ish"—The sheriff's deputies showed up and his pastor, Ray Shirley, showed up at about the same time. He gave his keys to one of the deputies and they went inside the house.

"4:30 ish"—He was put into an ambulance and checked for shock.

Sometime later—Ray Shirley took him to the sheriff's office, where he was taken into an interview room.

At the bottom of the form, Mike wrote, "This is the time line to the best of my ability to recall it. I am not positive of the times and order of the meetings at work, but I believe this is pretty accurate."

Chapter 3

Searching

Sergeant Wayne Weyler was a good man for the present interview with Mike Blagg. He had been in law enforcement for eighteen years and investigated sixty homicide cases, and more than four hundred unattended death cases. Weyler had dealt with thirty kidnappings and reported kidnappings as well. He'd also taught at the Law Enforcement Training Academy of Colorado (LETAC) and the Colorado Institute of Law Enforcement Training (CILET).

Investigator King was equally well-trained in his field. He had been in law enforcement for many years, and had taken refresher courses in crime scene analysis and had often been a witness on the stand in criminal court cases.

On November 14, Sergeant Weyler contacted both St. Mary's Hospital and Community Hospital in the Grand Junction area, and discovered that neither place had Jennifer or Abby Blagg as patients. Officers checked trains, planes, buses, and automobile rental agencies, but came up empty. Family and friends of Jennifer were contacted, and

Investigator Lisa Norcross, of MCSO, spoke with Jennifer's mother, Marilyn Conway. Mrs. Conway told Norcross that she'd been expecting a telephone call from Jennifer around 8:00 P.M. on November 13 concerning Marilyn's ongoing cancer treatment. Marilyn added that it was common for Jennifer to phone her before a cancer treatment so they could pray together.

Investigator Hebenstreit spoke with Diana Shirley, who Mike had said was one of Jennifer's best friends in the area. Diana told him that she'd spoken with Jennifer twice on November 12, but couldn't reach her on November 13. Diana said she'd phoned the first time at 8:45 A.M., but only got the answering machine.

Sergeant R. Rosales interviewed Helen West, a neighbor who lived across the street from the Blaggs. West had spoken with Jennifer at about 8:00 P.M. on November 12, just as Mike had written in his report. Sergeant Weyler interviewed another neighbor, Judy Currie, who said that between 3:00 and 3:30 P.M. on November 13, she saw a maroon/beige minivan driving toward the Blaggs' residence from Greenbelt Drive. Currie had been sitting in her sewing room at the time and had looked out the window. Currie said she didn't see the driver, but she was pretty sure it was the Blaggs' minivan. This seemed odd to the investigators, since the bloodstains in the minivan looked older than just the amount of time between 3:00 P.M. until Mike came home and discovered them. They wondered if the minivan that West saw was actually the Blaggs' minivan.

Several items from the Blagg home were taken into evidence, including the contents from the purse found in the master bedroom, the jewelry box from the floor, and clothing from the master bedroom that had been scattered on the floor. All of these items seemed to be in direct correlation to the possible crime scene, especially the jewelry box and purse.

The people in Grand Junction woke up on the morning of November 14, 2001, with bold headlines across the top of the main newspaper, the *Daily Sentinel,* proclaiming, MOTHER AND CHILD MISSING. Journalist Mike Wiggins reported that a thirty-four-year-old woman and her six-year-old daughter were missing and that there was a pool of blood in their house. No information was given as to the woman's name or the girl's name at that time. The sheriff's department, however, did say, "There have been some circumstances inside the house that lead us to believe they were in danger and may still be in danger."

It was reported that the husband was in shock, but was not being considered a suspect in his wife and daughter's disappearance at the present time. However, the husband was being questioned. Wiggins reported that a whole team of police had cordoned off the home on Pine Terrace Court, and they had walked around the neighborhood with flashlights on the night of November 13, looking for clues and talking to neighbors.

The next day's newspaper, November 15, added only a few more bits of information, with the headline of DISAPPEARANCE A MYSTERY, including a strange phone call that apparently came into the Bookcliff Christian School, on November 13, saying that Abby wouldn't be going to school that day. Janet Prell, spokesperson for the MCSO, told reporters that investigators didn't know who had called the school or for what reason, but did confirm that Abby had been in school on Monday, November 12, but not on November 13. Prell said, "It's a real mystery at this point what happened. The most important thing we can do right now is collect information about the people, their lifestyles, their habits, where they go, to allow a picture to emerge of what happened. Right now there are a lot more questions than answers."

By November 15, who the people were who lived on

Pine Terrace Court was no longer a mystery in the news-papers, and all of the Blagg family members' names had been printed, and a photo of Jennifer and Abby had ap-preared on the front page of the *Daily Sentinel*. Within the article, neighbors spoke of the Blaggs as secluded but friendly. On the rare occasions when neighbors saw the Blaggs, the family was usually all together, taking a walk in the neighborhood. One of these neighbors was Mesa County deputy district attorney (DA) Tammy Eret and she saw the Blaggs so infrequently, she thought their house might be vacant, even though the Blaggs had been renting the home for nearly a year.

Interestingly enough, Eret wasn't the only law enforce-ment official in the fourteen-home subdivision of Pine Ter-race. Marty Currie was a captain with the Grand Junction Police Department. Neighbor Don Opp, who lived two houses away, said the Blaggs kept their shades pulled down, even in the daytime, but were friendly whenever he saw them outside. Of course, like Eret, he had not seen them out on many occasions. They seemed to keep mostly to themselves.

All of it was very baffling. Pine Terrace was consid-ered to be a safe neighborhood with an active neighbor-hood crime watch program and low history of crime. Eret spoke for many others when she said that the disappear-ance had jarred her sense of security.

Tammy Eret recalled waving to Mike Blagg as he re-turned home from work on November 13, at around 4:15 P.M., as she got into her car and went to the gym. When she returned home sometime after 5:00 P.M., she was startled to see all the police cars blocking the street. She said later, "I think I was kind of in shock. All I could think of at the time was, 'I want to get home.'"

Janet Prell released information to the media that Mike Blagg had been very cooperative and was currently staying at the home of a local minister, whose church he and his wife sometimes attended. As a matter of fact, members of the Monument Baptist Church and New Hope Fellowship Church were already helping to search a nearby field for traces of Jennifer and Abby. Flyers with Jennifer's and Abby's photos were placed around the area, and the sheriff's office registered Abby with the National Center for Missing and Exploited Children.

On November 16, an intriguing meeting took place between Investigator Jim Hebenstreit and a woman named Louella Cross. The meeting took place because of information passed from the Grand Junction Police Department to MCSO. Officer LaCount, of the GJPD, told Deputy Mike Dillon, of MCSO, that Louella Cross worked for Colorado Rural Legal Services (CRLS) and she had told him that in early November two individuals matching Jennifer and Abby's description had been at her office. The woman who had come in had been frightened of her husband and said she was tired of domestic violence.

Investigator Hebenstreit visited Cross at her residence and she related to him, "I'm pretty sure it was her (Jennifer), because she said she was from South Carolina." [This, in fact, was the place where Jennifer, Mike, and Abby had lived before coming to Colorado.] "I don't want to say for sure that it was absolutely her."

Hebenstreit asked if the woman had given her name, and Cross said yes, but that she couldn't remember now what it was. Then Cross added, "The woman was very nervous."

Cross said at the time she didn't want to pursue anything with the woman unless she could get legal representation for her. Unfortunately, the office wasn't taking on any new cases at the time because of a shortage of attorneys. Once again, Cross stressed that the woman was from South Carolina, and this stuck in Cross's memory because she had family in South Carolina. Cross described the girl who had accompanied the woman as having short brown hair, and wearing bib overalls. Abby had short blond hair and on occasion wore bib overalls.

Cross stated, "She (the adult) said that she couldn't handle it anymore. She asked if we could help her and I asked her what she needed help on. She said, 'I can't take any more of this abuse!'

"So I asked her if there was domestic violence, and she said yes. She was about to cry and I suggested that she fill out an intake sheet and the attorneys would review it. She asked, 'I can't see an attorney now?'

"I answered, 'The attorneys will review your application and then let you know.' She replied, 'Oh, no, no, no!'"

Cross told Hebenstreit that the woman was "scared to death." Cross added that she had given the woman a paper about divorce and told her that she could get a restraining order the next morning at ten o'clock, but apparently the woman had not done so.

Hebenstreit asked Cross how tall the woman was, and Cross answered, "About five-four or five-five." Asked if the woman was fat or skinny, Cross said that the woman was slender, then added, "Her hair was kind of blond in color. It was a short haircut."

Asked if the woman wore glasses, Cross said that she didn't.

About the little girl, Cross remembered that she wore a blouse with puffy sleeves, which was white with a few stripes in it, along with the bib overalls. The girl didn't say anything, and only nodded her head when Cross asked her questions.

Hebenstreit asked Cross if she'd seen the flyers showing the photos of Jennifer and Abby, and Cross replied, "What flyers?"

At that moment, Louella Cross's husband came into the room and said, "You saw their pictures in the newspaper at your sister's house, and that's what drew your attention to call and mention this."

When shown the flyer of Jennifer and Abby, all Louella could say was, "I'm pretty sure it was her. I'm pretty sure." Then Louella spoke of passing a newspaper rack in Grand Junction and had exclaimed to her husband, "My God, Robert! That girl was in the Colorado Legal Services!"

Later that same day, Cross had looked at a newspaper more closely when visiting her sister's house and commented to Hebenstreit, "I'm not positive at all this is the person. I don't want to get somebody in trouble. I want to make sure that you guys know that. That I kinda feel that's the girl."

Asked if she knew what kind of vehicle the woman drove, Louella answered that she couldn't see the parking lot from her office window. Louella did add, however, that the woman said she lived in the Redlands—the same district that Jennifer lived in. Hebenstreit asked if the woman looked poor, and Cross answered no, she was neatly dressed and wore a little makeup. Cross added, "She was wearing a light-colored blouse." Then Louella related that she wondered why the woman said that she didn't have any money if she lived in the Redlands, which was a nice upper-middle-class part of town.

Cross said that she no longer worked for Colorado Rural Legal Services because she had a new manager who was "breathing down my neck," and telling her that she didn't need to go into such detail with prospective clients. Louella added, "If not for that new manager, I probably would have gotten the woman's name."

The interview was terminated between Hebenstreit and Louella Cross, but the next day she phoned back and said that she had been thinking more about the missing girl. Once again Hebenstreit drove to the Cross residence and showed Louella different photos of Jennifer and Abby

Blagg. As soon as Louella saw the new photo of Abby, she exclaimed, "That's her! That's the little girl!"

As far as the photo of the woman, Louella said that she was 99.9 percent certain that it was the same woman who had been in her office. Asked why she was so sure now, Louella said there was something about her eyes.

Cross added one more thing. "I almost asked the woman if we might be related, because I come from a large family in South Carolina. It was about that time that the secretary, Arlene Lyles, came in and said the attorney wasn't taking on any more domestic violence clients. I almost asked the woman to come home with me, but decided against it because I didn't think my husband would approve."

Meanwhile, on November 17, Sergeant Weyler checked the Blagg telephone records. It seemed strange to Weyler that there were no calls for a ransom demand. That certainly would have been a typical event in a kidnapping case. The *Daily Sentinel* ran an article around the same time headlined, CLUES, CONCERNS MOUNT IN JUNCTION DISAPPEARANCE. Janet Prell, MCSO spokesperson, admitted, "Every bit of information leads to two or three more questions."

Prell said that a special agent of the Denver office of the FBI had traveled to Grand Junction and was looking into the case, and sixteen members of the MCSO were searching for clues into the disappearance of Jennifer and Abby.

The leading headline of November 17, 2001, in large bold letters, stated, JUST LET THEM GO, followed by MAN SEEKS COMMUNITY'S HELP FINDING WIFE, CHILD. There was a large photo of Michael Blagg out in front of the Mesa County Sheriff's Office, surrounded by a bank of television and radio microphones. He was flanked by Harold and Marilyn Conway, Jennifer's stepfather and mother, who had come to the area from Texas.

Mike said, "Anyone who knows anything about my wife

and daughter, I pray that you'll come forward. Please just let them go. Just allow them to come home. My wife and daughter are the most loving people in the world. There's nobody in the world who could have any animosity towards them."

Asked why he hadn't phoned Abby's school to see if they were there, Mike answered that he had no reason to believe that Abby wasn't at school that day.

A *Daily Sentinel* reporter noted that Mike spoke "somberly and calmly throughout the news conference, standing with his hands clasped in front of him. He showed no emotion and answered all the reporters' questions."

By contrast, Marilyn Conway's voice was choked with emotion. She told the crowd, "Look into the face of people in the streets and pray for my daughter and granddaughter's return."

On November 20, Investigator Beverly Jarell interviewed Vona and Gary Murphy, who lived on Pine Terrace Court. The Murphys said that they had been leaving on a vacation to Las Vegas on November 13, around 7:15 A.M., when they spotted a white female between 5'2" and 5'4" walking from Greenbelt Drive to Pine Terrace Court. She wore a coat, a stocking cap, and had an "intense, deranged, cranky, angry look to her face." They said they were 98 to 99 percent sure it was Jennifer Blagg. And yet this sighting was another mystery. The supposition was that blood on the bed would indicate that Jennifer had never gotten out of bed that morning, much less would have been walking around in the neighborhood at 7:15 A.M.

In the Redlands, bloodhounds sniffed items belonging to Jennifer and Abby and then were allowed to try and follow the scent. A bloodhound unit from the Jefferson County Sheriff's Office (JCSO) joined the K-9 unit of the Grand Junction Police Department. Janet Prell told a reporter, "We were fortunate the trainer (of the Jefferson County Sheriff's

Office) was able to come over here and help us. Hopefully, they can give us some kind of track." Investigators with the dogs searched the Colorado River between Blue Heron Trail and the town of Fruita. One promising lead turned out to be a false lead. Blood had been reported to have been discovered on a river trail, but then it was proven that the blood had been there since Sunday, before the disappearance had taken place. So it obviously could not have been related to Jennifer and Abby. Another false lead was also disproved. There had been a contention that someone had phoned Abby's school on Tuesday, November 13, saying that she would not be going to school, but, in fact, this phone call had never taken place.

The entire area around the Blaggs' home was canvassed by investigators going door-to-door and asking about the missing woman and girl. And reporters talked to people who lived in the neighborhood. Helen West told *Denver Post* reporter Nancy Lofholm that she and Jennifer had planned to get together and have coffee sometime after Thanksgiving. Jennifer had told West that she missed South Carolina and her friends there. Then she added that she would bring Abby over on the day after Thanksgiving to play with some of West's relatives.

West said that she hadn't seen Jennifer very often in the neighborhood. Neighbor Leonard Wiedner agreed, and said, "She would mostly keep to herself." Both Wiedner and West saw Mike and Abby more often, because they rode their bikes in the area. Mike had even helped the Wests unload a truck when they first moved into the neighborhood.

Lofholm spoke with Ray Shirley, the Blaggs' pastor at the Monument Baptist Church. He told her, "We have been praying a lot. You can't go on without an answer." Shirley said that Mike would spend Thanksgiving Day at his home, and it would be a low-key affair.

Lofholm also spoke with investigators who were connected to the case of the missing woman and girl, and they had some interesting things to say. They were not ruling out the possibility that Jennifer had killed Abby and then herself. And they seemed to be downplaying the idea of a stranger abduction. Chris Franz, a spokesperson for the MCSO, told Lofholm, "We're not saying it couldn't be a stranger or some psychopath or any number of things, but the chances of that aren't good."

The CBI began doing lab work on the blood and fibers removed from the house. Phone calls flooded into the sheriff's office from local residents with tips about suspicious characters and possible sightings of Jennifer and Abby. And the investigators began a technique known as victimology, in which they gathered all the information they could about the supposed victims' friends, family, coworkers, employers, traits, and habits.

Victimology tries to assess if there was a connection between the victim and the perpetrator. The reason the victim had been at the crime scene, and the reason the perp had been at the crime scene, had to be taken into account. In his book *Urge to Kill,* Martin Edwards wrote, "The victim's past provides crucial data in many cases. If he or she had been prey to the attentions of a stalker, for instance, that will suggest an immediate line of inquiry. It may be that the victim's lifestyle or personal habits are significant."

Also of relevance were the victim's leisure activities and places she was known to frequent, as well as what contacts there were with friends and people around the community. As Edwards pointed out, "It is worth looking at the reactions of close family members to news of the murder, to see whether they yield any telltale signs of guilt." He also stated that too much shouldn't be read into a family member who reacted with an emotionless reaction. Everyone reacted differently to murder. The same could also hold true for "too much emotion." In the case of Jeremy Bumber, convicted of killing five family members and staging the scene, he had appeared to be very upset at the time of the crime, and had tried suggesting that his sister had been responsible.

Katherine Ramsland, Ph.D., added in her book *The Criminal Mind* that "risk factors must be identified as well as any potential relationship with the offenders. Among low-risk victims are those who lead fairly normal lives and are assaulted in daylight or in their homes." Jennifer Blagg certainly fit into the category of a seemingly low-risk victim, and she had been either kidnapped or murdered in her own home.

Mike Blagg spent the morning of November 20 appearing on ABC's *Good Morning America.* He said in part, "Anybody that's watching this—I know you have pictures of Jennifer and Abby. I just pray that if anybody has seen Jennifer or Abby, please, please, Lord, let them call the Mesa County Sheriff's Office."

Mike's sister, Clare Rochester, was also in town, having traveled from Louisiana, and she recalled of that period, "We were at the Holiday Inn on Horizon Drive, and they very graciously gave us a room for the actual taping to take place and a second little area where we could actually watch the interview. I don't remember the technical crew, how many people were there, but I think at least two were there and Marilyn Conway, my mother, myself, and, of course, Michael. There might have been assorted friends that were there, too. There was a rush by myself to get out of that little room where he was, and he cried. I mean, we hugged and there was a tremendous sense of relief because of the huge responsibility. There was so much emotion going into that moment to be able to be on national TV and to be able to carry his message that the girls (Jennifer and Abby) were missing, and to put this national plea forward.

He wanted to do his best to be able to get that message across. And so, afterwards, there was this rush of emotion and wanting, from us, to let him know that we loved him. I thought he did a very good job of doing what he needed to do to be able to find his wife and his daughter. We all hugged. We cried. Mike cried. My mom and I cried. Marilyn was there and she hugged us—it was just a very emotional time."

By now, six detectives of the Grand Junction Police Department and sixteen officers for MCSO were working on the case full-time. They spoke with 180 employees of AMETEK Dixson and members of the Monument Baptist Church and New Hope Fellowship Church.

Janet Prell said that investigators were looking at financial paperwork, personal paperwork, medical records, and other data to build up victim profiles and family profiles. No stone was left unturned in the case of the missing woman and girl.

On November 21, Investigator Steven King spoke with Michael Blagg at the MCSO building on Rice Street in Grand Junction, once again. Mike started by asking if there was any good news in the investigation so far. King replied that the only good news was that they should be getting some lab results back shortly. Then King asked if Abby ever had a safety card, which would assist in identifying her with a photo and fingerprints. Mike answered that she had done that at Learning Adventures Preschool in Simpsonville, South Carolina, but he was unsure where the card was now. He didn't remember if the preschool kept them on file, but he had their address and phone number in a silver address book at his home.

King asked Mike the top three things he loved about Jennifer. Mike answered that the number one thing was

Jennifer's love for the Lord. The second was her love for her family and the way she showed it every day in her smile and the way she talked about them. The third thing was her servant's heart, by which he meant she would do just about anything for anybody to the best of her ability, whether it was an inconvenience to her or not.

King asked what three things he hated most about Jennifer. Mike said he didn't think "hate" was a good word, but the three things he disliked about her were her perfectionist attitude, because he himself was not a perfectionist, and he used cleaning the automobiles as an example. If they weren't spotless, she would remind him. King asked if keeping the house clean was a similar situation, and Mike said it wasn't that big a deal, but that was another such instance.

The second thing he disliked was Jennifer's sometimes biting sense of humor. For instance, she would tease him about his age, but she didn't like it when she was teased about her age. He then added, he really couldn't think about a third thing.

King wondered who was responsible for taking out the trash, and did they have a company that came by to pick it up. Blagg said he thought BFI was the contractor that picked up the trash, and that both he and Jennifer took trash out to the trash can in the garage, but it was he who took the trash from the garage to the curb for pickup. It was Abby's job to take the trash bags out from the bathroom and set them at the back door.

King asked Mike what Jennifer normally wore when she went to Jazzercise or when she went to the park to meditate. Mike answered that she normally wore "black stretchy pants" and a top for Jazzercise. If the weather was warm, she wore shorter "stretchy pants" and just a T-shirt over the top. She went to the park during the day, so she basically just wore whatever she had on for the day, like jeans and a shirt. If it was cold, she wore a jacket.

King reminded Mike that he'd said that Jennifer had suffered for ten months from postpartum depression after Abby was born. King asked if Jennifer had spoken with a doctor about this, and Mike replied that he thought she'd discussed about her weight gain. Mike didn't remember the doctor's name, but was pretty sure it would be on Abby's birth certificate because it was the same doctor who had delivered Abby. Mike answered that he was not aware of Jennifer ever talking to a psychologist about this matter, or any other problem.

King questioned what happened if Mike was at work and Abby intentionally committed a spanking offense. Mike answered that Jennifer would often do noncorporal punishment, such as taking away privileges or treats like ice cream. Sometimes she would also say, "When your father comes home," there would be additional discipline. Asked if Jennifer ever spanked Abby, Mike said that she probably had, but not that he could remember. Mike added that this was the discipline pattern in his family while he was growing up, and his dad had done the spanking.

King queried about the discipline in Jennifer's family while she was growing up, and Mike said that Jennifer came from a family where the parents had divorced, so her mom had to be the disciplinarian. King mentioned that Jennifer seemed to be very close to her mom, and Mike agreed that she was. Asked if Jennifer was close to her dad, Mike said that she had not been close to her dad, and that he had passed away in 1999. Her dad had been a state trooper, and Jennifer attended his funeral, but Mike and Abby had not gone there. Asked how Jennifer had handled her father's death, Mike said that he'd gotten word later that Jennifer had broken down and cried hysterically at the funeral. Her brother had had to help her, and it was a very

emotional time. Jennifer had some problems with her
father, while growing up, and she and her father had never
been able to patch things up to Jennifer's satisfaction.

King told Mike that he'd heard Jennifer's father had a
problem with alcohol, and Mike answered that when Jennifer's parents were married, it was known that Jennifer's
dad liked to drink and "carouse." He was not a state
trooper at that point, and in Mike's words, "he was not
very settled." It was after the children were born, Jennifer
and her brother, David, that he had joined the state patrol
and worked his way up through the ranks. According to
Mike, Jennifer's dad eventually got help with his alco-
holism and became more respectable. After the divorce,
Jennifer's dad had remarried, to a woman named Linda,
and they had led a stable life until his death in his late
fifties.

King wondered if Jennifer had ever shared information
about spousal abuse between her parents that occurred
when she was a child. Mike said that Jennifer had told him
that it was rough. Then King asked Mike if Jennifer had
ever mentioned her dad physically abusing her as a child.
Mike said that Jennifer had told him that her dad would
punish her and David with a belt. Jennifer added that she
tried running away all over the house, but her dad hit her
with the belt as she ran. Mike said that the man he met,
after he and Jennifer had married, seemed to be a changed
person. [Jennifer had told some of her friends in South
Carolina that she had been molested as a child.]

King said that it appeared that Mike didn't like talking
about anything negative concerning Jennifer, but he wondered if Jennifer related anything else about the relationship with her father. Mike answered that Jennifer didn't
think her dad was a very loving person and that he almost
never had hugged her. Her dad had almost never said to
anyone, "I love you," and that she'd considered him a real

redneck. Asked if Jennifer had ever spoken of any inappropriate sexual activities with her father, Mike answered that she had not.

King questioned Mike as to who had potty trained Abby. Mike answered that he had after buying a book on how to train your child in one day. He and Jennifer had both read the book, and decided it was highly unlikely to work, but he'd gone ahead and decided to try the method. Jennifer had decided she would be a detriment to the plan, because she was afraid she'd laugh out loud at the procedure. So she left home to go shopping, and Mike had potty trained Abby. The method utilized a doll that when filled with water could be placed on a doll potty and would pee into the potty. In a very short time, Abby was trying to emulate the doll and was successfully potty trained.

King asked Mike if Jennifer's doctor had suggested anything else besides Ensure for her after Abby was born, and Mike answered no, and that only recently she'd started going to a nutritionist rather than a general practitioner. The nutritionist had provided Jennifer with a book that contained information on carbohydrates and all the other nutrients. Jennifer was to write down all the food she ate each day and record how many minutes she exercised per day. By doing this, she had lost six pounds within the first week. Mike also said that he and Jennifer drank a lot of distilled water, because he'd read somewhere that distilled water helped leach toxins out of the body. They bought a case at a time and it could usually be found on one of the chairs around the kitchen table.

Asked if Jennifer had made friends at Jazzercise, Mike answered that she and the lady who coached the class had become friends and that he would give King the woman's name.

King asked if Jennifer could possibly be a hypochondriac; Mike replied that even though it seemed like Jennifer suffered from a lot of ailments, there was always a diagnosable cause confirmed by a physician. King wondered if Mike knew if she'd ever told any of her friends she had a brain tumor, and Mike said that Jennifer had worried five or six months previously that she might have a brain tumor. She later found out it was a thyroid problem, as diagnosed by Dr. Reichs. Asked what Internet sites Jennifer used to research health problems, Mike answered, "ABOUT-dot-com and WEBMD."

King questioned if Jennifer ever related her health problems with her religious beliefs, as though possibly her health problems were a test of faith, and Mike answered that Jennifer sometimes wondered if the Lord was testing her to see if she would be faithful through sickness. Mike said they had prayed for guidance during those times, but more often than not, they went to a doctor for a diagnosis.

King asked if Mike thought that God tested people, and he said that he and Jennifer believed that the Lord allowed testing in their lives to see where you were going and what you were going to do.

Then King told Mike that he had to consider every possible scenario, and Mike said that he would like to ask a few questions of his own. He thought it might be helpful if he could go back into the house and see if he could find any more of Jennifer or Abby's possessions that were missing. King replied that while this might be an easy way to discover information, the detectives were already checking to see if Jennifer and Abby had left the area, and one of the easiest ways to do this was to try and follow a money trail. King said they would have noticed immediately if a credit card had been used or any activity on her bank account. He related that so far there had been no activity with her bank or any credit cards.

Mike reiterated it would not be like Jennifer to go anywhere without contacting her mother or other family members, even if she had decided to move away with Abby. She would never cause intentional pain to so many people.

King told Mike that it would be the first time in his career as a law enforcement officer that if someone decided to leave secretly, they had not created some kind of money trail. Especially since their story had been on *Good Morning America,* someone, somewhere, would have seen them or would have run one of Jennifer's credit cards.

Mike told King that he would never want to inflict pain and suffering on her family, so that fact, he claimed, didn't make him a plausible suspect. He said, "I'd never be so cruel as to cause such anguish to family and friends." King answered that even though he was getting to know Mike now, he still couldn't check that possibility off the scenario list. Everyone had to be looked at as a suspect.

Mike asked what kind of evidence had been submitted for examination and how it could affect things. King replied that if the blood tests came back and they weren't Jennifer and Abby's blood, that would change things considerably. Mike said that would be a good result, and would mean that "she beat the crap out of the bad guy." Then he quickly added, "If that's the case, though, where are Jennifer and Abby?"

Mike told King that all of the family members had different theories. Jennifer's mom thought that multiple people were involved, and that they had kidnappped Abby. Mike wasn't convinced, because multiple people would have left multiple bits of trace evidence. King said that nothing had been done right for a robbery—there had been too many items of value that weren't touched, and drawers that remained unopened. Mike then asked if this now led to a theory of sexual assault; King answered how that couldn't be ruled out and there were lab tests being done in that regard. In fact, nothing was being ruled out at the present time.

Mike asked if any conversations with John Blagg, his brother, had turned out to be helpful. John worked for the Department of State outside the United States. King answered that John didn't think so, because he didn't even have Mike's current address or phone number. The last time they had seen each other was in San Diego when Abby had been christened. Then Mike asked if they'd looked into any national database to see if there had been similar incidents, and King answered they had an investigator working on that aspect of the case. This, after all, was November 2001—barely two months after the harrowing events of 9/11. No one knew for sure what other terrorist atrocities might be perpetrated or upon whom. That John Blagg worked for the Department of State outside the country made this angle not totally without merit. It seemed somewhat far-fetched, but there was always the possibility that a terrorist could have snatched Jennifer and Abby, and would seek some kind of ransom or hostage exchange.

Mike mentioned that Jennifer had an extraordinary number of shoes and that it would be difficult for him to know if any were missing, unless they were shoes he saw regularly, like workout shoes, a plain pair of white canvas shoes, or a pair of Birkenstock sandals. Then Mike asked what evidence had been ruined in their search, and King told him a mattress and bedding would need to be replaced.

King asked why there were fans running in both Abby's room and the master bedroom on November 13 during such cool weather. Mike explained that the running fans created "white noise," which blocked out any traffic sounds in the neighborhood. It was Abby's job to turn off her fan and humidifier every morning when she got up, and the fact that they were still running seemed to indicate that whatever happened had happened before Abby ever got out of bed. This was usually at 6:30 A.M. on a school day.

* * *

The headline for the *Daily Sentinel* of November 21 was SHERIFF—BLAGG CASE BAFFLING. The *Sentinel* compared the case to a jigsaw puzzle where "what the investigators hold in their hands are square edges with round holes. Nothing fits."

MCSO sheriff Riecke Claussen told reporter Mike Wiggins, "I've been with the department for thirty years and have worked a lot of these cases myself. I can say it's certainly one of the most difficult or baffling cases I've seen."

Claussen added that it was still hard to determine if the case was a kidnapping/burglary/robbery/assault/homicide case, or some combination. Then he admitted that the baffling part was that they didn't have more information than they already had. Claussen said, "Everybody, including the pathologist and CBI, is out there saying, 'What does this mean?'"

On November 23, with so much information coming in, and so much that still needed to be kept under wraps, Deputy DA Andrew Peters asked that the search warrant for the Blagg home remain sealed to keep the contents from being disclosed by the press. This was granted by Judge Massaro with an addendum: "This motion and the warrant affidavit shall remain sealed for thirty days, except by order of the court."

A very curious phone call came into the MCSO the next day on November 24 from a woman named Katelin Bricker. She spoke with Deputy Hicks and said that she'd received a phone call at home at around 12:15 P.M. When she answered her phone, the incoming call registered as "anonymous" on her caller ID box. The person on the other end of the line was crying and had a young female voice. The person said, "I'm Abby Blagg and I need help."

Bricker asked the girl where she was calling from and

the girl answered, "Mexico." Bricker asked her where in Mexico, but the girl said she didn't know. Then the girl said, "I need my mom."

Bricker asked, "Is your mom there?"

The girl answered, "No."

"What's your mom's name?" Bricker asked.

The girl answered, "Jennifer." Then she said, "I gotta go," and hung up.

Bricker told Deputy Hicks she believed the call was real and not just someone trying to trick her by disguising her voice.

Investigator Glade Johnson followed up this lead and spoke personally with Katelin Bricker. Johnson asked if this call could have been a hoax, perpetrated on Bricker by one of her friends. Bricker said she thought the call was real, and didn't think any of her friends would do such a thing. Just who the anonymous caller was has never been ascertained.

Sergeant Weyler spoke with Mike Blagg again, on November 26, and Mike asked him about the DNA results at the lab. Weyler told him they hadn't come back yet, and Mike reiterated that he hoped the blood that had been found in the house belonged to someone besides Jennifer and Abby.

Weyler told Mike that they were looking for other items in the house that would contain Jennifer and Abby's DNA. Mike mentioned Jennifer's retainer box that held the retainer she used on her teeth every night. The retainer had not been found in the house, and he supposed she still had it in her mouth when she was abducted/hurt/killed. The retainer box might hold some of her DNA, though, Mike said.

Weyler noted, "The absence of the retainer indicates that

Jennifer was harmed or incapacitated before getting out of bed."

Mike suggested that Weyler take Jennifer's makeup kit, lipstick, sheets, and clothing for possible DNA; Weyler replied, "You know a lot about DNA."

Mike admitted that he did and that he had a degree in nuclear engineering from Georgia Tech.

On November 27, MCSO staff officer G. Clifton contacted the Blaggs' telephone company, Qwest Communications, and spoke to a representative of their security unit. The rep told Clifton it would be possible to get records of long-distance and toll calls, but not local incoming calls. Those would not show up on records.

The newspapers kept a running commentary on the investigators' activities, noting that search and rescue teams continued to scan the Colorado River for signs of bodies. Officer Chris Franz said, "These folks know the eddies and the deep spots. They know the river."

One investigator, searching along the river, found a black plastic bag taped up, but it contained no body or evidence that led to the Blaggs. He noted that on cool, cloudy days, it was harder to look into the depths of the river, and also that the cold would make a body take longer to rise to the surface. Franz noted, "The dynamics of the water changes from day to day. If we're not out there (every day), we may miss something."

The river wasn't the only place being searched. Sixteen members of the Mesa County Sheriff's Posse mounted horses and scanned the area from Connected Lakes to the Redlands Parkway. Horses and dogs were useful tools in the rugged areas around Redlands, but Chris Franz admitted, "[The bloodhounds] followed up on a lead, but it dropped off pretty quickly. In fact, the dogs had led the handlers toward the Colorado River, but the Blaggs had been in that area before." The fact that Mike, Jennifer, and

Abby had taken walks all over the neighborhood didn't help matters.

On November 28, Investigator Steven King had another interview with Mike Blagg at the Mesa County Sheriff's Office. After exchanging pleasantries, King asked him, "What haven't you told me about Jennifer?"

Mike said that she was a good mom and had battled off and on with depression over the years. Then he asked, "What kind of stuff do you need to know about Jennifer?"

King said, "I need to know the dark side, if there is a dark side." He told Mike that so far he'd painted a pretty rosy picture about their marriage, but that wasn't what he necessarily needed to know.

Mike said, "All right, I'll tell you about the embarrassing side of our relationship. For someone like me, it's going to be difficult, and I don't see how it has anything to do with what's going on. But I suppose it's not for me to make that decision.

"You know about Jennifer's health, and you've talked to enough doctors to know by now her vestibulitis and the problems it caused her sexually—that intercourse is difficult and painful for her. And so, because Jennifer is very outgoing, loving, serving-type person, she wanted to ensure we had, as it's listed biblically, a good sex life. The Bible says that you become one flesh and you do not withhold your body from your mate, except for time of prayer. She takes that very seriously, and I do, too. I think it's important for us to have a good sex life. But when intercourse is painful and difficult, not all the time, but a good portion of the time, you have to get creative and do other things.

"What she liked to do was oral. When we got married, neither one of us had any experience in that, and the first four years of our marriage—until the health problems came out—we didn't experiment with any of that, the different kinds of things. But when the vestibulitis appeared and it became increasingly difficult for her to make love, we had to start getting creative on how we did that. So she wanted to learn more about different things that we could do. As a result, we turned on the Internet. We went to various adult sites on the Internet to get some techniques and ideas, and that is how she learned various things to keep us sexually active.

"It's certainly not something I'm proud of, that we turned to that area, but to the best of my knowledge, the last six to eight months, we have not had to go there for any additional learning. We've worked things out and things are good. There is not a problem there anymore, but it is certainly embarrassing to talk about. If she knew I was talking about this, she would be mortified beyond belief. But you wanted to know everything, so that's one of the not-so-pretty things. Again, I don't see how this really pertains to this, but you need to know, I suppose."

In fact, it's not certain that this was what Steven King was looking for. He said that what he wanted to know was "the more human, the less flattering things that will let me get a better perspective of who Jennifer Blagg is. Until I know Jennifer, I will not be able to find Abby."

Mike then told King that Jennifer had an issue when they first got married—something he said she called her "rage." What this concerned was Jennifer's mom's systemic lupus, and while growing up, her mom had to be on prednisone. This made Marilyn have significant mood swings, according to Mike. "As Jennifer grew up, that was the sort of behavior she grew up with, some fairly drastic mood swings. During the first part of our marriage, Jennifer would exhibit these same emotional outbursts that she called her 'rage.' I could be fifteen minutes late coming home from work, and she'd scream at me. Thirty minutes later, she'd be okay."

Mike made a point of saying, "We made a habit of not letting the sun go down on our anger. In other words, not going to bed mad. We made an effort to talk about our problems before going to bed at night. Quite often, whether it was an hour or two hours, we'd work many problems out by talking before going to bed. And we were very big about sending notes back and forth about what was going on and our feelings toward each other."

King asked Mike where he had met his wife, and he said he'd met her while he was in the navy across from Coronado Island at an amphibious vehicle landing area where his company was having a beach party for friends and family. At first they were in San Diego, and then Mike was sent to Corpus Christi, Texas, as a flight instructor for the navy. At the time, Jennifer went to Arlington, Texas, to start planning for their wedding. After the wedding, they lived in Corpus Christi, then San Diego again, then headed to Phoenix, Arizona, and Simpsonville, South Carolina, before moving to Grand Junction.

On his second navy stint in San Diego, Mike's job was to launch and recover aircraft from the carrier *Kitty Hawk*. It was around this time, he said, he and Jennifer discussed his leaving the navy for the private sector. Mike said he spoke to a navy detailer for a couple of years about careers in the private sector versus the navy. Mike agreed he had a promising career in the navy, and enjoyed his job, but he and Jennifer were also talking about starting a family, and they weren't getting any younger. So he said he and Jennifer prayed for guidance.

The cruise on the *Kitty Hawk* took Mike away from Jennifer for a six-month period of time. The next job up the line for him would have been as helicopter squadron leader, which would have meant even more time away from Jennifer. It was at that point that he and Jennifer agreed that God wanted them to start a family, and they began trying to conceive a child. Mike said that he thought Jennifer got pregnant on their first try. While he was out on a six-month deployment, he found out that Jennifer was indeed pregnant. By the time he got home, Jennifer was six and a half months into her pregnancy. He was up for department head, but it would mean that he would have a five-year tour, with six months away from home each year. Mike said he could not, with good conscience, be away from a newborn child for that long. It was at that point that he and Jennifer made a mutual decision for him to leave the navy. He talked with the naval detailer again and was given an interview with Allied Signal.

Mike got a job with Allied Signal in the Phoenix area of Arizona, and it was connected to the aerospace industry. For the next two years, he was a quality engineer for Allied Signal.

After those two years, the company transferred him to Greer, South Carolina, at another Allied Signal complex as a continuous improvement engineer. He and his family lived in South Carolina until he got a job with AMETEK Dixson in Grand Junction. Both he and Jennifer liked the South Carolina area, but Mike did not get along with his boss there, and there were also rumors that the plant might shut down.

At that point, King and Mike began talking about the crime scene. Mike commented that he thought the blood was probably Jennifer's. King asked him why he thought that, and Mike replied that it was only logical. King asked him what the logic was, and Mike said that because Jennifer was gone for so long now without contacting anyone, the blood was probably hers. Then he added that he was willing to explore anything, and that his real desire was that it was some third party's blood, but he theorized if

Jennifer had hurt an intruder badly, how did that person then get Jennifer and Abby out of the house?

King asked Mike to return to talking about what Jennifer had called her "rage." Mike told him that Jennifer could fly off the handle and into a tantrum for the smallest of reasons. It was never a situation where she would be physically abusive, although one time, he said, she had thrown a pillow at him. Rather, he said she would yell at him and then stomp off in anger. Then, according to Mike, ten or fifteen minutes later, she would calm down and they would talk about what had triggered the rage in the first place. He said that Jennifer was not happy about this aspect of herself and wanted to change. These "rages" did not fit into her biblical understanding of how a wife and mother should act.

According to Mike, Jennifer thought it was caused by some kind of chemical imbalance, and Mike added that often these rages would occur three days after her menstrual cycle. So he felt it might be a PMS-induced rage. He said that Jennifer had tried various herbal medications to combat this problem, but these had not really helped much.

Mike said that it wasn't until Jennifer's hysterectomy that the whole situation changed, and these rages suddenly ceased. Mike added that he could tell the difference between October 5, 2000, and October 4, 2000, the date she had her operation. It was that sudden a shift, according to Mike, and she was a lot more emotionally stable, in his opinion, after the operation.

King asked Mike if Jennifer had ever directed any of her anger toward Abby. Mike said that she could get mad at Abby, but never as angry as she got at him during these episodes. Then he added that because of his work schedule, he may have missed some anger episodes between Jennifer and Abby during the daytime. King asked Mike if he was ever afraid of leaving Jennifer alone with Abby, and he answered no. King brought up about the "dark side," as Mike had put it, and was an allusion to the fact that Jennifer might have killed Abby and then herself.

King wanted to know if Mike spent time with Abby so that Jennifer could have a period of time away from their daughter. Mike agreed there were many times that Jennifer would go to the movies by herself, or say, "I'm going to the mall. . . . You've got Abby." It was her way of saying that she needed time away from Abby. Mike also said that he and Abby would often have a father/daughter playtime on the weekends so Jennifer could be alone for a while. At those times, Jennifer would stay home and do her Bible study by herself, while Mike and Abby spent time together. Asked how long these periods might last, Mike answered they were two or three hours, either on a Saturday or Sunday afternoon. Mike also said that he liked these father/daughter times together.

King asked Mike what the last thing was that he and Jennifer talked about on Monday night, November 12. Mike answered that they had been talking about his work and the lean manufacturing system project, that he was fairly excited about it, and at that time he was in the bedroom working on his laptop computer as a football game was on television in the background. Jennifer told him that she knew he would like teaching on the project, and he agreed.

King questioned Mike about a disagreement he and Jennifer had about a recruiter calling him at work, and Mike said he'd gotten a phone call from a recruiter about a job on the eastern slope of the Rockies, some days before the disappearance. Mike said he wasn't interested in the job, but he did listen to what the recruiter had to say, and mentioned this phone call to Jennifer. When he got home, according to Mike, she was angry because he had talked with a recruiter on a work phone. She thought he had put their livelihood at risk by talking on the work phone rather than at home. She was also angry that he had talked with a recruiter before talking about it with her first and before they could both pray about it together. They talked about it some more, he said, and then he apologized for upsetting her. He went on to say that the next day he had typed her a letter telling her that he was sorry, and that he hadn't intended to cause this situation. Mike said he wanted to get the situation resolved before the weekend, because he really cherished their time together then, and he didn't want a cloud hanging over the entire weekend.

King questioned Mike if there was a possibility that AMETEK Dixson would send the Blagg family to Mexico, and if that had caused any problems. Mike said that there had been some discussion about that with his supervisor, Wes Hardin, that he could be promoted to vice president in charge of production, in Reynosa, Mexico. That would entail him spending a lot of time at the Reynosa plant, however, and there had been an ongoing problem at the time with the manager of the Reynosa plant. Once that manager had been replaced, the Mexico idea had been tabled.

King asked Mike if Jennifer had a passport; he replied that she did. Then King wondered if Abby had a passport, and Mike said no. King questioned if Jennifer had ever been to Mexico, and Mike answered that she had when he was in the military. They had taken a trip to Mazatlan on the Pacific Coast of Mexico for a vacation, and he also thought she had gone across the border to Tijuana to shop, when they lived in San Diego even before they were married.

King questioned if while going down to Mexico on the AMETEK Dixson project, he'd had any particular problems. Mike said no, there hadn't been any particular problems about work or anything else connected with that. There had been no one who had given him any problems or acted strangely around him.

King wanted to know, on a scale of one to ten—one being the worst and ten the best—how did Mike rate himself as a husband and father. Mike said he would rate himself as an eight on both scores. Then as an employee he rated himself as an eight.

King asked Mike how long he had been married to his ex-wife, Gerri; Mike replied it was eleven months. They had done a summary dissolution of marriage in California, and the dissolution had been possible under California law because they had not been married for a full year.

King wondered if Mike thought that God talked to him, and Mike answered yes, but it wasn't necessarily in words, but rather in experiences that taught a lesson. Mike then gave an example about how he believed he came to get his job at AMETEK Dixson. It wasn't until after he and Jennifer had prayed, that they believed that coming to Grand Junction was the right thing to do. Mike went on to say, "So does God speak to me audibly? No. He speaks to me in other ways."

King asked Mike what God had said to him lately, and Mike replied, "Be patient—but I'm finding this hard to do. I want to know where Jennifer and Abby are, what has happened to them and why they're not in the house with me right now. As a result, I'm not being obedient. I'm being more rebellious in my prayer life with Him right now. Art (Blankenship) and Ray (Mike's pastors) are very good at grounding me. Yesterday I talked with Art for a long time about feeling like I'm not going to see Jennifer and Abby ever again. I've been told there still is a possibility we'll find Jennifer and Abby, and they'll be okay. But as time goes on, I'm feeling that I've heard their voices on earth for the last time.

"Yesterday was a very hard day for me. So Art prayed

with me and has been strong in helping recenter me each
time we talk and get to spend time together. I'm feeling a
little more encouraged today because of it, but I am not
dedicating the prayer time that I should be dedicating at
this particular moment to the Lord. Basically because I'm
mad. I want Jennifer and Abby to be here. I want them just
to be here. I don't want it to drag on. I know you're telling
me that these things take time, but that's not what I want to
happen."

King asked what he meant by "not talking to Him."
Mike responded, "I think I'm mad at Him and I just don't
understand it. If there had been some weirdo following us
around, and things like that, then I would have some form
of understanding. But right now, I'm mad and I'm confused and I don't understand, because it's my Jennifer and
Abby and there's no one I can think of that would cause
anybody to do anything to them. And I'm mad about that.
Maybe it's taken me two weeks to get to the point where
I'm mad about it. I know it's not your fault and not your
burden."

King said he didn't know what to say in reference to
that. Mike replied that Art had told him the Lord was in
control and the Lord is providing for Jennifer and Abby.
"These are things I know intellectually, but emotionally
I'm having a hard time with that. Jennifer used to always
say to me, 'Whenever we go through a trial and questions
would come up about trusting in the Lord, or being mad at
a problem . . .' Well, like when Jennifer's grandmother died
and we asked why she'd be taken from us—Jennifer would
say, 'His way is not our way.' There is a lesson to be
learned in everything the Lord provides for us. You can
learn that lesson easily or you can learn that lesson with
great difficulty. If the Lord is trying to get you to learn
something, He is going to continue to turn up the heat to
the point where you learn it.

"Art said that same type of thing to me over the last few days. But he said, 'You know Mike, the Lord is going to turn this to good. There is going to be some good that comes of this.'

"Maybe because I'm too close to it right now, or maybe because of whatever, I don't see the good that's leaping out at me. So I'm frustrated and yesterday I was so depressed. I'm tired of the roller-coaster ride. I'm tired of the whole thing. I want to find them. I want to know where they are. I want to know who did this to them, what they did to them and why."

King asked Mike if he pondered the fact that he might never have an answer to those questions and Mike answered, "Yes, I've thought about it, and I don't like that possibility at all. That's all part of the 'what-ifs.' I believe what Marilyn (Conway) told me, that this is a solvable case. Well, if it is a solvable case—those kinds of questions are going to be answered. We should be able to find that stuff out, right?"

King answered, "Yes."

Mike replied, "Good. Because I have a lot of hope in that. We'll solve this and find out where they are. It may not be solved to my satisfaction. My satisfaction is that Jennifer and Abby come home unharmed. I am realistic enough to understand that may not be the case. My daughter and wife are Christian. If the Lord has taken them home, they're in Heaven right now and I can take solace in that fact. But that's not my first choice. My first choice is that they come home to me."

King said, "So, Michael, you know that we're not gonna tell you anything about the blood, right?"

Mike answered, "No. I didn't know that. What I really don't want to have happen is for us to find stuff out through the media."

King said that they would not be telling the media. It was too sensitive an issue.

Mike then asked King if the back door to his home had been forced open and that he had a follow-up question. King asked what the follow-up question was, and Mike responded there had been a hanging alarm card system on the back door, and he didn't remember hearing it when he came into the house, nor did he remember seeing it hanging on the door. He wanted to know if the audible alarm system was still there, and if it had been, why it didn't go off. King said he couldn't talk about whether there was a forced entry or not, but he would look into whether the alarm was still there, and if it was functional.

It turned out that during the search of the Blagg home, a computer was seized with the permission of Mike Blagg, and Investigator Mike Piechota, of the MCSO, and Detective Julie Stogsdill, of the GJPD, searched the computer's hard drive and temporary files. They found numerous images of an adult-pornography nature in the deleted temporary files. Investigator Piechota discovered more than a thousand pornography images, and 250 adult-pornography references. Pornographic images and content were also found on Mike Blagg's laptop computer and on his work computer.

Also, on Mike's work computer at AMETEK Dixson, there was an e-mail written to Jennifer on November 13, 2001, at 3:58 P.M. It had not been sent. It stated: "Jennifer, I love you! I am sorry we have ruined this day and opportunity to spend our lunchtime together. I don't know what went wrong."

The e-mail went on to say he wanted to spend time with her and also get some Christmas shopping done. "That obviously went horribly astray. The Lord tells me not to let the sun go down on my anger, and so I won't."

The rest of the e-mail stated that she was the light of his life, and that he asked her for forgiveness. He said he did not want to waste a future weekend being angry with one another—he wanted to spend some time for them to talk things out. Mike made reference to Paul in Ephesians 4:26-27: "Do not let the sun go down on your anger and do not make room for the devil."

Mike added to this, "I am sorry if I have given the devil a foothold." Just what the problem was, was not addressed in the e-mail.

Mike was allowed back into his home on Thursday, November 29, after more than two weeks. By that point, the investigators had collected all the items they deemed necessary and Janet Prell told reporters, "We've finished processing the house and so there's not need for us to maintain custody of the house." As to Mike's plans, Prell added, "I imagine it would be a difficult place to reside in, but I don't know what his plans are."

Due to a spate of sexual assaults in the county, the MCSO scaled back the Blagg investigative task force from sixteen to nine. Prell said, "We have an obligation to all victims of crime. While the Blagg case is important, and we're concerned about Jennifer and Abby, it's a continual balance of the needs of all the cases."

One person who was with Mike when he returned home to the residence on Pine Terrace Court was his sister, Clare Rochester. She recalled, "Around that time, Marilyn Conway and Michael and I had been staying at a bed-and-breakfast, and we made hundreds, maybe thousands, of little pins for Abby and Jennifer. And once the house was turned back over to Michael, I wanted to be helpful. We knew that he was not going to want to bring the girls (Jennifer and Abby) back to that house, figuring that it would be a very traumatic thing, so the house needed to be packed up in order for him to be able to move. Recognizing that the most emotional thing that was going to happen in that house would be to pack Abby's room and the master bedroom, I volunteered to do that. And so my mom and Marilyn stayed at the bed-and-breakfast and my brother and I went over to the house, and that was my job.

"One of the things I noticed was that they kept the house extremely organized. It was a very neat house. And so, thinking to myself that Jennifer was going to come back and she was going to be getting those boxes and she was going to want to know where her things were, where Abby's things were, I was very careful in the way I packed the boxes to make sure that everything was very neatly organized as items were put into the boxes. Things in her bathroom, which was in the master bedroom, everything from there would be together and it would be very carefully labeled on the box as to what it was, so that she would be able to get it and know exactly where the things were and she'd be able to pull them out.

"I packed the master bedroom closet. I packed up the nightstands and everything from in there. I packed up everything that was in the dresser as you enter the room. I packed up the entire master bath, everything that was under the bed, and a lot of stuff from the closet. In Abby's room, I didn't move any furniture, other than to look under it, and I left all the furniture, but I packed up all of the other items. The same thing in the guest bedroom upstairs, and two closets that were on the landing at the top of the stairs.

"I went into the under-the-stairs closet, really looking to see if there was anything loose in there that needed to be packed up and primarily everything under there was already boxed up.

"Later in the day, my mom and Marilyn joined us. They worked in the kitchen while I worked in the master bedroom. I didn't find any kind of jewelry of silver or gold. The dresser just had very neatly folded clothes. In the bathroom of the master bedroom, there was shampoo and creme rinse, but the shaving things were in the bathroom off the kitchen."

One item of interest that Clare discovered was an emergency planning book, and it had a friend of Mike's name on it—Homer Frasure. The emergency planning book dealt with things such as how Jennifer and Abby should be taken care of, if something suddenly happened to Mike. Mike later told reporter Nancy Lofholm that he had started this emergency planning book after the terrorist attacks of September 11 because he routinely traveled by plane for his managerial job. He carefully had included in the book such things as information about their insurance, bank accounts, savings plans, and a list of numbers of people to call. On the cover of the book, he had written, "I love you Jennifer. This should be all the information you need in case of a disaster."

Besides the emergency planning book, Clare discovered an ornate jewelry box under the master bedroom bed. Clare recalled, "There were pearls in the jewelry box, and they were my main focus of interest because they were so beautiful. I wasn't sure where all those pearls were acquired, but if I'm not mistaken, they were Mikimoto pearls, which were like the nicest and very expensive strands of pearls. He got those while he was in the navy. He had been in places like Hong Kong, the Philippines, and ports like that."

Lofholm interviewed Mike and Marilyn, Jennifer's mom, one morning in Grand Junction as they both had breakfast. Mike told Lofholm of the last night that both Jennifer and Abby were in their house. Abby had been singing to herself before going to bed that evening. Her voice had drifted down the stairs to where he and Jennifer were watching television.

Mike said, "We miss them desperately. We beg for a miracle every day. The truth is we've had a miracle having them in our lives. And we beg for a miracle to bring the two of them back."

Marilyn was teary-eyed as she spoke to Lofholm. "Tuesday will be a month. It's hard to keep open the idea that Jennifer and Abby are okay somewhere and just not able to get home to us yet."

Yet both Mike and Marilyn still spoke of Jennifer and Abby in the present tense, and they were not giving up hope. And as they spoke about Jennifer and Abby, they spoke of their qualities as if they were still among the living. Marilyn said that Jennifer was her own worst critic and would sometimes be down on herself. Yet she always seemed to rebound and was very outgoing. Marilyn even joked about one of Jennifer's quirks—she would only eat whole potato chips from a bag.

As for Abby, Mike and Marilym said that she liked to collect rocks and jewelry. She loved sweets, especially cookies-and-cream ice cream. She was terrible about keeping secrets and always liked to be in the middle of things.

Mike recalled fondly an incident where Abby wanted to have a formal dinner at home. So she put on a dress and had Mike put on a coat and tie. The whole family ate by candlelight that evening.

On December 7, 2001, an anonymous phone call came into the MCSO that was a blockbuster. The female caller said that Mike Blagg had been visiting a local escort service in Grand Junction. Detective Kevin Imbriaco was able to identify who the caller was—twenty-seven-year-old Julie House, who lived in the Grand Junction area. Detective Imbriaco interviewed Julie and she told him that she'd seen Mike Blagg on TV and believed he was someone who had visited her escort service several times. The person who looked like Blagg had said his name was Steve or Steven. When shown two photo lineups, the first being without Mike Blagg in it, she picked no one out of the lineup. When she looked at the second photo lineup, with Mike's photo in it, she immediately picked out a photo of Mike Blagg.

Julie said that Mike had visited the escort service several times between December 2000 and April 2001. He generally came in two or three times a month, she said. He would usually come in between 11:00 A.M. and 2:00 P.M., wearing business attire. He'd ask for a topless massage and then ask the girls to give him a "hand job." Julie said she saw him twice, and possibly four other girls saw him during that time period. It was her opinion that this man was shopping around for a girl who would do "illegal things" for him. She said she only gave him a topless massage, and had not done the other things that he was asking for.

Julie declared that she'd seen him once at her residence, and once at a Motel 6. He usually gave her $60 for a session. She remembered he said he had a daughter with an old-fashioned name. Something with a *Y* in it, or an *IE*. One of the last times he came in, he was upset with his wife over a shoe box she'd found in the closet. The shoe box had either receipts or letters in it. She wondered if the letters might have been from a woman who was not his wife.

This information from Julie House, and all the pornographic Web sites that had been discovered on Mike's computers, made the investigators look at Mike in a whole new light.

Chapter 4

Stealing

Because of some of the inconsistencies in Mike Blagg's statements, and the things that Louella Cross and Julie House had said, Captain Bill Gardner, of MCSO, and Sergeant Wayne Weyler contacted retired FBI agent Ron Walker. Walker had been the special agent in charge of the FBI Denver office from 1989 until 2000. He'd also been supervisor of the Evidence Response Team and supervisor of the Violent Crimes/Fugitive Task Force. Walker had a Master of Arts in counseling and psychology, and had spent thousands of hours in profiling violent criminals. With this knowledge, he'd often been on the stand in court cases around the world.

In the not too distant past, Agent Walker had been asked by Boulder, Colorado, detective commander John Eller to come in on the murder of University of Colorado student Susannah Chase. She had been beaten to death, and there seemed to be a sexual context to the murder. Eller wondered if the killer had been responsible for the sexual attacks on other women in the area, and had advanced to murder in the case concerning Chase.

Eller asked Walker to develop a psychological profile of the attacker who had beaten twenty-three-year-old Chase and left her in a pool of blood not far from her residence. She had died of head injuries the day after being discovered. Another FBI profiler, Gregg McCrary, who knew of Walker's background and experience, said that he was good at what he did, and explained, "We're probably about eighty to eighty-five percent accurate with our profiles. It begins with victimology and we put the victim in a continuum of risk, from low to moderate to high. We're tying to find out what, if anything, elevated that victim's risk of being the victim of a violent crime. If there are patterns in the attacks, that's something a profiler can help determine."

McCrary added that profilers looked for signature aspects in the crimes, and in the case with Chase and the others, it could be of a sexual nature. This didn't necessarily have to do with the genital area alone—it could be the victim's breasts, buttocks, or anything else the perpetrator sexualized. And in the case of a personalized attack, the perp often used his hands as the weapon. McCrary added one more thing that may have been an aspect in the possible murder of Jennifer Blagg. He said, "Typically, there's some situational stress in the lives of the perpetrator or something that triggers it." Whether Mike Blagg had situational stress was something that Agent Ron Walker intended to find out.

By 2001, Walker was employed as senior analyst for Threat Assessment Group, Inc. and Park Dietz & Associates, Inc., as a criminologist in the Personality Research Project and special agent in charge of the National Center for the Analysis of Violent Crime at the FBI Academy in Quantico, Virginia.

To some degree, most profilers used a kind of matrix

to develop certain basic information about who, what, when, where, how, and why of the crime:

Who—Was the victim a man, woman, child, certain ethnicity, or have a certain religious background?

What—What was the cause of death or circumstances of a kidnapping? Was there anything unusual about it?

When—What time of day, time of month, time of year, did the crime occur? Was there anything special about that date?

Where—Where did the crime occur? Outside, inside, in a particular room or area?

How—How was the crime committed? Was there anything unusual about the method?

Why—Did the crime appear to be sexual in nature? Was it profit-motivated, spontaneously planned and executed, out of anger or passion?

Roughly speaking, profilers would put the criminal into an organized or disorganized category. Organized criminals would personalize the victim, control the crime scene, move the body, remove the weapon, and leave little evidence. A disorganized criminal would act spontaneously, depersonalize the victim, create a chaotic crime scene, leave the body, leave the weapon, and often leave other evidence.

The crime scene at the Blagg residence suggested a more organized crime scene than not, with no body in evidence, no weapon, and very little evidence left around as to why there was a pool of blood near the master bedroom bed. This suggested an organized criminal who was probably highly intelligent, might have gone to college, had social and sexual competence, lived with a partner, and had suffered harsh discipline as a child. The criminal could also be charming, had variable moods, and was geographically and occupationally mobile and followed media coverage about the crime.

Captain Gardner gave Walker a brief outline of the Blagg case, including a description of the crime scene and statements of witnesses. In addition, Walker watched and read some of the media reports about the Blagg case, including the news conference at which Michael Blagg had spoken. After watching this, Walker said, "I saw red flags waving around Mr. Blagg."

Walker told Gardner and Weyler that based upon his training and experience, law enforcement detectives should focus a lot of their attention on Michael Blagg. Walker added that he was 99 percent certain that the case was not a random kidnapping/murder. He based part of his analysis on the fact that crime scene cleanup and removal of a body took time, and random killers did not usually operate in that manner. Then Walker rhetorically asked who would be comfortable being in the house for a prolonged period of time cleaning up the crime scene. His answer was, of course, Michael Blagg.

Secondly, Walker pointed out that burglars and rapists do not move or transport bodies from a house, since their perception of risk rises with the time it takes to remove a body. The neighborhood in general was a relatively crime-free area, and the crimes that had been perpetrated were usually property crimes, not violent crimes. When violent crimes happened in "safe neighborhoods," the victims usually had been targeted beforehand, often by spouses.

Walker said a question usually arises about the victims as to "Why here, why now?" He said that Jennifer and Abby were low-risk victims, and low-risk victims are generally targeted victims, and prone to "personalized attack." Walker added, "Upper-middle-class victims killed in their

own home bedrooms equate to an intimate partner killer."
The Blagg case, he said, "is the result of intertwined intimate relationships." In cases like this, "the intimate partner has almost always done the killing."

Walker was asked if the case could possibly be a professional hit. He answered that a professional would "at least
want Jennifer's body found, possibly with a ransom note.
The hired killer would not want both bodies missing."

Walker then detailed what the crime scene had to tell
them. He said that the blood found in the most intimate
room in the home, the master bedroom, on the victim's
side of the bed, was not coincidence. That crime took a lot
of time to commit and cover up. Whoever had done the
crime had a big comfort level in the home. The pooling of
blood and lack of high-velocity blood spatter suggested
that the victim had been asleep when she was killed, and
there were no signs of a struggle. The scene also spoke of
the execution taking place while Jennifer was asleep, with
the bedcovers drawn up to her neck. Walker suggested that
a pillow had been placed over Jennifer's head and either
her throat had been slit, or she had been shot at close range
by a gun. The blood flow was not consistent with blunt-
force trauma, and one of the pillows was missing. It may
have been the pillow used to cover Jennifer's face.

Walker concluded that the crime was not a spontaneous
event, but rather planned and meticulously executed. He
said, "The crime scene is staged, and it's the classic case
of ineffectual staging." He said that noncriminals did not
know what a burglary scene looked like, and the jewelry
box/emptied purse contents were a classic staged scenario.
Walker added that an actual burglar, turned killer, would
have canvassed the entire home. There were plenty of valuable things left untouched in the Blagg home.

Foremost, Walker stated that the body removal most
likely meant that Michael Blagg had committed the

murder, and not someone else. Body removal took time, and the bodies had to be "bagged." By this point, Walker concluded that Abby was also killed, and she may have been killed before Jennifer. He said the blood evidence in the van indicated incidental transfer that the killer did not spot. The water droplets in the foyer he suggested were the remnants of the killer's attempt to clean up blood that had dripped there. Walker said that if the blood in the bed turned out to be Jennifer's, then Abby probably had been killed elsewhere and possibly in a different manner.

In early December, members of the New Hope Fellowship Church searched for traces of Jennifer and Abby along the river front trail of the Colorado River. Nothing new of importance was found. The pastor of the church put out a statement: "The church family and many Christians continue to pray for the safe return of Jennifer and Abby. We serve a God of restoration and healing and we will not grow faint in our prayers on behalf of the entire Blagg family."

The pastor noted that Mike would soon have his computer back, and that church members could e-mail their prayers to him. The pastor reassured his flock that God knew where Jennifer and Abby were, and that nothing was impossible for Him. The pastor did not say that they were alive, rather that only God knew that as well.

On December 14 Investigator King and Sergeant Rusty Callow went to the MCSO Impound Lot to determine how much fuel it would take to fill the gas tank of the Blaggs' Ford minivan's gas tank. Investigator King started the minivan and gave Callow the odometer reading, which was 8,619.5, prior to driving the minivan to a gas station on North First Street and Grand Avenue. Sergeant Callow followed behind the minivan, and when they reached the sta-

tion, King said that the odometer reading was now 8,619.8.
Sergeant Rusty Callow filled the gas tank of the Blaggs'
minivan and the pump reading showed that it took seven
gallons to fill the tank. King meanwhile looked at the
minivan's onboard computer, and noted that it was getting 17.9 miles to the gallon. Sergeant Callow concluded
that the minivan had traveled 125 miles since the last time
it had been filled.

King told Sergeant Callow that he was able to determine
that Jennifer Blagg fueled the van on November 9, 2001.
This was derived from a statement Michael Blagg had
made, and corroborated by a credit card statement. Mike
Blagg's statements also pointed out what destinations the
minivan had been to between the fill-up on November 9
and the time he reported Jennifer and Abby missing on
November 13. King checked the distance of all the known
destinations and gave the information to Sergeant Callow.
Callow noted that the known trips would have amounted
to thirty-four miles—so ninety-one miles were unaccounted for. A round trip of the unaccounted miles would
be 45.5 miles out and 45.5 miles back.

In December, Sergeant Callow spoke with FBI special
agent Gerard Downes, who was the supervising agent of
the FBI's Critical Incident Response Group, which was af-
filiated with the National Center for the Analysis of Violent Crime. In fact, Downes recently had helped in another
Grand Junction murder case. He helped investigators for-
mulate a plan of action against Robert Spangler, who was
believed to have murdered his entire first family, and then
murdered his third wife by pushing her over the edge of
the Grand Canyon. Downes was able to profile Spangler
in such a manner that it gave the investigators a good idea
of how to make him confess to his crimes. Downes was so
perceptive, that Spangler did eventually confess to the

murders in an interview room at the Mesa County Sheriff's Office in October 2000.

The conversation with Downes in the Blagg case was conducted from the MCSO conference room, and included Callow, Grand Junction FBI special agent Ron Baker, Lieutenant Richard Dillon, of the MCSO, and Captain Bill Gardner. After the conference was over, Downes said that the crime was highly suspicious and most of the detectives' efforts needed to be concentrated on Michael Blagg. He was in agreement with Agent Ron Walker: the one person who would have been most comfortable in a murder and cleanup effort in the Blagg home would have been Mike Blagg.

It wasn't until December 10, 2001, that several items of blood analyzed by the CBI for DNA were proven consistent with DNA from Jennifer Blagg. Also, a latent fingerprint on the jewelry box was positive to a fingerprint from Michael Blagg. Assorted contents from the purse matched fingerprints to Michael Blagg. No blood anywhere was found to match that of Abby Blagg.

Around Christmas, Mike placed wrapped presents underneath his Christmas tree. The presents included a set of gold earrings for Jennifer and a Barbie nightgown for Abby. He set the presents out as if they were still coming home, and would eventually unwrap them. Mike spoke of how excited Abby was about opening Christmas presents.

During this period, Mike handed out hundreds of homemade cardboard and ribbon pins that read, "Hope—Jennifer and Abby." When he went out around town, he generally wore one of these pins on his shirt. The members of his church were still loyal to him, and they held prayer sessions together. Mike told a reporter, "I know that Jennifer and Abby are totally in the hands of God." It was also around this time that he told the investigators, "All I need to know from you is that you guys don't think I'm a suspect and that you've moved on to other things. At that point, I'm cool."

By January 2002, Mike Blagg did some very curious things. Right after he moved to a new town house on North Club Court, he went to a local chain store and bought some expensive stereo equipment, a large-screen television, and a new computer. He was able to buy these things because he had just received a large insurance settlement concerning the supposedly stolen jewelry items that Jennifer had once owned.

One day in January, two AMETEK Dixson employees became suspicious of Mike when they saw a company pickup truck backed into a space between the loading dock and the Dumpster. They thought the man at the wheel was Mike, but weren't sure, because it was fairly dark out. These two contacted the plant manager, Wes Hardin, and they all went inside the plant. By then, they noticed that the pickup truck was gone from the area. Once inside the facility, they saw that a new paper shredder, which had been in the shipping and receiving area, was now missing, and a workbench had been moved on a dolly to a spot near the loading dock.

Hardin marked the underside of the workbench so that it could be identified if it was taken. By the next morning, the workbench was indeed missing. Trying to find out who the thief was, the two employees circled around the plant area in vans, and one of them noticed a suspicious-looking car that was parked near the plant. They would have been amazed to know that the car was actually an unmarked police car, and the man inside was a police officer who was conducting a surveillance on Mike Blagg. He was just as suspicious of them, as they were of him.

This officer was one of four from the Grand Junction Police Department keeping tabs on Mike Blagg. Like the employees, they, too, had witnessed Mike's suspicious activity around the AMETEK Dixson plant. After it was closed for the day, they had watched as Mike drove a company pickup to the plant and hauled some kind of furniture from the plant to his town house. Then he had returned the company pickup and left in his own car, which he had parked in a space between other vehicles on the edge of the parking lot.

An officer, on stakeout near Mike's town house, noticed that Mike discarded a cardboard box into a construction Dumpster near the town house. When the officer checked, he discovered that the cardboard box had contained a new paper shredder, and it had a delivery address to AMETEK Dixson.

On January 21, Hardin told police that there had been a yard sale at AMETEK Dixson recently, and Mike had been in charge of it. There was a desk at the yard sale that was not supposed to be sold, and a Not for Sale sign had been placed on it. An employee, however, saw Mike replace the sign with one of his own that read, "Sold—MB." Soon after, Mike borrowed a pickup truck, drove to AMETEK Dixson after the yard sale, and took the desk to his own residence.

By now, investigators had installed a video camera near Mike's new residence on North Club Court, and a videotape showed Mike taking the desk into his residence. Hardin said that none of the missing items were supposed to be in Mike's possession.

Two search warrants were asked for and granted, on February 5, 2002, to search Mike's new residence for the allegedly stolen items at his apartment on North Club Court, Grand Junction. Deputy Scott Ehlers, Investigator Glade Johnson, and crime scene technician Mike Piechota executed the search warrant on North Club Court to look for stolen property from AMETEK Dixson. Mike's residence was a single-story dwelling, and as the officers entered the foyer, they could see the general layout. Before starting the search, they activated a video camera and also took still photos of the residence.

Johnson wrote later, "Among the items listed in the search warrant that we were looking for were a computer desk, a paper shredder, a workbench, a small white table, and proof of occupancy." They did find a computer desk in the living room and beside it was a paper shredder. They found a workbench in the garage. Ehlers told Johnson that the computer desk should have the serial numbers A11NFYS written in red ink on the underside. When they turned the desk over, those numbers were there.

Johnson videotaped the entire residence, showing in what shape they left the dwelling. Then Scott Ehlers left a copy of the search warrant inside the residence and locked the doors. The search and seizure had taken about three hours. Johnson transported the seized items down to the MCSO Alternative Storage building, where they were unloaded and placed into storage by evidence custodian Gordon Smith.

That same evening, Mike was asked to come down to the Mesa County Sheriff's Office for an interview and polygraph test, and he complied. FBI agent Bill Irwin was there when the polygraph test was administered to Mike, and the questions concerned the disappearance of Jennifer and Abby. Before becoming an FBI agent, Irwin had been a police officer in Sherman, Texas, for five years, and Denison, Texas, for three years. He'd conducted interviews nearly his entire law enforcement career, and estimated that by 2001, these had numbered into the thousands. He had also conducted numerous polygraph tests.

The interview started off in a very general way, and the topic got around to how Mike was feeling, and was he taking any medication. Mike admitted that he was having trouble sleeping and he was taking Klonopin for a sleep disorder and Celebrex for arthritis. Mike added that he was not currently seeing a mental-health specialist, but that he had done so in Simpsonville, South Carolina, on issues concerning his marriage to Jennifer. He also said that he had a Bachelor of Science degree from Georgia Tech University and that he'd been a helicopter pilot and officer in the navy.

Mike was administered the polygraph test, and the results indicated that he was either being evasive or lying. After the test was over, since some indicators pointed to the fact that Mike had failed the test, Irwin point-blank told Mike that he thought he was lying, and that he had killed both Jennifer and Abby.

Agent Irwin recalled later, "There was a determination to confront Mr. Blagg. I went back into the room and I told him that he knew where his wife and his daughter were and that he could take us to them. And then I began talking to him about reasons why he should do that. I told him that this was his opportunity to have some control in what happened from here on out. The investigation was going forward and there wasn't a whole lot that he could provide, but there was some information that we needed and one was the location of their bodies. I described the investigation as being like a jigsaw puzzle. And I said that the jigsaw puzzle had been dumped out on the table. When you looked at it at first, you couldn't tell what it was. You couldn't tell what the picture was. But the investigators have slowly and methodically been putting the pieces of this puzzle together and that a picture was now getting very, very clear. And the picture was that Michael Blagg had killed his wife and daughter. There were only a few pieces missing. And those pieces were the locations of where Jennifer and Abby Blagg were."

Mike vehemently denied that he had harmed Jennifer and Abby, but one thing was for certain now, he had gone there in the hopes of clearing his name once and for all. Instead, now more than ever, he looked like the main suspect in the disappearance of his wife and daughter.

What followed was an interview that became a marathon event, lasting more than ten hours. The interviewers included FBI agent Bill Irwin, Investigator George Barley, Investigator Steven King, and Sergeant Wayne Weyler. The interview, over time, changed gears from the stolen goods at AMETEK Dixson to the crime scene at the Blagg residence, and then back again to the stolen goods. During the interview, Mike continually denied having anything to do with Jennifer and Abby's disappearance. He kept saying that he thought the act was a robbery gone bad or perpetrated by some people who wanted children, and had taken Abby. The investigators initially made very little headway on anything concerning Jennifer and Abby. All questions and allegations that Mike had a part in their disappearance were met with stout denials.

Agent Irwin asked Mike about the evening before Jennifer and Abby disappeared. Mike said that it had been a usual dinner, and afterward he worked on a laptop computer he'd brought home from work. He and Jennifer watched a little bit of the Monday-night football game on TV, until Jennifer received a phone call from a neighbor at around 8:30 P.M. The phone call was about a lunch date for the next day.

Mike said that Jennifer was still ill from a sinus headache and allergy symptoms that she had been suffering from since Sunday. According to him, she had been so sick on the previous Sunday that she had not gone to church. Her lunch date with the woman had been originally scheduled for Monday, but since she hadn't felt good that day, they decided to go to lunch on Tuesday.

Asked when he got up on Tuesday, Mike said that he had awakened at 5:30 A.M. This was counter to an employee seeing him at AMETEK Dixson at around 5:40 A.M. He could hardly have awakened at 5:30, and been at work by 5:40 A.M.

Irwin asked about a fight that Mike and Jennifer had sometime on the previous Friday. Mike initially denied that he and Jennifer had a fight, but then hedged on this and said that it might have been a minor occurrence on the Friday in question. He did not call it a fight, but rather a disagreement. As time went on, he said he recollected that their disagreement had occurred because he'd been looking at Web sites at different real estate locations. The locations included Chicago, Illinois, Dallas, Texas, and Longmont, Colorado. Jennifer became upset about this last one because a recruiter from Longmont had spoken with Mike about a job there, and Jennifer did not want to move to Longmont.

Agent Irwin zeroed in on this so-called recruiter, and Mike could not remember his name or even what company he worked for. As they spoke about this issue, Mike's story changed once again, and he said the argument between himself and Jennifer had not occurred on Friday night, but rather at noon on Friday, November 9. He had gone home for lunch and the argument had ensued at that time.

Moving back to the stolen items from AMETEK Dixson, the detectives wanted to know why he had taken them. Mike denied stealing anything, and said that he thought the items were going to be sold by the company in a yard sale. When he was confronted with testimony that people had seen him stealing the items, Mike finally admitted that he had stolen the paper shredder and office furniture, only to recant this later and state that he hadn't stolen them, and it was all a mistake.

The interview now turned to the fact that the detectives had found more than eighteen hundred items of pornography on his personal and work computers. Mike denied for a short while that he had been viewing that much pornography. However, the investigators were able to prove to him that he had been viewing a large amount of porn, and, in fact, they said that on the night of November 12, 2001, he had been looking at photographs of oral sex on his home computer in the upstairs computer room—the room that adjoined Abby's bedroom. This scenario opened up new and even darker aspects of what might have happened that night of November 12. There were suspicions that Jennifer had been incensed that Mike had viewed porn so close to Abby's room. Having spoken about molestation in her own childhood, this was bound to be a very sore point with Jennifer.

Mike vehemently denied that he had been looking at Internet porn on the night of November 12, and that this had sparked his murderous rage when Jennifer confronted him about it and led to him killing her. In fact, he denied using his home computer at any time on November 12, but rather said that he'd only used the laptop he brought home from work to do things related to AMETEK Dixson.

After a while, Mike admitted that the crime scene in the master bedroom looked staged, but he denied having actually staged it. When shown a photograph of his side of the bed, he denied that he hadn't slept in it on the night of November 12 to 13. Mike insisted that he closed and locked all doors before going to work each day, but he could not explain why the alarm on the back door was not functioning properly on November 13.

Mike acknowledged that he'd had an impressive naval career and had been somewhat disappointed by his civilian jobs since leaving the navy. He conceded that he'd given up a lot for Jennifer by leaving the navy.

Once again, the subject moved back to porn on his computers. Mike didn't think he'd spent a great deal of time looking at porn on the computers, but he acknowledged that Jennifer might have thought that he did. Then he added that because Jennifer had such a painful medical condition in her genital area, it made normal sex painful for her, and they had both gone on the computer looking for alternative sexual situations that they could perform.

Irwin asked Mike if they would find his semen underneath the computer in the upstairs computer room, and Mike answered yes. Then Irwin pressed Mike about how many times Jennifer actually looked at the computer with him, and he finally came up with a number of about a dozen times. Mike said on those occasions they would look at the act being performed on the computer screen and then they would do that act. According to Mike, this included him ejaculating on her face.

Agent Irwin asked Mike when was the last time that he and Jennifer had sex, and Mike said it was on the weekend before she disappeared—in other words, the weekend of November 10 and 11. Pressed about how often he looked at the Internet porn without her present, Mike acknowledged it was a lot more times without her than with her. He finally admitted that he might have an addiction to Internet porn. Irwin and the other investigators kept asking if this was a problem with Jennifer, and Mike first said that it wasn't, but then his story changed and he said that one time she caught him alone looking at pornography and she had become very upset. He said this had occurred four or five months before she disappeared. According to Mike, "She felt betrayed by me doing this, because if I was going to do it, she wanted us to do it together." Irwin asked if she felt like she was being cheated on, and Mike agreed that might be a possibility.

Sergeant Weyler and Investigator Barley confronted

Mike by saying that Jennifer probably didn't like him viewing photos of men ejaculating on women's faces at all. They said, knowing the type of woman Jennifer was, she probably did not look upon those kinds of activities with pleasure. Mike, however, declared that they would view that kind of activity and he would perform it on her, and that she didn't mind. In fact, he said, she was a willing participant. At one point, he even said that she enjoyed it when he ejaculated on her face. Mike declared, "Strangely enough, she did like it. She would perform oral sex and would do this for me. I didn't have to ask her. It was her idea, basically."

Asked when they would do this kind of activity, Mike answered it was usually between 8:00 and 10:00 P.M. The investigators wondered why that wasn't a problem, since Abby's room was right next door to the computer room. Mike insisted that it wasn't a problem, because Abby was always asleep, and they closed the door.

He did admit that they had argued about him going on the computer on Friday night, November 9, not about the move to Longmont, as he had suggested before, but about porn. However, not long after he admitted to this, he would change his story once again, and say that the argument of November 9 had nothing to do with porn. Then, once again, Mike claimed that Jennifer enjoyed looking at photos of men ejaculating on the faces of women as much as he did.

Mike said they tried to have some form of sex every weekend. He did admit that they had different sex drives, which was why he viewed porn on the Internet more often than she did. He even had made collages of photos depicting women performing oral sex—and these collages were on two different computers. Whether Jennifer had seen these collages, he didn't say.

Mike also claimed that Jennifer had never had any worries about him having sexual contact with Abby, nor had she ever talked to him about divorce, though he admitted they had discussed the need to separate when they had lived in Phoenix, Arizona.

Mike admitted that Jennifer might have gone recently to a legal aid place in Grand Junction, because a friend of hers named Stacy was thinking about divorce. He claimed, however, that his marriage to Jennifer was a good one prior to her disappearance and he didn't think that Abby had any perception that he and Jennifer fought. He insisted that Jennifer would not have gone to a legal aid place to seek a divorce from him. Once again, he claimed that their marriage had been a strong one, and there was no talk of divorce on her part.

The investigators keyed in on why Mike had bought so many new electronic items after he had received money from a settlement on an insurance claim dealing with Jennifer's "stolen" jewelry. He said that he had bought a new computer because the police had seized his old one, and that he bought stereo equipment and a big-screen television from Circuit City to help him deal with the stress of the present situation.

Of the very lengthy interview, Agent Irwin said later, "A great deal of what happened was extemely repetitive. I spent about four hours saying the same things over and over again. I did most of the talking during that time frame."

Over and over was indeed how things went as Mike denied harming either Jennifer or Abby, or knowing where their bodies were at the current time. The investigators kept insisting that he tell the truth, and they wanted to know if he believed in the statement "The truth will set you free." Mike declared that "only God knows the truth." By now, ten hours had elapsed since the interview had begun. Mike's eyes began to fill with tears and his lower lip began to quiver.

Weyler said, "Tell us what happened to Jennifer and Abby."

Mike responded, "I can't." And then once again he denied any knowledge of where they or their bodies might be found. He reiterated that he loved them both, though he admitted that he was afraid of going to jail.

As Agent Irwin remembered this part of the interview, "Investigators Barley and Weyler were encouraging him to tell the truth about what happened. This was very late in the interrogation. Mr. Blagg had his head on Investigator Weyler's shoulder and appeared to be crying. Investigator Weyler was encouraging him to tell the truth, and Michael was saying, 'I can't. I can't tell the truth.'"

At that point, Mike asked about different scenarios and what might happen to him if he said certain things. He vehemently denied having sex with Abby or even thinking about it. He posited that one reason this might have come up is that Jennifer claimed to have been sexually molested as a child, and had bottled that anger up ever since. As far as certain physical evidence went, Mike said that both he and Jennifer used the minivan, so his DNA would probably be there, as well as hers.

Going over what scenarios might occur, if he spoke about certain things relating to Jennifer and Abby, Mike said that he knew the difference between pre-meditated murder and heat of passion. He asked to pray for several minutes, which he did, and then said that if he told the truth, he wanted to have a lawyer present to advise him "what telling the truth will mean." Since he asked to talk to a lawyer, the interview was finally over after more than ten hours of questioning.

Just before he left, Mike was asked about his mental state, and if he had thoughts of suicide. He answered that he wouldn't harm himself or commit suicide.

* * *

The next day, February 6, 2002, at around 10:00 A.M., Scott Ehlers and Investigator Barley and technician Piechota went by Mike's residence on North Club Court to retrieve some of the stolen property that was still there. When they got to the North Club Court residence, they knocked on the door several times and announced their presence, but no one came to the door. Talking to the undercover surveillance crew, who had the residence staked out, they learned that Michael Blagg had not left the residence.

At around that point, Sergeant Rosales phoned Ehlers and asked if they'd made contact with Mike. Ehlers said that they hadn't, and Rosales told him to stay in the area and that he was coming over to the residence. Rosales also said he was going to contact the Grand Junction Police Department, and he was going to conduct a "welfare check." By a welfare check, he meant a check to see if Mike was all right and had not harmed himself.

At around 10:45 A.M., Ehlers contacted Jeannie Kloberdanz, who worked for the property management company from which Mike was renting. Kloberdanz brought a key along with her so the officers could enter Mike's residence, and at 11:00 A.M., Ehlers used the key on the front door, and he and Officer D. Oswalt, Sergeant Rosales, and Investigators Art Smith and Dave Rowe entered the residence. Once inside, Sergeant Rosales yelled out several times, "Michael, this is the Mesa County Sheriff's Office!" He got no response.

Once inside the place, they all smelled a strong odor that had not been in the residence the day before. Rosales and Ehlers cleared the living room and kitchen, and Rosales headed down the hallway. As he did, Ehlers noticed what looked to be blood on the floor. Investigator Smith moved into the master bedroom and then the master bedroom's bathroom. As soon as he did, he saw Mike lying naked in a tub of bloody water, and his wrists were slashed. A photo of Jennifer and Abby lay on the edge of the tub, along with a Bible. Smith immediately asked for a rescue squad.

Ehlers came into the bathroom and noted all the bloody water in the tub, and that Mike was not coherent. Since Smith and Rosales were already in there talking to Mike, Ehlers exited and tried to track down the strange odor. He traced it to the garage and determined that it was the smell from an exhaust pipe. Ehlers surmised that this may have been Mike's initial attempt at suicide.

Far away in Texas, Officer Lisa Norcross had met with Jennifer's mother, Marilyn Conway, to discuss the interrogation that had been going on with Mike in Grand Junction. Conway agreed that she would phone Mike on the morning of February 6 and allow the conversation to be recorded. Around 7:00 A.M., she phoned Mike's residence three times, but only got his message machine. She never did talk to him directly, and had no idea that he might be planning to commit suicide.

The first newspaper article to reveal that Mike Blagg might be something other than a grieving husband and father came out in the *Grand Junction Daily Sentinel* on February 6, 2002. The headline stated, BLAGG QUESTIONED IN THEFTS. Janet Prell, the MCSO spokesperson, addressed questions about whether the thefts had anything to do with Jennifer and Abby. She told a reporter, "He (Mike) is someone we have been looking at very closely in connection with Jennifer and Abby's disappearance. I would say this activity (the thefts) certainly raised additional red flags concerning Mr. Blagg's involvement in the disappearance of his wife and daughter."

The newspaper account went on to detail Mike's ten-hour interview at MCSO and that he had been under surveillance for a long period of time before that meeting. The story about the thefts was nothing compared to February 7's *Daily Sentinel* edition: BLAGG ATTEMPTS SUICIDE AT HOME. It reported that only hours after being questioned at MCSO for ten hours, Mike had gone home and slashed his wrists while in the bathtub. He had to be rushed to St. Mary's Hospital in an ambulance. The article added that he was conscious and breathing on his own while placed on a gurney for the ride to the hospital. A police spokesperson said that Mike was in "critical condition on Wednesday night."

The next day, it was reported that Mike had left a suicide note in his residence. The note stated, "God love you all! I have tried to do the right thing throughout my life. I have made many mistakes along the way, and I am sorry for any of those mistakes that have harmed any of you out there now."

It went on to say that the sheriff's office was going to say many things about him in the coming weeks, and that he wasn't perfect, but neither was he a murderer. He said that he loved his wife and daughter and that he planned to see them in Heaven someday. Mike declared that the investigators now made him believe that Jennifer and Abby were dead, and that he couldn't live without them. There was a postscript at the end: "My Lord of Hope and Peace is now my Lord of Comfort."

Around this same time, a short statement written by the pastor of the New Hope Fellowship Church about Mike's suicide attempt appeared. In part, it read, "Please pray with us that Satan will not be allowed to take his life, but that he will be saved and that God's will WILL be done. Pray that we will love as Christ loved, and that we will not grow faint in our commitment to do what Christ would have us do."

It went on to ask that people not rush to judgment about Mike's guilt, but rather be "guilty" of loving unconditionally. Even from this horrible situation, the pastor held out hope that something good would come of it all.

By February 8, 2002, Mike was upgraded from critical to serious condition. Janet Prell stated, however, "Our focus is on Jennifer and Abby. They are the victims in this situation. While we are concerned for Mr. Blagg's welfare, this is not distracting the investigation's goal of finding Jennifer and Abby."

Then she added rather darkly that the investigation had suspicions about Mike's involvement in Jennifer and Abby's disappearance, and that further investigations were ongoing by MCSO and other agencies.

On February 12, it was reported that Mike was "saddened" by his suicide attempt. Art Blankenship, Mike's pastor at the New Hope Fellowship Church, told a reporter, "He's saddened by all these developments. He feels like he did the wrong thing in regards to this suicide attempt." And Blankenship added that when he visited Mike, his eyes were glazed over and he was deeply depressed.

Many of Mike's fellow church members were still supportive of him and believed in his innocence. Even some who knew Mike, far outside the area, still believed in him. A reporter spoke with a friend of Mike's from Simpsonville, South Carolina, named Lydia. She said, "The Mike I knew wouldn't have stolen anything. My husband and I love and care for Mike and still have faith in him and his innocence." She chalked up his suicide attempt to allegations from the police that he might somehow be involved in Jennifer and Abby's disappearance.

A friend of Mike's named Spence, who lived in Arizona and who had known him from his navy days, said, "I think stress and distress can make people do weird things, but I don't think he had anything to do with Jennifer and Abby's disappearance."

One person who had grown more skeptical about Mike's innocence was Jennifer's mom, Marilyn Conway. At one time, she had told a reporter, "Michael is as much a son to me as Jennifer is a daughter." Now, when asked about these latest developments, she answered, "I just don't think I have anything to say."

Mike was released from the hospital after a few days and allowed to go back home. He was joined by his mom from Georgia and sister from Louisiana.

Clare Rochester remembered of this whole chaotic period, "I arranged for my transportation within a forty-eight-hour period from when I heard about Michael. I don't like my mother to travel alone, so it wasn't as quick as jumping on an airplane and going straight there. I went to meet her in Atlanta, even though I live in Louisiana, and then we flew up there (to Colorado) together.

"We were stunned that the allegations had been made against my brother. We were aware there were receipts for the furniture (that was supposedly stolen from AMETEK Dixson), and so my mother and I had a conversation on the way back from the hospital about these receipts and where they would be if they were in the house. And when we got back to the apartment from the hospital, we looked for them and my mother walked into the bathroom. I followed her, and in that bathroom there was a little waste basket and the receipts were in the waste basket.

"I kept my mother out of that bathroom, while all the blood was there, and I cleaned the bathroom and the carpet and through the master bedroom and the utility room into the garage of all the blood drops."

The very next day, after he was released from the hospital, Mike retained the services of Grand Junction defense attorney Stephan Schweissing, who told investigators that if they wanted to talk to Mike, they had to go through him first. Clare Rochester recalled, "We took the receipts to Stephan Schweissing and asked him to be sure they were delivered to the sheriff's department so that they would know."

* * *

On February 21, 2002, Special Agent Jeffrey Newton, of the FBI, spoke with Edith "Edie" Melson in Simpsonville, South Carolina. Melson told Newton that she had met the Blaggs in 1998 and became friends with Jennifer, though not with Michael. Melson originally had met Jennifer at the First Baptist Church of Simpsonville, and they quickly became friends.

While the Blaggs lived in Simpsonville, she and Jennifer got together at least three times a week, and spoke with each other on the telephone practically every day. Much of their activities were church related, and they met regularly at church on Sunday morning, and Wednesday evening and Thursday mornings for Women's Bible Studies.

Melson described Jennifer as a pretty woman who suffered from self-esteem problems. Melson also said that Jennifer had confessed to her and various members of the church that she had been sexually molested by an older male relative when she was twelve years old. Even though these memories bothered her greatly, she felt compelled to be a sexual abuse survivor advocate to others who she could help. For that reason, she spoke up about being abused as a child. Melson said that Jennifer also had struggled with anorexia for most of her adult life.

Melson recalled that over the last few years Jennifer had suffered with various health problems, including gallbladder surgery as well as endometriosis, which eventually led to a hysterectomy. On top of these, Jennifer began to have thyroid problems, and her medication led to tiredness and weight gain, which further diminished her self-image and led to despair.

As if that weren't enough, Jennifer began to have chronic fatigue syndrome. When this was at its worst, Jennifer would retreat from the world for a week to ten days.

Melson said that whenever she phoned the Blagg home in the evening, it was Michael who would answer the phone. He would tell Melson that Jennifer was too tired, and to call again later. Asked if she thought Jennifer was being physically abused by Mike, Melson said she didn't think so.

Agent Newton asked about Jennifer and Mike's personalities. Melson said that Jennifer was warm, outgoing, and a spiritual person. Jennifer's faith was strong and unwavering, and she tried her best to live her life as a Christian person. Jennifer was kind and considerate of others, and she was a good, if somewhat overprotective, mother to Abby.

Asked if Jennifer ever spoke about Mike's navy career, Melson said that Jennifer had told her that he'd been a helicopter pilot. Jennifer also told Melson that she'd been "warned off" about Mike early on, because of his lifestyle and the reputation surrounding hard-drinking, carousing naval aviators. She had gone out with him, nonetheless. Jennifer added that in civilian life Mike never seemed to find a job as satisfying as that which he'd had in the navy. It made him restless and unsatisfied with his lot in life, and he seemed to keep his family moving around a lot as he searched for the perfect job.

Melson stated that even though Jennifer was a loving mother, neither she nor Mike had ever wanted children. Melson added that Abby was an "accident" and one of the reasons why Mike left the navy. (The part about Abby being an "accident" contradicted Mike's statements about how he and Jennifer purposefully had tried to conceive a child just before his last cruise.)

Shortly after Abby was born, Jennifer underwent surgery to prevent her from having any more children. Melson declared that Jennifer had undergone a difficult pregnancy and suffered greatly with postpartum depression after Abby was born, and had been prone to hormonal-based mood swings all her adult life.

Jennifer was very protective of Abby because of the sexual molestation she had suffered as a child. Jennifer had been very nervous about placing Abby in a "Mother's Day Out" program at a local church. (This was a program to give young mothers some time away from their children.) Melson admitted that as time went on, Jennifer had begun to relax with Abby and enjoy her more.

Melson said that Michael was quiet, very private, and somewhat aloof. Even though she was best friends with Jennifer, she said she didn't know Mike very well. In fact, she said she often felt uncomfortable being around him, but couldn't really say why she felt that way. He was a large and imposing man, whose size seemed to intimidate her.

Melson agreed that Mike was a good father to Abby and that she had never noticed any unusual or inappropriate behavior by him around Abby. Even though Mike was superficially polite and charming, underneath she saw him as being arrogant and unapproachable.

Newton asked Melson about the Blaggs' lifestyle, and she said they were both very involved in the church and their religion. In fact, she couldn't think of any other sports, hobbies, or activities that they were involved in. Melson added, the more she thought about Mike, the more she perceived him as seeing the world in black-and-white terms, with no gray areas. She said he was very conservative on his views about religion, morality, and politics. Her vast majority of interactions with him concerned church-related topics. Even though her own husband, Kirk, and Mike were engineers, neither man seemed to have much in common and they didn't socialize.

Melson related that several years before, Mike's very conservative views had gotten him into trouble with their church. During the year before the Blaggs transferred to

Colorado, Mike had taught a Sunday-school class at the church for young adults. Mike had made some statements about social issues that offended several members of his Sunday-school class, and they complained to the church administration. Mike was asked to step down from his position. Later, Jennifer told Melson that she was embarrassed by the affair, but she supported Mike in his beliefs, because he was her husband.

Melson insisted that Mike was the dominant member of the marriage, but for the most part Jennifer went along with that, because she believed a father should be the head of a family unit. Melson added that Mike was controlling, but not a "control freak." In other words, he would not go so far as to dictate Jennifer's dress, hairstyle, and other facets of her life.

Melson admitted that she never phoned Jennifer at home if she thought Mike would pick up the phone first. Whenever she got him on the line, he would tell her that Jennifer was either busy or not feeling good, so she would phone Jennifer when she knew that Mike wasn't home. Melson just generally felt uncomfortable being around him or talking to him.

During the whole time the Blaggs were in Simpsonville, Melson only visited the Blaggs' home on two or three occasions, while Jennifer and Abby came to her home numerous times. In fact, Melson said that Jennifer often made excuses why she couldn't come over to the Blaggs' home. The underlying reason, Melson believed, was that Mike didn't want people over at the house. She believed this stemmed from Mike's reclusive and controlling nature.

Jennifer had told Melson over the phone that they had experienced financial problems when first moving to Grand Junction. They had been unable to sell their home in South Carolina before moving, and it had created a financial burden. According to Jennifer, they had depleted their savings account before the South Carolina home finally sold. All of that only added to her stress.

Melson noted that while living in South Carolina, the Blaggs had been fairly well off, and that both of them drove BMWs. Later, they had sold these off and bought Dodge Neons. As an explanation for doing this, Jennifer had told Melson that she thought the BMWs were too ostentatious if she and Mike were going to be witnesses as Christians, and driving Neons was more in line with a humble lifestyle.

Asked about any unusual behavior exhibited by either Mike or Jennifer, Melson told Newton that on several different occasions Jennifer told her she was praying for Melson's sex life. This made Melson very uncomfortable. Melson had never told her about her sex life, and Jennifer had not volunteered about her own sex life with Mike. Why this had suddenly become a topic for discussion from Jennifer upset Melson very much.

Another thing Jennifer said was that she hoped Melson would never experience what she had experienced and felt. Melson assumed she was talking about her sexual molestation as a child, and she had no knowledge of any sex problems between Mike and Jennifer.

Asked if she knew of any serious marital problems that Mike and Jennifer had experienced, Melson said that Jennifer once had threatened to leave Mike when they were living in California. (She may have meant Arizona, which others spoke of as the place where Mike and Jennifer had talked about a separation.) The crux of the problem, according to Jennifer, was Mike's partying and drinking. Mike had agreed to reform his behavior, and she didn't leave. Other than that, Melson didn't know of any other marital problems.

Jennifer on occasion asked Melson to pray for her, albeit she wouldn't say what the problem was that she wanted prayers to concern. Melson hadn't been too concerned about this, because she said she realized everyone had problems.

Melson related that while living in South Carolina Jennifer had been very happy, and Mike was unhappy. Jennifer loved Simpsonville and their church, but Mike hated his job because of his boss. Once they moved to Grand Junction, the opposite became true—Jennifer was not happy there, while Mike liked his new job. Later, Jennifer asked Melson, "Why has God put me down in the wilderness?" Jennifer was not a high desert fan—she loved the greenery of South Carolina. Then with a sigh, Jennifer related that as long as Mike was happy in Grand Junction, "I can tolerate it."

Melson said that Jennifer and Mike were having a hard time picking a church in the Grand Junction area. Jennifer had become depressed when Mike turned down a job in North Carolina so that he could stay in Colorado. It seemed to her, more and more, that she was becoming trapped within her own marriage and had to tolerate whatever Mike wanted.

When asked about how she had heard of Jennifer and Abby's disappearance, Melson stated she had learned about it from Kim Genoble, the wife of the associate pastor of her church. Genoble had awakened her at 6:00 A.M., November 14, with the bad news. Genoble had gotten the news from Art Blankenship, the Blaggs' pastor in Grand Junction.

When Melson phoned Mike later in the day on November 14, he seemed to be in a genuine state of shock, and his reaction seemed normal for such an event. He did, however, decline her offer to fly out to Colorado to help in the search for Jennifer and Abby. Ever since November 14, Melson and her husband had offered to fly out to Colorado to support Mike on numerous occasions, and he turned down their offer every time. She did think this was in keeping with his reserved and private nature, and not for some more sinister reason.

Mike did tell her that at one point he thought he was being considered as a suspect by the investigators. He said that he was frustrated that they were spending time on him, "instead of looking for the real culprit."

Melson had spoken with Mike shortly before he was accused of stealing furniture from work and his suicide attempt. Up until that time, he told her that he was optimistic about Jennifer and Abby's safe return, and "they will have a celebration and a big party."

Melson added that she'd spoken with Jennifer ten days before her disappearance, and Jennifer told her two things that had haunted her ever since. The first of these was: Jennifer had asked Melson to pray for her concerning a problem she was having, and that she had something to tell her, but couldn't do so at the present time. Jennifer then added that what she had to say would be very upsetting.

The second important news was that Jennifer planned to take a trip to see Melson in South Carolina, and she would be bringing Abby with her. Mike would not be coming along with them. Melson told Agent Newton that this upset her more than the first comment, since Mike always went everywhere with his family. Melson became certain that the reason for Jennifer's visit was that she and Mike were having serious marital problems that might have been leading to divorce.

Ten days later, Jennifer and Abby were missing and there was a lot of blood in the house where Jennifer once had slept. Whatever Jennifer was trying to tell her friend in South Carolina vanished, just as she had.

Chapter 5

Discovery

With all these latest developments swirling around, there was a new push in trying to discover Jennifer and Abby's remains. The authorities were no longer holding out any hope that they were alive. On April 16, 2002, the MCSO officially asked for volunteers at a town hall meeting in Grand Junction. The Fellowship Church on Road 24 became the headquarters of the volunteer effort, and more than twenty-two hundred people would eventually responded to the appeal. The range of tasks of the volunteers went from manning a checkout table to assembling first aid kits for those in the field, distributing maps, and actual ground searchers.

Janet Prell told reporters that the initial areas of search would concentrate on public lands, and private lands, whose owners gave permission for searches. Special areas to be looked at would be ditches, gullies, ravines, bushy areas, and anyplace where the ground looked disturbed.

The backgrounds of those who joined in the search effort were as diverse as the area itself. They were housewives, off-duty police officers, store clerks, retirees, doctors, auto mechanics. Some small businesses in the area even shut down for the day so that all the employees could join in the search. They strapped on boots and backpacks and orange-colored vests before heading into the countryside. Pastor Ray Shirley told a reporter, "This is very tough. I think a lot of people are fearful they'll be the ones to find them. This is really about giving some closure to this thing—giving closure and bringing justice."

The searchers not only came from the Grand Junction area, but from locales across the nation. Patty Powel came from Houston, Texas, and told a reporter, "I want these people to know that these two women are worth every ounce of effort that is going into this."

Ed McNevin, of Chicago, who lost a daughter in a car accident, was there, as was Mona Blee, whose daughter had been missing for twenty-two years. Don Cleveland, a Vietnam veteran, was there as well, and said, "I volunteered for Afghanistan, but they wouldn't take me. I'm too old. So this is the best thing I can do now to help make the world a safer place."

The search effort was being helped by the Laura Recovery Center, a nonprofit organization from Friendswood, Texas. The center had been created in 1997 when twelve-year-old Laura Smither was abducted and murdered. More than five thousand people had volunteered to help search for her, and by the time they were done, they'd covered an eight-hundred-square-mile area. In the present Blagg case, the Laura Recovery Center admitted that the searchers would be covering the most rugged terrain the group had ever dealt with.

Coordinating the effort between searchers and the MCSO was Investigator George Barley. He manned a trailer that had been set up as a headquarters for the search, at the Fellowship Church. A large map of the area covered one wall of the trailer. Barley said that the searchers initially would key in on an area eleven miles south of the Redlands, where the Blaggs were known to have mountain biked and explored. They would also search areas that could be reached by low clearance vehicles, such as a Ford Windstar minivan.

By the third day of the operation, searchers had flagged more than a dozen suspicious sites in the dry piñon-covered area south of the Redlands. These sites included ten rock-covered mounds that appeared to be small graves, as well as areas where bits of clothing and small bones were discovered. Investigator Barley said, "My gut feeling is they are nothing." In fact, most of the sites turned out to be places where family pets had been buried.

Investigator Barley was known as "Big Daddy" by his colleagues in the law enforcement community, for his size and genial nature. He had been headed for a barbershop in the area on November 13, 2001, when he heard over his police radio, "Missing mother and daughter. Blood in the home." He was off-duty at the time, but something told him to forget his haircut and head for Pine Terrace Court in the Redlands.

Now at the headquarters for the search, Investigator Barley arrived each morning at seven-thirty, and would often still be there at seven-thirty in the evening. His supervisor had to send him home to rest at times, after Barley had been out all day hiking around the backcountry at suspicious sites the searchers had discovered.

Bob Walcutt, of the Laura Recovery Center, said of Barley, "Good investigators are always bulldogs, but George is better than that. He's a very amiable bulldog." And Investigator Steven King agreed, saying, "He's a down-to-earth person. He is good to his family, loves the Rockies and Cracker Barrel restaurants. But he is not the kind of person you would want after you."

Every day of the search was difficult, both for Barley and the searchers. High winds and blowing dust hampered efforts in the hills, mesas, and canyons. And there was also the emotional toll, knowing that if Jennifer or Abby were found, they would probably not be alive. Investigator Barley told a reporter, "I believe I have a clear understanding of what happened. I believe they are deceased. Where are their bodies? I don't know. But I'm making sure all areas are covered."

Barley was also making sure that Jennifer's family was being taken care of as well. He had real compassion for them, and Jennifer's brother, David, said of Investigator Barley, "George understands to the core of his being how I feel."

Another local person right in the middle of the search effort was stay-at-home mom Connie Flukey, who had eight kids ranging in age from six to nineteen. By April 2002, she was the civilian coordinator of the search effort and liaison to the Laura Recovery Center. Speaking to reporter Lori Cumpson, Flukey said, "It is not a depressing situation. You do what needs to be done. You come back, you're tired; it doesn't matter. You go back out, you don't want to leave. You just want to help bring them home."

By April 21, the Laura Recovery Center volunteers had flown back to Texas and left the volunteer effort in the hands of local people. David Dannemiller, a spokesman for the center, said, "I don't think any of us have any qualms about leaving at this point and knowing that this effort is in good hands." Then he added that he knew the local search organization had good maps, good administration, and plenty of searchers. He noted, "If you don't keep track of where you've searched and what you've found, what you've done is wasted."

On April 21, a Sunday, 160 volunteers were broken up into thirty-one teams that included a search dog and horseback riders. Janet Prell, of the MCSO, said, "We've found a couple more hot spots investigators are checking out. They continue to be animal remains. Some objects are suspicious, like rolls of carpet, and we've been checking those things. But nothing significant so far."

During this period, Marilyn Conway and her husband went over to Mike's residence and noticed that he had some crystal stemware that had been passed down to Jennifer from her grandmother. Marilyn wanted them back, and Mike agreed. Harold and Marilyn met Mike in his garage area and loaded up the stemware, and she went into the town house and talked with Mike for a few minutes. When the Conways got back home to Texas, she discovered that Mike also had packed some of Jennifer's books, college papers, and high-school papers in the box with the stemware.

Even as all of this went on, an important meeting took place between Investigator Henry Stoffel and Joan Cordova, an employee of AMETEK Dixson. Cordova had worked for AMTEK Dixson for twenty-two years and was a quality inspector by 2002. She said that on November 13, 2001, she had arrived to work at 5:35 A.M., and as she approached the facility, she spoke with another employee, Karen Walker. Walker was sitting outside the building near the employee entryway, smoking a cigarette. Walker informed Cordova that she would not have to use her security card to get into the building, because it had been unlocked the entire night. Cordova was surprised at this security breach.

Cordova said that only about five people were usually at AMETEK Dixson at that time of day, and as she walked through the building, initially she didn't see anyone at the facility. As she turned a corner in the hallway, however,

Mike Blagg was walking toward her. The immediate reaction on his face was one of complete surprise. She asked him why the security system had been off all night, and he initially didn't respond. Cordova told Investigator Stoffel, "He looked dazed. I was surprised by his reaction to my question. I expected him to be upset over the door being left open. But he wasn't. Also, he was never there that early in the past."

Cordova said, "Throughout the day, Michael acted very strangely. Since he started working there, on an average day I would see him once or twice a day, if at all. But on the thirteenth, he came out onto the loading dock over twenty times. Each time Mike went out to the loading dock, he looked at a truck that contained assembly line components for another AMETEK Dixson plant in Mexico." Cordova thought he looked very nervous each time he gazed at the truck.

The truck was to be sealed with a numbered metal strip, and once it was sealed, the strip would have to be cut away to get the door open once again. The truck had been scheduled to be sealed on November 12, but that had not happened. Cordova said that she didn't see Mike talk to anyone out on the loading dock that day, and she avoided him because he was acting so strangely.

Investigator Stoffel asked Cordova if a large amount of trash was created in her work area. She said that the only trash items usually collected were made of cardboard. The cardboard was taken to another area to be recycled or stored. Any other trash was taken to a Dumpster or compactor on the side of the building, and she couldn't see those from her work area.

Stoffel asked Cordova why Mike was at the facility so early on November 13, and she said it was very unusual for him to be there that early. In fact, she had not seen him there at that time of day on any other occasion. Asked why

she had not told investigators about all this before, she said
that she was worried that she might be terminated if she
spoke negatively about Mike or the company.

Because of this revelation, and other evidence not
recorded at the time within public documents, a search
warrant was obtained to search the Mesa County Landfill.
On May 15, two days after the search of the landfill began,
Mike suddenly left Grand Junction and moved to Warner
Robins, Georgia, into his mother's house. Of this move, Investigator George Barley said, "I let him move, but I'm
going to keep track of where he is."

The reason Mike gave a reporter for moving was that he
could not find work in the Grand Junction area. He also
may have found it hard to go around town—by this time,
most residents of the area looked on him as a suspect, not
as a victim.

It was determined by the investigators and landfill staff
that they would be able to set off an area that was most
likely to contain trash from November 2001. An excavator
was brought in to remove refuse from a specific area, and
then investigators searched more closely through the excavated material using rakes and shovels. They also used
global positioning system coordinates and detailed landfill records. Lieutenant Dan Dillon said that the records
were so accurate, they could zero in on certain trucks that
had driven on certain routes, and then dumped their loads.

Even so, it was a mammoth job for the investigators. Reporter Nancy Lofholm noted, "Wielding rakes and shovels and steeling themselves against a powerful stench,
investigators chopped and poked at hundreds of tons of
trash as the search continued at a landfill for the bodies
of Jennifer and Abby Blagg." She said that in a single day
they sorted through three hundred tons of garbage by using
machines and hand tools. Backhoes and loaders dug the
trash out of the immense pile of garbage, and spread it out

in an area about a foot deep. Then the investigators searched through the foot-high "plume of trash" before it was carted off and reburied.

The investigators had pitched a large tent at the landfill and used it as a command post. With grim humor, they hung a sign outside the tent that declared, BIG DADDY AND THE SOGGY BOTTOM GANG. Big Daddy, of course, referred to Investigator George Barley, and the Soggy Bottom Gang referred to the loads of dirty diapers they had uncovered. In a vast understatement about how the work was progressing, Investigator Barley said, "It's a chore."

While looking through the specific area of the landfill, searchers found several newspapers from the week of November 13, and several items from AMETEK Dixson were also found in the general area. It was in an area that the investigators later would refer to as a "plume of trash," or a "swath of trash." The advent of finding the newspapers was a good sign. They knew they were on the right track.

The twenty-third day of the search, June 4, 2002, began like every other. It was hot, dusty, and the stench of the landfill filled the air. Then at 10:15 A.M., the excavator pulled a bucket of refuse from the area and was about to dump it when Investigator Stoffel suddenly yelled for the operator to stop. He had seen what he thought was a human leg and foot dangling out from the excavator's bucket.

All operations immediately ceased and it was discovered that the leg was partially covered in a nylon-type material. No further digging was done and a forensic team from the MCSO, FBI, and CBI was called in to complete the search. Dr. Robert Kurtzman, of the Mesa County Coroner's Office, also arrived on the scene and confirmed that what they were looking at was the right leg of an adult female.

The day after the leg was found, the decomposing body of an adult female was discovered, minus a left leg, in the same area of trash. The upper torso was found within what was later discovered to be a red-and-black tent. The badly decomposed body was taken to the Mesa County Coroner's Office, and later, a left leg was found in a hole near where the bucket had first pulled the right leg out of the trash. Near this leg were found numerous plastic gauge punch-outs similar to those produced at AMETEK Dixson.

The whole Grand Junction area was stunned by the news in the *Daily Sentinel,* under the headline REMAINS MAY BE BLAGGS! Reporter Mike Wiggins noted, "Mesa County sheriff's deputies found a leg with a foot attached while digging through a swimming-pool sized area at the landfill. Authorities believe they found the remains of only one person."

Janet Prell told reporters, "We don't know that we have Jennifer and Abby until we do a lot more work on this case."

Mike Blagg's attorney was contacted and he made a short statement. "Michael will likely return to Grand Junction if the remains belong to his family."

Reporters were heading in all directions by this point, and one spoke with an official at AMETEK Dixson who said that Mike did have access to the trash compactor during November 2001. Then the man added that everyone at the facility also had access to the same trash compactor.

Investigator Norcross and Hebenstreit attended a postmortem examination of the decomposed body found at the landfill. The postmortem itself was done by Dr. Dean Havlik at the Community Hospital Morgue, along with Dr. Kurtzman. Also in attendance were CBI agent Kevin Humphreys and FBI agent Arnold Bellmer. Investigator Hebenstreit had a dental X-ray of Jennifer Blagg, which he obtained from the evidence section at MCSO. The X-ray of Jennifer Blagg had been taken in 1990, before she married Michael Blagg, and was under her maiden name of Jennifer Loman. Hebenstreit gave the 1990 X-ray to John Bull, D.D.S., and Bull compared it to a dental X-ray from the decomposed body. Based on the X-rays, Bull pronounced that the body and Jennifer Loman Blagg were one and the same. A retainer was also found from the teeth in the body, and was identified by Bull as the lower retainer that Jennifer Blagg had worn.

As the day went on and the postmortem progressed, Dr. Havlik removed a bullet and bullet fragments from Jennifer Blagg's brain. Havlik noted that there was an entry wound in the left eye. CBI special agent Kevin Humphreys did a brief examination of the bullet and indicated that in all likelihood it had been fired from a handgun. He noted the size of the bullet was probably a nine-millimeter or similar size. At 12:20 P.M., Dr. Havlik ruled that the cause of death was a gunshot wound to the head and the manner of death was homicide.

The *Daily Sentinel* soon told the Grand Junction area that it was indeed Jennifer Blagg's body that had been found, cast away in the landfill like so much garbage. Sheriff Riecke Clausen told reporters, "There was still a lot of flesh attached to the bones. A backhoe had just dug up a section of garbage at about ten-fifteen A.M., when an investigator spotted what he believed to be human body parts. The operator was just getting ready to swing it around and dump it, when one of the investigators yelled, 'Hey, I think I see something!' Investigators laid down a tarp, set the bucket load on the tarp, and located a leg and foot."

Then Clausen added that the whole character of the search was going to change from that point. He said, "You go from taking big scoops of refuse and dumping them, to doing more of an archaeological dig, when you're working with some minutiae."

Mesa County DA Frank Daniels weighed in as well, stating, "Instead of taking it out by the bucketful, they'll take it out by the spoonful. We have at least one human being to be treated with respect."

Miles away, in Georgia, Elizabeth Blagg, Mike's mother, was contacted by a reporter and she said, "Right now we are terribly distressed, although pleased the sheriff's department is working so hard. We're just trying to assimilate what we heard." When pressed as to where Mike was, she wouldn't say, or even answer if he was living with her at the time.

Marilyn Conway, Jennifer's mom, was terse to the point of being laconic. All she would tell a reporter was "The situation is not okay, but we've been given something to deal with, and we'll deal with it."

Neighbors of the Blagg family in the Redlands were also contacted by reporters, and for the most part they thought that Mike Blagg was responsible for his wife's death. Don Opp said, "I think it's painfully obvious that he (Mike) is involved. We would sure like to get some closure and find out who is responsible. Let's hope this doesn't turn into another JonBenet Ramsey thing."

Young Colorado resident, and beauty contestant, JonBenet Ramsey had met a very mysterious death. Even by 2002, rumors still swirled around that her father had murdered her, or her mother had done it, or a stranger had been the culprit. No one knew for sure, although the tabloids constantly came up with new theories.

Art Blankenship, the pastor of New Hope Fellowship Church, was one of the few people still holding out hope that Mike Blagg was innocent. He told a reporter, "We care about this young man and his family. All we want is the truth."

By June 6, 2002, nearly the entire front page of the *Daily Sentinel* was filled with Blagg-related stories, under the lead headline of MICHAEL BLAGG ARRESTED. The body of the story attested to the fact that Mike Blagg had been arrested at his mother's home in Warner Robins, Georgia, at 11:45 P.M., local time. Lieutenant Joe Wethering, of the Warner Robins Police Department (WRPD), said that Blagg was being quiet and cooperative. His mother told a reporter, "He did nothing to hurt his wife and child, that I can tell you."

It turned out that Mike had been under FBI surveillance the whole time he had been in Georgia, and he wasn't going anywhere without their knowing. Mike's Georgia neighbors were flabbergasted by the news of his arrest. One neighbor recalled Mike as a teenager often washing his car in the driveway. The neighbor said, "He was in ROTC, he was a good student, and I just don't believe it!"

Another Georgia neighbor told a reporter, "Mike always helped out in the neighborhood. He was always very nice to everybody. I think something else will come out. You want to believe the good in people. I just believe Mike is innocent."

More and more details were starting to surface now about the Blaggs and the landfill. Investigators said that they were searching for Abby in a part of the landfill that was one hundred feet long, by twenty feet wide and twenty-five feet high. Sheriff's lieutenant Stan Hilley stated, "Until we find Abby, we are going to exhaust that area as much as possible." This was easier said than done. Finding the body of one small girl in that mountain of trash was akin to finding a needle in a haystack.

Investigators were bracing themselves for some tough days ahead. The temperature was supposed to get up to 99 degrees, and gusting winds were certain to swirl around the landfill as the air heated up in the afternoon hours.

Jennifer Loman met and married Michael Blagg while he was in the Navy, stationed in San Diego, California. *(High school photo)*

In 1995, Jennifer and Mike had their only child, Abby Blagg, who was a bright, inquisitive girl.

While living in Grand Junction, Colorado, Abby loved the statues of children that were placed on downtown street corners.
(Author photo)

MISSING

Jennifer Blagg - 34
(DOB 1-8-1967)
white female, sandy blonde hair, brown eyes, 5'3", 118 lbs.

Abby Blagg - 6
(DOB 3-21-1995)
white female, blonde

Jennifer and Abby Blagg were reported missing Tuesday, November 13, 2001 from their home at 2253 Pine Terrace Court, Grand Junction, Colorado.

Circumstances surrounding Jennifer and Abby's disappearance have led investigators to believe they may be in danger.

Anyone who has seen Jennifer or Abby Blagg or has information concerning their whereabouts is encouraged to contact the Mesa County Sheriff's Office at 244-3500 or anonymously call Crime Stoppers at 241-STOP.

On November 13, 2001, Mike Blagg reported Jennifer and Abby missing from their home.
(Photo courtesy of Mesa County Sheriff's Office)

Mike was a highly respected industrial parts engineer and manager at the AMETEK Dixson plant in Grand Junction. *(Photo courtesy of Mesa County Sheriff's Office)*

The alleged disappearance of Jennifer and Abby occurred at their home in the Redlands district, below the towering red walls of Colorado National Monument. *(Photo courtesy of Mesa County Sheriff's Office)*

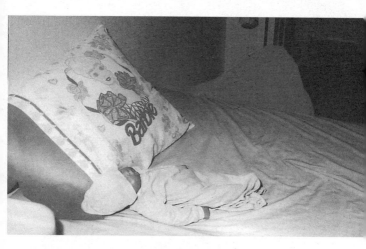

MCSO investigators found Abby's sheets pulled down on her bed and a doll lying on her pillow. *(Photo courtesy of Mesa County Sheriff's Office)*

In the master bedroom of the Blagg home, a large pool of blood ran from Jennifer's side of the bed onto the floor. *(Photo courtesy of Mesa County Sheriff's Office)*

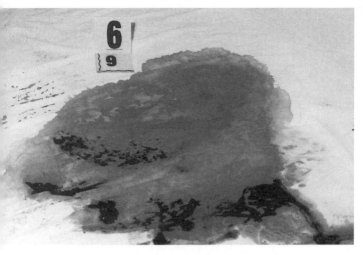

There was a large bloodstain in the area where Jennifer slept on the bed. *(Photo courtesy of Mesa County Sheriff's Office)*

Jennifer's purse lay on the floor of the master bedroom. *(Photo courtesy of Mesa County Sheriff's Office)*

Contents from Jennifer's purse were scattered on the bedroom floor. *(Photo courtesy of Mesa County Sheriff's Office)*

Jennifer's minivan was still parked in the Blagg residence garage when investigators checked. *(Photo courtesy of Mesa County Sheriff's Office)*

Seats in the rear of the minivan lay flat, as if something or someone had been placed there. *(Photo courtesy of Mesa County Sheriff's Office)*

Small blood smears were present in the minivan.
(Photo courtesy of Mesa County Sheriff's Office)

A large area in the hills near the Blagg residence was searched by investigators. These mysterious bricks were discovered during the search. Written on them were the words "Mediocrity," "Excuses," and "Laziness." *(Photo courtesy of Mesa County Sheriff's Office)*

As time passed by and Jennifer and Abby were not found, MCSO created an "age progression" computerized photo of Abby. *(Photo courtesy of Mesa County Sheriff's Office)*

Investigators learned that Mike Blagg had viewed a lot of Internet porn on his home computer. *(Photo courtesy of Mesa County Sheriff's Office)*

As Mike became more of a suspect, his guns were tested by the authorities. *(Photo courtesy of Mesa County Sheriff's Office)*

One of Mike's coworkers told investigators that Mike had made many trips to the AMETEK Dixson Dumpster on November 13, 2001, the day he said that Jennifer and Abby had disappeared. *(Photo courtesy of Mesa County Sheriff's Office)*

Investigators started searching the Mesa County Landfill, looking for the bodies of Jennifer and Abby. *(Photo courtesy of Mesa County Sheriff's Office)*

It was hard, grueling work in hot, windy conditions for the investigators at the landfill. *(Photo courtesy of Mesa County Sheriff's Office)*

A backhoe operator dug down more than twenty feet into the trash, searching for signs of Jennifer and Abby. *(Photo courtesy of Mesa County Sheriff's Office)*

After many days of digging, a newspaper from mid-November, 2001, was discovered in the landfill. This was the time period when Jennifer and Abby disappeared. *(Photo courtesy of Mesa County Sheriff's Office)*

On June 4, 2002, an investigator suddenly spotted a human leg dangling out of the backhoe's bucket. *(Photo courtesy of Mesa County Sheriff's Office)*

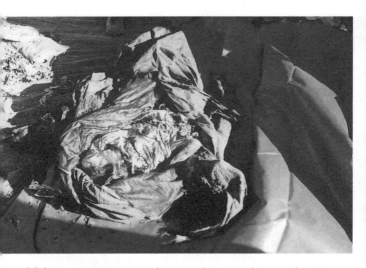

Adult human remains were discovered wrapped in a red tent at the landfill. *(Photo courtesy of Mesa County Sheriff's Office)*

Jennifer Blagg's mummified leg was part of the remains.
(Photo courtesy of Mesa County Sheriff's Office)

Michael Blagg was arrested at his mother's home in Georgia, on June 5, 2002. He was extradited to stand trial for murder in Grand Junction, Colorado. *(Photo courtesy of Mesa County Sheriff's Office)*

Steven King was a key member of the investigation team that had questioned Mike Blagg and then helped dig through the landfill. *(Courtesy of Steven King)*

The team of investigators that searched through the landfill endured days of very meticulous searching through tons of trash under difficult conditions. *(Photo courtesy of Mesa County Sheriff's Office)*

Mike Blagg's trial began in March 2004 with a charge of
first-degree murder at the Mesa County Courthouse. *(Author photo)*

An MCSO investigator always spoke with Jennifer Blagg's family
members as the trial progressed, until Mike was convicted on
April 16, 2004. *(Photo courtesy of Mesa County Sheriff's Office)*

Investigator Steven King related that more AMETEK Dixson material was being found near the spot where Jennifer was discovered, and he said that they would go back to using a backhoe, since digging with only hands and shovels wasn't enough. He related, "We have to go back to using the equipment most suited for creating a break in the case, and two or three people digging in that hole aren't going to do it."

Investigator King told reporters, "I think when Mike was arrested, and once Jennifer's body was identified, you have to get back into that mental toughness to say this is for the long run. It's not the finish line. There really isn't a lot of time to dwell on the accomplishments. It's very important that Jennifer was recovered, but I think whenever you're dealing with the disappearance of a child, that hits very close to home because of the innocence, because of the lack of time to enjoy life. The story is not complete, and the puzzle is not put together without Abby."

Marilyn Conway was a little more responsive by June 6, and she said, "I believe her (Jennifer's) pain is over with, and that is a blessing. We have prayed individually, and churches have prayed for us, to have an earthly closure."

Because of Mike's suicide attempt, or at least pretense at one, MCSO expressed concern that he might try it again and stated that he was under a constant suicide watch at the Georgia jail, where he was being held. They also related that he wasn't going to return to Colorado without a fight. Mike refused to sign extradition papers and seemed to be digging in his heels. DA Frank Daniels said, "He can make us jump through hoops." Daniels also indicated that he would take each "hoop" one step at a time and make sure the correct legal process brought Mike Blagg back to Colorado to stand trial for the murder of Jennifer Blagg.

The first hoop Daniels and the others would have to jump through was sending a letter to Georgia's governor asking him to extradite Mike Blagg. To that end, Daniels began putting together an extensive report about the crimes, crime scene photos, and even reproductions of fingerprints. After Georgia's governor reviewed and signed the report, it would wind its way to the Houston County DA's Office in Georgia, for further review. Mike Blagg would appear in court before a judge in an extradition hearing and a bond would be set. The bond in this type of crime was expected to be at least $1,000,000. Georgia authorities could hold Mike up to ninety days in their state.

For whatever reason, Mike eventually decided to waive an extradition hearing, and return to Colorado. Soon there was another twist, however. For some reason, Mike's Colorado lawyer, Stephan Schweissing, said he had been denied phone access to Mike while he was in a Georgia jail, and Schweissing contacted another lawyer for him. This was a Georgia lawyer, Michael Moore, and perhaps he was retained because he was more readily available in the area where Mike was being detained. Moore had been a Georgia state senator and former prosecutor.

Schweissing put the best face on things by telling a reporter, "Mike still maintains hope that Abby will be found and is safe and well."

At court in Perry, Georgia, Mike made an appearance before Judge L. A. McConnell. Mike's mother mouthed words of encouragement to him as his sister, Clare, and brother sat nearby. Mike was led into the courtroom, wearing an orange jumpsuit, his feet and hands shackled. Because of the shackles, he had a hard time trying to sign the extradition papers. Finally his hand shackles were removed momentarily so that he could sign the waiver for extradition. He uttered not a word the whole time he was in court, although he did smile at his mother and sister.

Soon thereafter, Mike and investigators from Mesa County took a flight from Macon, Georgia, to Atlanta. From there, they got on a flight to Salt Lake City, and finally a short hop from Utah to the airport at Grand Junction. Once he was in the Mesa County Jail, Mike was immediately placed in solitary confinement on a suicide watch. Law enforcement authorities were taking no chances with him now. Solitary confinement was to protect Mike from other prisoners in the county jail. There were some of these who viewed Mike as a child killer, and authorities worried about Mike's safety, as far as these inmates were concerned.

Talk of the Blagg case seemed to be on everyone's lips in the Grand Junction area that week. Reporter Andrea Price wrote, "Necks craned over kitchen tables, and eyebrows raised between sips of mocha, as more than a few people said, 'Well, you know what I heard.' Abuzz with speculation about his guilt, and his six-year-old daughter Abby, who is still missing, the Blagg case was the topic of the day everywhere from office cubicles to the Lincoln Park Moyer Swimming Pool."

Courtney Rebord, who was watching her kids in that pool, told Price, "We've been saying that he did it since the first week they disappeared. From day one he showed zero remorse. He just didn't seem as concerned as he should have been."

Nearby, Sunday Montgomery added, "They must have a ton of evidence against him by now."

Even one of Blagg's neighbors, Norman Sherwood, joined in by saying, "We all kind of wondered why they let him leave Colorado. Nice quiet guys are often the most screwed up."

Much of the news coming out of the investigation now concerned Abby. Lead investigator George Barley admitted that Abby's body might not be found near Jennifer's. He said, "It's a possibility, watching the way they move that heavy equipment out there at the landfill, that Abby's body could be pushed quite a way."

The landfill search was all very frustrating, and Sheriff Clausen noted, "There's no rhyme nor reason to the way the trash containing Jennifer's body was compacted." The searchers had been following a promising path of papers from AMETEK Dixson, but that eventually played out. One reason for there being no set path to follow was that when the garbage was first dumped, the front loader would push it in a pattern that somewhat resembled a bird's foot—left, right, and center. The investigators were searching in an area that contained a huge area of trash. They had to dig not only outward, but down to a depth of twenty-five feet in hot, miserable weather.

Just how tough the work was, physically and mentally for those who were there, was testified to by backhoe operator Mike Doyenhard. He was the operator who initially had pulled a bucketful of trash from the landfill that contained Jennifer Blagg's right leg. He later said, "I'd never experienced anything like that! I had a few sleepless nights. Nobody looks forward to this. The dig, though, is a necessity for the people involved and for the community. So you put the smells and the heat and the nasty stuff behind you."

Every bucketful was a strain on Doyenhard's nerves, and the material itself was tough and recalcitrant. He spoke of it as being almost like "engineered soil," which put a severe strain on the machine's hydraulic system. Every once in a while, he would dig into some suspicious material, like a rolled-up carpet, which would have to be unrolled and searched by hand. Doyenhard spoke of the investigators with their rakes and shovels as "bulldogs on the chase."

Across town, church leaders were planning a memorial service for Jennifer Blagg, and the whole community was invited, especially those who had spent long hours out searching for the missing woman and girl. Memorial services were also planned for Simpsonville, South Carolina, and Ardmore, Oklahoma, where Jennifer had grown up.

News media throughout the region were seeking information on the case, which was initially sealed by Judge M. Osuan, but when the case was assigned to Judge David Bottger, he unsealed much of the material and it hit Grand Valley like a bombshell.

The *Rocky Mountain News* headlined, AFFIDAVIT SHOWS SECRET LIFE, while the *Daily Sentinel* headlines stated, JENNIFER CLAIMED ABUSE, BLAGG SOUGHT PORN ON NET. All of the newspaper accounts told of Mike Blagg's double life—one as a supposed loving Christian husband and father, and the other as a man who had downloaded more than a thousand pornographic images onto his computer. There were stories about his visits to the escort service, where one woman said she gave him a topless massage, and he wanted sex as well. Mike's image as a pious family man was blown sky-high.

Just as damning as all the stories about pornography was a report that on November 13, 2001, one employee at AMETEK Dixson said he saw Mike pushing two large cardboard boxes toward the company's loading dock. When the person said he would help, Mike allegedly said sternly, "Nope! Just get away!"

Another report stated that on November 13, someone at AMETEK Dixson phoned BFI trash services to make a special trip to pick up a Dumpster at the facility. BFI did so on November 14. The caller was never identified, but the implication was that it was Mike Blagg who had called them to make sure that Jennifer and Abby's bodies were hauled out to the landfill.

Another revelation came out in the *Rocky Mountain News* that "Jennifer Blagg was likely asleep when she was shot in the face in what one investigator called an 'execution.'" The newspaper also reported about FBI profiler

Ron Walker and his thoughts that the crime scene looked staged. He said that the contents of a purse being dumped on the floor and the empty jewelry box appeared to be the efforts of an amateur who didn't really know what a burglary scene looked like.

Speaking to the *Daily Sentinel*, Dr. Havlik said that death for Jennifer was either instantaneous or within seconds as the bullet entered her brain. Within days, however, a new wrinkle only added to the mystery of the case. It was reported that in the search of Mike Blagg's residence, a Ruger .22-caliber handgun, a Ruger .22-caliber rifle, and a Remington shotgun had been seized, but the bullet that had killed Jennifer Blagg was most likely a 9mm bullet. Of course, it was hypothesized by many that Mike Blagg had shot her and then discarded the firearm elsewhere. A 9mm handgun had not been found.

It was reported that on the night of November 12, 2001, Jennifer did have a fight with Mike, and it wasn't about a move to Longmont, Colorado. This revelation was found within a book that Jennifer had been reading titled *Love Your God with All Your Mind,* where she had stashed a note about an argument that she and Mike had recently experienced. Other evidence tended to back up Mike's contention that Jennifer was distraught during much of 2001, leading to the possibility that she might have harmed Abby and then killed herself. At least that had been some authorities' thoughts for a period of time, before Mike became the main suspect. Investigators found medication belonging to Jennifer that treated anxiety, panic disorders, and depression.

Out at the landfill, conditions went from bad to worse. Hot, gusting winds made digging cease for a while because searchers were threatened by flying objects, such as plywood and other debris. Lieutenant Dick Dillon said in disgust, "Everything that blew west this morning, blew back this afternoon."

By now, legal pundits were adding their voices to the general clamor about the Blagg case. Mimi Wesson, a University of Colorado law professor, told a reporter, "Motive is a key part of the case. Though the law doesn't require motive, most jurors do. Unless they (the prosecution) can hypothesize a motive, they will have a hard time with a conviction."

Attorney John Baker, who specialized in criminal law, related, "You have to give jurors a very strong reason to make a leap from circumstances to conviction. It is the glue that brings it all together for them." He did admit that the MCSO did have a lot of circumstantial evidence that helped their case. Jennifer's body had been found in an area that contained AMETEK Dixson trash, and DNA found in the van matched her blood DNA. Mike suddenly had moved to Georgia two days after the landfill search began, and his suicide attempt was highly suspicious. Perhaps worst of all, the contention that Mike had visited an escort service asking for sex, and had more than a thousand porn images on his computer, destroyed his credibility as a spotless family man.

Within the DA's office, Frank Daniels was contemplating whether to seek the death penalty against Mike or not. Former DA Terry Farina noted, "If Frank decides to do it, he will have to wrestle long and hard with the decision." Colorado law required prosecutors to prove at least one of several aggravating factors to make a murder a death penalty case:

1. Killing a witness to a crime.
2. Killing someone in an especially heinous, cruel, or depraved manner.
3. The killing of two or more people during the same episode.
4. The killing of someone who was younger than twelve years old.

This last factor was going to be hard to prove if Abby's body was not found.

Mitigating factors might also come into play, such as Mike's lack of a criminal history, his stint in the navy, or a lack of murderous intent before the murder was committed—in other words, if it was committed in the heat of passion rather than with premeditation.

Farina admitted it might be tough to get a death penalty conviction against Mike Blagg, because "the death penalty should be used sparingly. People have a sense when something is out-of-bounds."

Memorials and remembrances of Jennifer and Abby were held in several states that June, including South Carolina, which they once had called home. Traci Danley, who had lived near the Blaggs in Simpsonville, spoke of them as "warm, caring, God-loving people. I think to everyone here they seemed to be very happy."

The Blaggs' pastor at the First Baptist Church in South Carolina, Randy Harling, particularly remembered Abby. He told a reporter, "She had a real unambiguous desire to know more about God. She, in some ways, had depth of understanding that a five-year-old should not have had. She was beyond her years."

Abby had wanted to be baptized fully into the church at a very early age. Harling had asked her why she wanted to become a Christian so early in life, and Abby answered, "Because God told me it's time."

Harling admitted in the summer of 2002, "when Abby professed her belief and trust in Jesus at such a young age, we thought, 'Wow, that's pretty early!' Well, maybe now, we know why."

Harling said of Jennifer that she had a deeply spiritual nature and an upbeat, positive approach to life. Even with this attitude, she could empathize with people who were having some kind of crisis or pain in their lives. In fact, Pastor Harling told a reporter that Jennifer had come to him several times before the move to Grand Junction for counseling. He said that it had not been over marital problems, but rather about other issues. One of the issues was the move itself. He regarded this as an "I hate to leave my friends" kind of thing, rather than "I hate to move to Colorado" kind of thing. He also recalled her saying, "I'm married to Mike, and this is my lot in life."

One of Jennifer's friends at the First Baptist Church in South Carolina was Nita Lyda, who taught women's Bible study classes along with Jennifer. Lyda said that Jennifer had a gentle, sweet personality, and made a person feel as if they mattered. Lyda accentuated what many others had said, that Jennifer had an infectious way of laughing. "She would just roar until tears rolled down her cheeks." Lyda also related, "Jennifer had an uncanny ability to connect with people. She had a serious side, but she loved her family and loved her friends."

Lyda recalled of Abby that she was a girl with a strong personality and an abundance of energy. "She was always inquisitive and would talk until your ears ached." She loved to swim and visit animals at the zoo.

Interestingly enough, Lyda's husband, Jeff, still had good things to say about Mike Blagg. He related that Mike was one of the most godly people he had ever met, always humble and meek. Jeff said, "I heard Mike talk and I said I wish I could love Nita the way he loved Jennifer. I found myself envious about the way he spoke about her."

Both Jeff and Nita Lyda agreed that Mike was very protective of Jennifer and Abby, and they found it unbelievable that Mike would have harmed them.

Another First Baptist Church member, Jennifer Coker, recalled Jennifer Blagg's spirituality as being very deep.

Whenever there was a weighty issue to be discussed, Jennifer would be very quiet for a while before saying a word. At times, Coker would ask her what she thought about a subject, and Jennifer would answer, "I don't know, I'm going to have to pray about it first."

Kirk and Edie Melson, who also knew the Blaggs, especially Jennifer, weighed in about them as well. Speaking of any marital discord, Kirk said, "We were completely unaware of anything like that. They were really affectionate toward one another, and he was doting on both of them all the time. What I felt about Michael was that if I needed anything, I could call on him."

Edie Melson told one newspaper reporter for the *Denver Post* that Jennifer had told her ten days before her disappearance, "I've finally had it. I'm miserable, we are going to hop a plane and we're coming back (to South Carolina)." Edie contended that Jennifer "had no friends, felt very alone, cut off and abandoned." Edie said that Jennifer had only acquiesced to the move to Colorado because Mike had put so much pressure on her. Edie declared, "I know Jennifer made friends and ties to people in Simpsonville like she had never made in her life."

Edie declared that Mike always had problems with his jobs. She said that he would have a honeymoon period for about six months and then things would go sour for him. She said this happened wherever he was, and then he would want to move on.

Edie told the reporter, "I feel like the Mesa County Sheriff's Office and the FBI have done a phenomenal job."

Strangely enough, Edie Melson, by this time, seemed to have some problem with the *Daily Sentinel,* and would not speak to its reporter. She issued a terse statement to them, saying while Jennifer had planned a trip to South Carolina, it was just to be a short visit. And the reason Edie Melson now gave that only Jennifer and Abby would be coming was that Mike was too busy at his job for AMETEK Dixson. There was no mention now about how afraid for her friend Edie had been at the time because Mike was not coming along with Jennifer, and Edie knew there had to be a serious marital problem because of his absence. What she related to them was very much at odds with what she had told FBI agent Newton, and the reporter for the *Denver Post*.

Even Kirk Melson's statement of why the Blaggs had moved to Grand Junction seemed at odds with Jennifer's own statements. He said that the Blaggs liked the West better than the East, and both looked forward to moving to Colorado. Jennifer, however, had written about how she longed for South Carolina, and she did not enjoy the prospect of moving back to the arid West. And Edie Melson adamantly told the *Denver Post* reporter, "Jennifer did not want to go to Colorado."

Reporter Charlie Brennan, for the *Rocky Mountain News,* asked Pastor Harling to play a word-association game, wherein he would associate just a few words with each member of the Blagg family. For Mike, Harling said, "Quiet sincerity"; for Jennifer, he said, "Spiritual depth"; and for Abby, "Joyful exuberance."

Friends from Jennifer's high-school days in Oklahoma also told reporters about the girl they had known. Jennifer Finley, who had been Jennifer Blackwood in high school, and knew Jennifer Loman Blagg at Ardmore High School in Oklahoma, told reporter Rachel Sauer of the *Grand Junction Sentinel,* "She was like one of the cooler older girls that you kind of idolized. She was likeable, she didn't have any enemies, and everyone liked her. She was pleasant, friendly, real popular, but she wasn't snobby at all. She was always nice to me."

Fellow classmate from those days, Bret Flatt agreed. "I didn't know of anybody that didn't like her," he said. "She was a nice girl and a real good friend."

During her high-school years, Jennifer had been on the drill team, the pep club, and in a jazz choir called The Group. She went to football and basketball games and even played on a girls' football team called "powderpuff football." As might have been expected for someone who was so religious later in life, Jennifer attended church regularly and sang in the choir.

More than anyone, it was her brother, David, and mother, Marilyn, who remembered Jennifer most vividly. David Loman said, "She was a typical young lady, who did everything that normal girls do at that age. She socialized; she went to church; she had reasonable boys for boyfriends." David also recalled that Jennifer loved talking on the phone, and after their mom went to bed, she would sit on the kitchen sink talking on the phone so that anyone walking by the kitchen couldn't see her.

More than anything, brother and sister liked sitting in a boat in the middle of a pond and fishing together. They would talk, relax, and not even care if they caught any fish or not. David said, "We always referred to it as the best place for us to be."

David said that Abby was a thoughtful, loving little girl. She loved to sing and often made up words to songs that she knew. She was learning to ride a bike with her parents at Canyon View Park in the days before she disappeared.

Marilyn Conway remembered her daughter, Jennifer, as loving to have a good time. Jennifer was born on January 8, 1967, in southern Oklahoma, three years after brother David. Jennifer's father, Roy Loman, divorced her mom when Jennifer was still very young. The family, in essence, became Marilyn, David, and Jennifer. As they grew up, David recalled, he traded in playing with Hot Wheels for pitching a baseball, and Jennifer would sit on a woodpile and watch him throw. On Saturday mornings, the whole family would congregate on the couch and watch cartoons together.

Marilyn said that Jennifer was very protective of Abby, but not to the point of smothering her. In a way, it reflected the way that Marilyn had brought up David and Jennifer. David recalled, "Mom would let you know pretty quickly if you were making some tragic mistake, but she let us grow up and let us learn right and wrong."

In the same manner, Jennifer instilled in Abby the difference between right and wrong, and the way people should be treated—with fairness and compassion. David referred to Jennifer as a "hands-on Mom," who loved to play with Abby, and even volunteered at the school that Abby attended in Grand Junction. He spoke of Jennifer, Abby, and Mike taking hikes in Colorado National Monument, riding bikes, and reading the Bible together. It had seemed like a very close, loving family, as far as David could tell.

And then, something had gone terribly wrong sometime on the night of November 12, or early morning hours of November 13, 2001. Marilyn Conway said, "Abby was a sweet little girl and Jennifer was my best friend. I miss them. I miss them desperately!"

Marilyn Conway attended a memorial service for Jennifer and Abby at the Northwest Baptist Church in Ardmore. Marilyn, Jennifer, and David had attended that church for ten years when they lived in the area. More than one hundred people attended the service, and Marilyn told them, "You lose a child and it's the wrong sequence in life. Watching Abby grow up and watching Jennifer grow up has been robbed from me. I will regret that to a certain degree for the rest of my life. It's been an evil thing that has happened to my children."

Jennifer's cousin, Kendall Evans, said, "My heart will be filled with her. There will not be a hole, and I encourage you not to have a void in your lives."

Pastor Phil Christopher picked up on this theme and told the audience, "She is not missing—not missing from your heart, not missing from your memory, and not missing from the reach of God."

On June 29, 2002, a memorial service for Jennifer Blagg was held at Canyon View Vineyard Church in Grand Junction. The more than 150 attendees came from all walks of life and backgrounds. Some had known about her only since they volunteered to search for Jennifer and Abby in April 2002. Others had been family members or lifelong friends. Jennifer's brother, David, came from Oklahoma, and her mom and stepfather came from Texas. Even Elizabeth Blagg, and Mike's sister, Clare, worked up the nerve to attend the memorial.

Pastor Art Blankenship spoke of Jennifer's presence at the New Hope Fellowship Church and all the work she had done at its school. Friend Stacee Baker read e-mails from Jennifer's other friends in South Carolina. Photographs of Jennifer, Abby, and the eleven-day-long search in April were shown on an overhead screen. The one glaring absence was the fact that no photos of Mike Blagg were shown.

Also in attendance were several law enforcement investigators and personnel. Janet Prell told a reporter, "Every case is hard, when you get to know the victims and their families, and this case has been particularly hard. When you're in law enforcement, the focus is on the case and putting the pieces together. This was a moment to think about Jennifer and Abby and what their lives were about."

Chapter 6

Jennifer's Journal

After high school, Jennifer had attended Oklahoma State University in Stillwater, Oklahoma. Perhaps missing her mom, she moved to San Diego, where Marilyn was now living with her new husband, Harold Conway. Jennifer enrolled in National University while living in the San Diego area and got a degree in business administration. It was in San Diego that fate intervened, and Jennifer met Michael Blagg.

One of Mike's best friends was dating one of Jennifer's best friends, and Jennifer and Mike met at a party. Mike later got her phone number through a friend, and he and Jennifer went out on a movie date on July 4, 1988. They watched *Who Framed Roger Rabbit*, went out to eat at a Japanese restaurant, and then watched fireworks from the top of Mount Carmel.

Mike had also come a long way from his childhood home to be in San Diego, California. Born in Texas to John and Elizabeth Blagg, Mike's father was a colonel in the air force and became a judge advocate general (JAG) attorney.

The family moved around a lot, from base to base, including one in Georgia and one in Hawaii. They eventually settled down in Warner Robins, Georgia, near Atlanta. Mike went to Warner Robins High School, where he was good in sports, and later he got a degree at Georgia Tech University in nuclear engineering. After Georgia Tech, Mike entered the navy's pilot program at Pensacola, Florida, where he learned to fly helicopters. He was in the Gulf region during Operation Desert Storm, where he saw duty in the combat zone and was decorated for his actions. From there, he was stationed to the San Diego area, where he met Jennifer.

Mike and Jennifer dated for three years, while he served in the navy at various locations. On November 16, 1991, they were married in Fort Worth, Texas. David Loman would later say that Jennifer dated for so long before getting married, because she wanted to make sure it was the right thing to do. Loman explained, "She wasn't someone who rushed into things."

Not rushing into things also was evident in the birth of their first and only child, Abby, who was conceived when Mike and Jennifer were discussing his leaving the navy for a civilian job in 1995. Mike was gone on a cruise in the Pacific throughout most of Jennifer's pregnancy. When Mike finally resigned from the navy in 1995, he held the rank of lieutenant commander. The young family moved from the San Diego area to Arizona, where Mike got a job with Allied Signal, which manufactured jet engines. During this Arizona period, there were rocky times in the marriage and even talk of a separation at one point.

There was still a restlessness in Mike, however, and it wasn't long before they packed up and headed clear across country to South Carolina, where Mike began working for Allied Signal there. Perhaps around this time, because Jennifer was fed up with his drinking problems, Mike began to go to church regularly with her. It was in South Carolina where he began to be active in church membership, and he and Jennifer formed a layperson's Intercessory Prayer Ministry, which was available twenty-four hours a day. It was for couples who were having some kind of crisis in their lives and marriages. It was also in South Carolina where Jennifer began keeping a journal in earnest—something she would do for the rest of her life.

Just what Jennifer's life was all about can be discerned from her extensive journals, which detailed everything from her relationship with Mike and Abby, to everyday occurrences and her declining health. Jennifer was a prolific writer, and she kept meticulous journals, especially during the 1990s. This habit especially came to the fore in 1998, when her physical problems started to increase, and there were more problematic issues with Mike and Abby as well. In January 1998, Jennifer wrote that she was having the flu once again, and reading The Left Behind series, which she found to be interesting. She worried that Mike and Abby might get her flu, and added, "Thank you Lord for my family you so graciously gave to me. What praise to you and a blessing from you."

Jennifer's journal was mainly about the issues of the day and her relationship with God. In fact, the journal was written as if these were letters directly to God—not a dialogue, but more of a soliloquy. All of the writing was not to someone who was distant, but rather, right there in her life. In the notation from the early weeks of January 1999, Jennifer wrote that she knew that God desired to communicate with her on a daily basis, and the journal was her best means of doing so. She thanked Him for always being there in spirit, and she knew that He always wanted to be by her side. She said she desired to worship, pray, praise, thank, question, ask, know, love, and cry with Him. "You are awesome Father," she wrote, and she thanked Him for her friends. Jennifer was always thankful for the blessings bestowed upon her, and her journals reflected this even when she complained about her health.

The January 14, 1999, entry dealt with a very divisive issue in the Blagg home—the question of whether they would stay in South Carolina or not. Jennifer wrote that she and Mike had been doing a lot of praying on the matter, and noted that someone from Phoenix, Arizona, had phoned about a job offer there. She said that she would leave it in God's hands, and prayed for wisdom in the matter. And then so typical of her, she ended with, "Help me to care for others."

By January 21, Jennifer complained of having the flu again, and admitted that she was not a good patient. She said that she despised, with every bone in her body, being sick. Even though she was sick, she wrote that she loved God for all His mercies, and "Praise your name, for giving me the most wonderful husband." Jennifer said that Mike had stayed home to take care of her, and she was thankful for it.

A few days later, she was still sick, but thankful that God continued to communicate with her and give direction in her life. She fretted about whether she would go to Oklahoma to see her dad, who was very ill, and then added, "Whatever you say, I'll do. Please give me the wisdom, desire and strength to do it."

The next day, the move issue was still bothering her, and she added that Mike had supposedly received an answer to his prayers from God saying to relax, don't worry, because everything would work out for the best.

A few days later, another issue popped up when a friend of Jennifer's found out that she was pregnant. Jennifer surmised that Abby would now start pestering her and Mike for a baby brother or sister—and Jennifer drew an unhappy face in the margin of the journal. Another child, after the last difficult pregnancy, was the last thing she wanted.

Her premonitions seemed to come true—the very next day she noted that she had blown up at Abby, and these were the least of her complaints. CMA, a company to which they owed money, was threatening to send them to a collection agency; Mike never seemed to be at his desk, and he wasn't answering his e-mails in a timely manner. Jennifer drew three faces on the page this time—a puzzled-looking face, a disgruntled face, and a third one that showed fear. Then she noted, "I'm mad and I can't believe someone is going to send us to a collection agency!"

At least by the next entry, Jennifer noted that it had been a much better day, saying that the Lord's voice was clear and quiet, and that she wished for her ears, eyes, heart, and life to be bent completely toward Him. As always, she prayed for others who were ill at the time. And there was a small notation that displayed her unconventional streak—"Remember to be uncommon," she wrote.

Jennifer also noted that she had been depressed since the new year began, and she had a hard time shaking the depression. As to the journal itself, she said it was a way to see God's love for her and His ways and desire to grow within her.

Trying to overcome her depression, she focused the entire next week's entries on the blessings in her life. There was a blessing that the Lord was in her life, a blessing for the friendship of Edie Melson, Kim Genoble, Tom Rucker, Glenn Bolt, and "countless others." Then she wrote that she especially felt blessed for "my adoring husband."

The blessing categories lasted until the next entries of worry about Mike's job situation, and a possible move, and the fact that Mike and Abby were sick as well. Abby got a "time out" soon thereafter, and Jennifer nearly cried out, "Lord, I simply don't know what to do anymore!"

If January was bad, February was worse. Jennifer noted on February 5, "Didn't sleep after Mike went to work. Stomach attack. I looked in medical book."

She tried to make the most of life a few days later, by thanking God for a beautiful cloudless day, and a walk in the park with Abby, but her physical ailments continued and seemed to grow worse with time.

Jennifer flew to Texas on February 10, to see her mom, who was having cancer treatments, and they went out to a movie and saw Kevin Costner in *Message in a Bottle*. She thought it was a beautiful movie, and wanted Mike to go see it with her when she got back home.

Jennifer noted that she and her mom were talking about weight loss and other issues, especially about not treating others negatively as they might treat you. She turned to Psalm 15, citing, "Who shall dwell in My house? Those who don't gossip or have a slur on their lips for their neighbors."

Jennifer was always a perfectionist and very hard on herself. She prayed to take that Scripture to heart, and become more "Christ-like, not man like." In a lesser person, it might be seen as overblown piety, or even arrogance, but Jennifer put her money where her mouth was. She earnestly tried to be a better person, and often went out of her way to help others. Having suffered a great deal, emotionally and physically, she wouldn't do anything to repeat those offenses on others. She took her Christianity, not as a canting display of self-advertisement, but a means of doing good within her family and within the world. And there is never any doubt in her journal entries how she felt about her relationship with God. She called him a caretaker, life giver, compassionate father, and miracle giver. She thanked God for her friends and for Mike and Abby.

Turning philosophical, she wondered, when in Heaven,

would she talk to God directly, and would she get to hug Him? Would her friends be there? She thanked God for making her a curious person, and she thanked God for her safe and smooth flight back home.

Jennifer returned home to find that Mike had painted and finished the garage, given her chocolates and a hundred roses, two snake chain necklaces, and then took her out to dinner. She said he saved the best for last. "He's the best part of me," she wrote.

Home, however, was a handful for Jennifer, when it came to Abby. Abby got into trouble at school by painting some of the chairs—and Jennifer was furious. It was a miserable time—Abby had bronchitis and Jennifer had worsening stomach problems. On one day in particular, Abby got five "time outs," and Jennifer wrote in amazement, "How can this be!"

As it turned out, Abby had asthma. It made her very cranky, and Jennifer was relieved when Mike took Abby to the mall, so she could have time away from her sick and unruly daughter. Jennifer prayed that Abby would fall "head over heels" in love with God, the same way she had. Yet, turmoil dogged them all—Mike's job situation got no better and he was very discouraged about it. He and his boss did not get along. Mike sent his résumé to a plant in Ohio, and Jennifer secretly wished for a move there, even though she said she would have to get used to the snow and cold. She did not want to move out West again.

Jennifer's entry of March 18, 1999, stated that Mike's manager at work, frankly, did not like him, and she was surprised, saying it was the first time he'd been in that situation. She said that his boss was missing out by not knowing Mike the way she did. Typical of Jennifer, however, she said that she wished his boss no ill will. Then there was a curious notation that she hadn't spoken to Mike all day long, and she realized how dependent she was on him. It may have even gone further than that. Mike called her several times a day to see what she was doing. It bordered on paranoia, rather than concern for her happiness.

At least a party for Abby was a good day, and Jennifer wrote, "Abby is a precious gift and I thank you for her," followed the next day by "Abby is truly unbelievable!!! She's such a joy to us!!"

It didn't take long for the attitude to change, however— five days later, Abby was "horribly trying—the worst day we've had in weeks!" Abby was a rambunctious little girl, not mean-spirited or petty, and full of energy, but it was very tiring for Jennifer at times, especially when she wasn't feeling well.

Jennifer's physical ailments were a constant problem, and she tried the drug Effexor, to which she had a terrible reaction. She tried Wellbutrin, and it left her dizzy and sleepy for much of the day. The next day, she tried something else. In desperation, she wrote, "Let something work, Lord!"

Jennifer's entry of March 24 was one of her most extensive. She had been nervous because she had an appointment with a doctor, and admitted that she had difficulty talking about all her ailments. The appointment went well, however, even though she noted that her PMS symptoms were getting worse all the time. At least she had taken care of her anxiety and depression to some degree. As always, she looked to God for guidance and help.

It was a chaotic time of ailments, misbehavior by Abby, and Mike's continual job search, which left Jennifer increasingly tired and worn-out, both mentally and physically. Mike left for Ohio, but said he wasn't hopeful about the prospects there. He was also thinking about a job in Escondido, California, and Euless, Texas. At least when the Ohio job did not come through, Jennifer admitted that she was glad that they weren't moving there. The thought of cold and snow must have gotten the better of her, after enjoying the sunnier climates of South Carolina.

Jennifer took a revelatory journey in June of that year to her father's funeral, and it was very hard for her. At the end of it, she noted that he was never going to be the dad she wanted or deserved. Through daydreams and visions, she said, she had come to some kind of acceptance about what had happened between them in her life. She said that her earthly father had been a big disappointment, but that her heavenly father was everything she wanted and needed.

The job search for Mike went on and on and extended to New Mexico, and other places—and in the midst of all this, Jennifer was truly rocked by the school shootings at Columbine High in Littleton, Colorado. "Horrible tragedy!" she wrote. "I've been scared and haven't trusted in You to keep me or my family safe."

Mike might have been suffering at work, but Jennifer noted that she and Mike had a wonderful, romantic evening on June 24. "He's awesome, Lord," she wrote. "Thank you."

The job search seemed to go on and on—Waterloo, Iowa, Delavan, North Carolina, and San Diego, California. Jennifer's head swam with all of the possibilities. She loved South Carolina and her friends there, and any major move seemed like a type of exile. At least she was immensely proud on November 28, 1999, when Abby walked down the aisle at their church and was baptized. Jennifer drew a huge smiling face on the page of her journal.

Jennifer's stomach problems continued to get worse and worse, and on February 1, 2000, the reason became apparent. Dr. Moore found a cyst in her abdomen and it was serious business, followed by the fact that Mike got a job offer in Colorado.

Perhaps to cheer her up, Mike took Jennifer on a "treasure hunt." She was led along a path, and at the end of the search was a brand-new minivan. She wrote of Mike, "He is a gift straight from Your hands. I don't deserve him!"

There was bad news for Jennifer soon thereafter that February, however. A doctor told her that her thyroid would fail at some point, but until her numbers got into a worse range, he wouldn't treat her. While Mike and Jennifer sat in a car, she said that they were both devastated by the news. Then she listed all the people who were praying for her.

Jennifer got a second opinion from a different doctor, who treated her with some medication, and she admitted in her journal that she'd been scared, then mad, then finally willing to place it all in God's hands. She was even apologetic to God for having thrown a tantrum and doubting Him for a while. She admitted that she was scared and asked, "Help me realize I'm well-taken care of in your hands. Why do I have such little faith?"

By March 2000, she started taking 88mg of Synthyroid and she felt drugged and almost in a stupor all day long. Her notation was interesting, however. She wrote, "I was drugged," and put a little smiley face next to that sentence. The drug seemed to do her some good—she slept better, ate better, had more energy, and she said that she was less fearful. She wrote, "Don't choose depression, fear, worry and anxiety."

Despite feeling somewhat better, Jennifer still had a lot of dizziness from the Synthyroid and was scared that it might be hurting her in some ways. She wrote of her family, "We are all suffering from me being sick again." As to her sickness, she tried to be philosophical about it and stated that she saw it as suffering, but she was sure God saw it as glory. It was in the overcoming of suffering that one matured.

April 2 was an important day in the Blaggs' lives—Jennifer wrote that Mike was moved by the Lazarus story, death and resurrection, to decide upon a move to Grand Junction, Colorado, as a rebirth of his career. Jennifer was very skeptical about this move, and leaving all her friends behind, but she admitted that prayer had led her and Mike to accept what seemed best. The Blagg family would make their new home in Grand Junction, Colorado. Once again, they would pull up stakes and take off for a destination that Mike chose.

Grand Junction, Colorado, lies in western Colorado at the junction of the Colorado River and Gunnison River. The official visitor guide described the area as a place "that takes you beyond the ski resorts of the Rocky Mountains into the mystery and majesty of the Grand Valley. Here's a town that hasn't lost its charming western hospitality even though it's the largest regional hub between Denver and Salt Lake City. Frontiersmen and early settlers were drawn to the area for its moderate climate and fertile soil, a bounty that our winemakers and peach growers cherish today."

In fact, by 2000, the surrounding area had more than a dozen wineries and acre upon acre of orchards devoted to cherries, peaches, and apples. The dominant backdrop to the area was Colorado National Monument, covering twenty-three thousand acres of colorful sandstone cliffs. In time, the Blagg family would move to the Redlands, right below the cliffs, and take advantage of the monument's hiking trails. It was a wilderness next door, with deer, hawks, and an occasional mountain lion roaming the mesas and canyons.

Jennifer, however, didn't feel immediately like she fit into the community of the Grand Valley. Perhaps, after having already lived in an arid climate in Arizona, she still longed for the lush greenery of South Carolina. She and Mike tried some new churches, and at least by their second week there, Jennifer had made a few new friends. She noted on May 27, 2000, that she'd been in Grand Junction for two weeks and connected with a woman named Sherri King and she'd begun to be involved in a Bible-study class.

This feeling of well-being was short-lived, however. On June 17, she wrote that she and Mike were having very serious communication problems. He seemed to be at work a lot, he wasn't being very affectionate, and she wrote, "I feel hopeless!" She was often stuck in the house alone or with Abby, who was sometimes a chore to handle. Abby was a very exuberant child, and Jennifer was a perfectionist and sometimes they mixed like oil and water. More and more, as solace, Jennifer turned to the journal, with a Bible verse for each day's topic. She wrote in the margins whatever situation was troubling her that day—and her troubles seemed to be many. The Bible verses were a way for her to deal with specific problems.

Jennifer's topics included the following:

"I'm Beautiful"—Apparently, Jennifer was still self-conscious about her weight, and she wrote down this passage to remind herself that she was still desirable. It also gave an insight on how she might have viewed Mike in the scheme of things.

Psalm 45:10–11

*Hear, O daughter, consider and incline your
    ear;
forget your people and your father's house,
and the king will desire your beauty.*

"Belief and trust"—This seems to allude not only to rest from her anxiety about ill health, but about trust in Mike as well, and perhaps some solitude away from Abby's rambunctious nature.

Isaiah 30:15

In returning and rest you shall be saved,
in quietness and in trust shall be your strength.

"Depression"—As Mike noted, Jennifer suffered with bouts of depression through most of the 1990s and even into the new century.

Isaiah 57:15

I dwell in the high and holy place,
and also with him who is of a contrite and
    humble spirit,
to revive the spirit of the humble,
and to revive the heart of the contrite.

Once again, this was also an admonition to be humble and not too proud in her knowledge of verse and Scripture. Jennifer was never one to display with ostentation her piety.

"Setting a Captive Free"—By this verse, there already must have been some thought on Jennifer's part about wanting to escape from what she deemed a crumbling marriage. The impetus of that view was Mike's continuing viewing of Internet porn, which had become a very sore subject between her and Mike.

Isaiah 61

The Spirit of the Lord God is upon me,
because the Lord has annointed me to bring
    good tidings to the afflicted;
He has sent me to bind up the brokenhearted,
to proclaim liberty to the captives,

and the opening of the prison to those who are
*   bound.*

"Tumor"—What came as a new and unwelcome revelation to Jennifer was addressed in the following Scripture.

Romans 15:13

May the God of hope fill you with all joy and
*   peace*
in believing, so by the power of the Holy Spirit
*   you may abound in hope.*

This last notation entered the journal because Jennifer started worrying that she might have a brain tumor. Just how she came to this conclusion at the time was not noted in her journal.

To try and do something meaningful in the Grand Junction area, Jennifer, along with Mike, started working as a team in something called a Prayer Warrior Group. By that, they meant taking on life's problems in a warrior fashion, rather than just sulking and avoiding them. Part of the structure included such things as "start claiming like a victor," and to think of God as the vine, and themselves as the branches. In this group, they and the others were to pour out themselves for others, and to be aware of ambition when it turned into self-destructive pride. They were to pour out their bitterness—"bitterness is spiritual cancer."

Increasingly during this time, Jennifer had problems in her genital area. As Mike had noted, she often referred to it as "sitting on hot coals." It was very pervasive, frustrating, and definitely interfered with Mike and Jennifer's sex lives. The prospect of having a hysterectomy became one of the options for Jennifer to deal with this problem.

Jennifer noted with relief that the hysterectomy surgery went very well, and within a few hours of the surgery, she was back home. Her mom had been there with her, and she was happy for the company. Yet nothing ever seemed to go smoothly, as far as Jennifer's physical problems went. Suffering from a bad yeast infection, she took three doses of medication by accident, instead of the one prescribed. When she found out that she'd taken too many, she panicked and went to a hospital emergency room. She was "very depressed, weary, heart-broken and confused." For the first time, there is a note of disbelief in God's power to heal, and she even admitted, "I didn't feel it. Believing isn't about emotions, it's about believing He can do something. That is power."

Jennifer spoke of the bleeding woman in the New Testament who touched Jesus's cloak and was cured. The reason she was cured was because she had faith that he could indeed cure her. At the moment, however, Jennifer's faith was being sorely tested.

Mike might have been satisfied in his job and life in Grand Junction, but Jennifer was not. She was sick a lot, she missed her friends in South Carolina, and Mike seemed more distant than ever. One of her notations was from Zephaniah 3:17:

> *The Lord, your God, is in your midst,*
> *a warrior who gives victory.*
> *He will rejoice over you with gladness,*
> *He will renew you in His love.*

She attributed this verse to a friend of hers named Beth "breaking free." What the breaking free refers to isn't spelled out, but it may have meant breaking free from a bad marriage or relationship. Then Jennifer wrote that "It's taken me so long to see the <u>light</u>." She may have been referring to her own marriage with that line.

And so it went throughout 2001—everything from "I was sick on Mike's birthday. I gave him a card, but nothing else" to "stop lying to make others feel good. I plant seeds of discouragement and reap a fruitless crop. No one else is perfect. Why do I want others to see me as flawless?"

Jennifer and Mike's ten-year wedding anniversary was coming up in November 2001, and perhaps to try and rekindle what they had once felt, she wrote him a letter. She stated that she was glad they had married and that she wouldn't have wanted to spend her life with anyone else. They couldn't know what the future held, but she hoped it would be better and better every day. Jennifer said that, like Jesus, they had to pick up their personal crosses every day and struggle on. Then she wrote, "I'm your beloved wife, who adores you. Thank you for being my husband and for loving me the way you do. I'll be waiting for you at home w/open arms and an open heart. All my love, Jennifer, your bride."

Yet, by 2001, it was no longer a fairy-tale marriage, and every so often, Jennifer would have a flash of insight. She wrote in her journal that she made Mike pay for everything that her father didn't give her, and she wondered if she was too demanding of him, because her father had been so much less than perfect. "Straining toward what is ahead, I press on toward the goal to win the prize for which God has called me heavenward."

By the last days of October 2001, Jennifer was in a deep malaise, as far as Mike and she were concerned, as well as their whole experience in Grand Junction. She hopefully wrote that they would move from Grand Junction within a year's time. Everything since they moved there had seemed to go downhill in their marriage and communication between each other.

Jennifer spoke of God smoothing her rough edges and making her stronger. She bought a book entitled *Love God with All Your Mind*, and hoped it would give her courage. A few days later, she went to a prayer group, where she felt "everyone else's praying was dead but mine." She was so annoyed by the others' dryness in their prayers, as if they were just going through the motions, that afterward she went outside and cried. A short time later, she felt bad for judging the others and realized that God gave people different gifts. Jennifer continuously fought against feeling too proud about herself, or feelings of being superior to others.

Sometime in the earliest part of November, Jennifer and Abby most likely took a trip across town to the Colorado Rural Legal Sevices. None of this would come to light until later. It must have been one of the most painful, soul-searching events that Jennifer ever had endured. As it turned out, the agency was not helpful because of understaffing. Asked to leave her name and number, Jennifer said, "No, no!" She was clearly afraid what would happen if Mike found out she was there.

And then on November 9, she and Mike had an argument so profound, that she would be writing about it for days to come. Jennifer never explicitly spelled out what the argument was about, but it had affected her deeply. To have been that disturbed by whatever happened suggests more than what Mike later would say, how the argument had only been about a job recruiter phoning him at work.

On November 11, 2001, Jennifer entered the last entry that would ever go into her journal. She put a title by it— "Sunday in Colo." This was unusual, for she generally never put notations as to place. It may have been placed there because she was planning to take a trip to South

Carolina with Abby, as Edie Melson suggested. "Sunday in Colo" would help differentiate in the journal the place of her writing, as opposed to any future writing in South Carolina.

The last notation included, "I watched Dr. Stanley. <u>The Key to Peace</u>. I learned Jesus holds the <u>key</u> to life and death. He knows when you're gonna be born and die. But He left us some keys as well. Health key, financial, material, relationships, future desires keys. I must give Him all these keys. I had some prayer time. I prayed and acted like I was picking up keys. Health key, future key, reached out next to me, and handed Jesus the keys. I may have to do it every day, but for today, He's got the keys and I've got peace. Thank you Father."

Feeling sick on Sunday, and irritated with Mike, perhaps because of their recent argument, Jennifer did not go to church with Mike and Abby. (And even Abby would tell her Sunday-school teacher that her mom and dad recently had had an argument about something.) Instead, Jennifer watched a religious program on television, and underlined some lines in a book entitled *Winning Over Worry*. A few of the lines she underscored stated, "I give God the things in my life—my home, my possessions, my time, my body and my mind. We are to make a plan for the day, pray over that plan and then proceed with that plan."

In her own handwriting, she noted on the pages of the book: "Fought with Mike on Friday. I unexpectedly got sick this weekend."

Around this same time, she also wrote directly on the pages of a Bible at Psalm 142:

> *I cry aloud to the Lord;*
> *I lift up my voice to the Lord*
> *for mercy.*
> *I pour out my complaint before*

Him;
before Him I tell my trouble.
When my spirit grows faint
within me,
it is to You who know my way.
In the path where I walk
men have hidden a snare for me.
Look to my right and see
no one is concerned for me.
I have no refuge;
no one cares for my life.

I cry to You, O Lord;
I say, You are my refuge;
my portion in the land of the living.
Listen to my cry
for I am in desperate need;
rescue me from those who pursue me,
for they are too strong for me.

Right next to these lines, she wrote, "Mike and I had a <u>very</u> serious talk about our lack of effective communication. You gave me this Psalm of when David was in the cave. It was a very dark time for him. I relate to tonight. I feel scared, numb, frustrated, almost desperate. Lord, tell me how to pray for Mike, myself and our marriage."

A few days later, Jennifer and Abby were gone, and only a large bloodstain lay upon the bed where Jennifer had once rested her head. Indeed, as she had written, "I am in desperate need . . . for they are too strong for me."

Chapter 7

Bird on a Balcony

Even though the search for Jennifer was through, some residents of the Grand Junction area wanted to keep alive her memory and that of Abby by creating an organization that helped search for lost children. They asked Marilyn Conway and David Loman, Jennifer's brother, if it was okay. In fact, it was more than okay with those two, and Loman agreed to be its president. The organization was named the Abby and Jennifer Recovery Foundation (AJRF), and it became an adjunct of the Texas-based Laura Recovery Center Foundation.

In one of their early statements, the foundation related, "When authorities called it quits after eleven days of looking for the bodies . . . more than 2,000 people shed their orange vests, and dropped their walking sticks and maps." There were others, however, who said they wanted to keep on doing something for missing children and have an organization in place that could quickly align itself with the authorities to help out when time was of the essence.

Executive director Connie Flukey told a reporter for the

Daily Sentinel, "We now feel like Abby is our child." Flukey, a mother of eight, had participated every day in the search during April 2002. While most volunteers had gone home after the search ended on April 27, a hard-core group remained. Of these, two hundred signed up to become part of the Abby and Jennifer Recovery Foundation. "There were a lot of volunteers out there that didn't want to see it end," Flukey said. The organization drew up legal papers with the IRS, and became a nonprofit organization.

Almost immediately, the organization was called upon to put its expertise to work. In Salt Lake City, fourteen-year-old Elizabeth Smart was kidnapped from her home on June 5, and four volunteers from the Abby and Jennifer Recovery Foundation drove to that city to assist in the search effort. In fact, the Smart family donated some computers to the organization to be used for mapping and searcher registration. Other sponsors were from the Grand Junction area, and as far away as Oklahoma City.

Over time, the AJRF hoped to create fifteen committees to focus on various aspects of missing children's cases, including being a contact to law enforcement, a helpful resource for the parents, and a place to train volunteers who would go out on the actual searches. They set up a twenty-four-hour emergency hotline, and set a goal of being able to go into action on very short notice. Flukey said, "The idea is that there is a perpetrator out there who should be scared, and maybe we can deter them if they know there is a huge community ready to go out within hours of a child being reported missing."

The motto for the organization was "Let it shine"— a phrase that came from one of Jennifer and Abby's favorite songs, "This Little Light of Mine," which contained those words.

Across town, the defense team for Michael Blagg, consisting of David Eisner and Kenneth Singer, had their hands full in 2002, stating in a document that they had just been provided with fourteen thousand pages of discovery from the DA's office, and they were going to need more time to digest it all. Besides written court documents, there were fifty audiotapes, fifty videotapes, crime scene photos, and lab reports. The CBI files hadn't even come in yet, and one of the defense attorneys wrote Judge Bottger, "In order to be on even footing with the prosecution, the defense needs to have the opportunity prior to the preliminary hearing to meaningfully view and examine those pieces of evidence." He then added that CBI agent Kevin Humphreys told them that they could not use CBI facilities to view evidence, but had to do so at the MCSO in Grand Junction. Items being tested at CBI wouldn't even reach the MCSO until the end of July.

One of the main issues for Eisner and Singer was that "every first-degree murder case is considered to be a capital case and death is a possible penalty." Although the DA's office wasn't required to declare their intention to seek the death penalty, until sixty days after arraignment, both Eisner and Singer had to plan for such a contingency. To that end, they asked Judge Bottger for more time before scheduling the preliminary hearing, and they cited several cases from around the country to back up their contentions.

On a more macabre note, DA Frank Daniels sent David Eisner a letter stating that the coroner's office had finished their work on Jennifer Blagg's body, and that work included the removal of her hands so that fingerprints could be obtained. The hands had been sent to the CBI office in Montrose, but were now back at the coroner's office.

District Attorney Frank Daniels noted, "Jennifer's mother is beginning to make plans for a proper burial. Of course, she would like the remains to be intact as much as possible for the burial. Jennifer's mother has become increasingly impatient with the inability to provide Jennifer a proper burial, and understandably so." Daniels said that if Eisner insisted on "thwarting the release of the body," then he should file an expedited motion for a court order.

Eisner and Singer were correct in their belief that the DA was "going to throw the book" at Mike Blagg. In September 2002, the DA's office filed additional charges against Blagg, accusing him of stealing from his home insurance company and from AMETEK Dixson. One of the four new charges alleged that Mike filed and collected on a false insurance claim regarding the jewelry that was supposedly stolen from the home on Pine Terrace Court. Another charge dealt with committing abuse and violence on a corpse, along with two additional counts of theft.

The crime of abusing a corpse was a sentence-enhancing charge. This could come into play if a jury did not find Mike guilty of first-degree murder, with its mandatory life sentence—but rather found him guilty of second-degree murder. Then the corpse abuse charge could garner him more prison time, as could findings of guilt for the theft charges.

The theft charges dealt with Mike allegedly stealing office furniture from AMETEK Dixson and defrauding the United States Automobile Association, the company that had insured his home. That felony theft charge alleged that he had swindled them out of $15,000.

David Eisner, the lead defense attorney, was the head of the Grand Junction office of the state public defender. Defense attorney Steve Laiche said of Eisner, "From the lowest-class felony to the most serious charge, he gives them everything he's got." Just how much he threw himself into these cases could be ascertained by his defense in the Santana-Figuracion murder trial. The victim died after suffering twenty-six stab wounds, but what might have looked like an open-and-shut case did not seem that way to Eisner. Working behind the scenes, Eisner helped shape the jury

instructions in such a manner that the jurors did not vote for
first-degree murder charges against the alleged perpetrator.
Fellow lawyer in the case, Steve Laiche said, "His fashion-
ing of jury instructions contributed to the verdict in that
case." And another attorney, Colleen Scissors, agreed.
"Dave had cutting-edge instructions and a marvelous and
complete understanding of where he wanted to go."

Eisner also was not timid about standing up for his
clients when he believed that the prosecutor was taking advantage of a situation. This side of him was highlighted
in the first-degree murder case against Deon Caballero.
Several witnesses could identify Caballero, but there was
a problem—the *Daily Sentinel* had prematurely run a mug
shot photo of Caballero, and Eisner questioned how many
of these witnesses had seen the photo in the newspaper. In
a hearing, long before the murder trial, Eisner questioned
these witnesses over a long period of time. Prosecutor Pete
Hautzinger later admitted, "In all honesty, I got frustrated
and a little bored. I will confess that I might have arched
my eyebrows and made faces." Seeing this, Eisner filed a
motion that Hautzinger be held in contempt. The judge
denied this motion.

Now it remained to be seen just how contentious the
Blagg trial might become between David Eisner and DA
Frank Daniels. This was sure to be one of Mesa County's
most potentially explosive cases.

On the one-year anniversary of Mike's 911 call of November 13, 2001, the *Daily Sentinel* did a retrospective on
the case, and questioned various members connected to it.
One of these was Investigator Steven King, who had been
preparing to leave work for home on that fateful day, when
he suddenly heard a tense voice over the police radio:
"Wife and young daughter missing. Blood in the house."

King told the reporter that he could discern the tension in the dispatcher's voice: "It was as if the faster she spoke, the faster police would respond."

The reporter noted that this crime scene wasn't like most others that the MCSO responded to. King said, "Ninety-eight percent of the cases you handle, you've seen it all before. He (the perpetrator) got drunk and he shot him (the victim) and now he's confessing and he's sorry. It's not the challenge that a complex case like this has with all its twists and turns."

There had been intense scrutiny from the public that November, the press, and even national television networks, along with *People* magazine, who sent a photographer to the region. King believed that all that outside scrutiny helped the officers of MCSO band more tightly together, even though they were pulling down long shifts. King realized early on that none of them could slip up and release protected information that might be critical later on.

Mesa County sheriff Riecke Claussen agreed about the case helping the sheriff's personnel pull together. He spoke of the sixteen officers assigned to the case who had worked full-time for weeks, from sunup to sundown. Claussen said that many of them had a hard time sleeping, because the case was still being viewed as a missing persons case at the time.

Captain Bill Gardner, of MCSO, told a reporter, "From a management vantage point, we had to carefully monitor hours and days and workload that people were willingly bearing—coordinating it and making certain that at some point people got adequate relief. I think it tested our abilities to communicate and ensure we remained productive through the weeks."

Gardner said that the personnel had passed the test, but had suffered a great deal of physical and emotional strain during the long hours of police work. Deputies had been pulled off other assignments to assist in the crime, and some criminal investigations in the area had been postponed and even canceled. The Blagg case had become the number one priority in the area.

Both Gardner and King agreed that the media focus on them had been intense. Media outlets from around the nation had focused on the Grand Junction area in general, and the MCSO in particular. *Unsolved Mysteries* and *Inside Edition* made inquiries about the case, *Good Morning America* had Michael Blagg do a live segment. King said, "I think what was unique to this case, unlike others, was the intensity of the public and media focus."

One of the early breaks was actually witnessing Mike Blagg stealing office furniture from AMETEK Dixson. It gave the investigators impetus to question him again, which led to his ten-hour interview and his "suicide attempt" the next day. King said that early on they knew that Mike was trying to lead them astray, and that he was an intelligent suspect. "This wasn't checkers," King told the reporter, "this was chess. This was multilevel chess."

One of the unusual steps taken, according to King, was MCSO actually asking for public support in the search. By doing this, they disclosed some information that would normally have remained sealed, but they thought it was worth the risk. One of the unexpected outcomes of this was a closer relationship between MCSO and many of the citizens of the region, who saw the office in a whole new light. A spokesperson for MCSO said, "We had been working for years embracing and welcoming the community into the sheriff's department, and I think this case took the department and the community to a whole new level in that effort."

In many ways, even though the community search had not turned up traces of Jennifer and Abby, it helped in an unforeseen way—it let the MCSO and other authorities concentrate on the landfill, rather than spending so much time and effort elsewhere out in the countryside. Finding Jennifer's body in the landfill had been a big boost to the case, but King admitted, "I would like to think there will come a day when I'll go through a whole day and I won't think of Abby Blagg. Whether it's seeing a girl the same age, or you see a flyer on your desk, it just doesn't go away. Someday it might go away. It hasn't yet."

It certainly hadn't gone away for Jennifer's brother, David Loman. He said, "Most days, the simple memory of a smile or the statement of 'I love you' rings in my mind, but some days the horror is more than I want to imagine. Jennifer and Abby will always be in my heart, and they are about God's work now."

If most of the focus in the community still centered on the missing girl, that was not the case in the law office of Stephan Schweissing, who also had represented Mike Blagg. Schweissing noted that he had represented Mike from early February 2002 through mid-June 2002, and in December 2002 he wrote an Affidavit in Support of Motion for Bond Reduction. Schweissing gave several reasons for this, starting with the fact that he had notified Investigator George Barley, of MCSO, well in advance of Mike Blagg leaving town in April 2002. Schweissing said that Mike's reason for leaving Grand Junction had nothing to do with the search at the landfill, but rather because he couldn't find employment in the Grand Junction area and his lease had expired on the place he had been renting on North Club Court. Mike allegedly also needed a close support system, which was provided by his family in Georgia. To that end, Mike had moved back to Warner Robins, Georgia, according to Schweissing.

Schweissing wrote that Mike had stayed in touch with him during his stay in Georgia, and that Mike never professed any intent to leave the country or avoid law enforcement. Then in the early evening hours of June 4, 2002, Schweissing learned some details about a discovery at the landfill connected to Jennifer Blagg, and on June 5, the discovery was confirmed as being the body of Jennifer. He immediately contacted Mike in Georgia.

Schweissing said that Mike attempted to make reservations to return to Grand Junction on June 5, but no flights were available. He was able to e-mail Schweissing his flight itinerary for June 6. On June 5, however, Mike's mother phoned Schweissing and told him that Mike had been arrested at her Georgia home. She said that he had been arrested in his pajamas while he was trying to get some rest for his journey back to Grand Junction.

Schweissing wrote that he was able to speak with Mike around 11 P.M., on June 5, and that Mike was in custody at the Warner Robins Jail. Schweissing spoke with Mike again on the morning of June 6 at the jail, and at no time did Mike ever state that he did not intend to return to Colorado. For those reasons, Schweissing contested that Mike Blagg's bail should be reduced from $1,000,000 to a lesser amount.

This document was minor compared to the one sent soon thereafter by Mike's new lawyers, David Eisner and Kenneth Singer. The document had the incredibly long title of "Motion for Sanctions, Either to Dismiss or Exclude from Introduction into Evidence at Trial Any Reference to the Ten and One Half Hour Interrogation of Mr. Blagg Conducted by the Federal Bureau of Investigation and the Mesa County Sheriff on February 5, 2002, on the Grounds of Failure to Record, the Utilization of Totally Unreliable Procedures, the Destruction of Exculpatory Evidence and Outrageous Governmental Conduct." This behemoth title was followed by point after point to Judge Bottger that ran a gamut of issues:

1. Mr. Blagg was suspected by law enforcement from the beginning, and MCSO allegedly assigned Steven King to befriend him and gain his trust. Supposedly, King and others told Mike that he should talk to them without an attorney being present, as a sign of his goodwill, and to gain their acceptance that he was not involved in the crime.

2. Sometime long before February 5, 2002, MCSO had consulted with FBI agent William Irwin Jr. to utilize his expertise in interrogating techniques, even though this case was entirely within control of MCSO, and not an FBI case. It was decided, according to Eisner and Singer, that Irwin would conduct a polygraph test with Mike and then subject him to an extensive and aggressive post-test interrogation in an attempt to get him to confess to the disappearance of Jennifer and Abby. MCSO investigators Barley, Weyler, and King were to be present and join in the interrogation.

3. Eisner and Singer alleged that Mike had been invited to the meeting at MCSO on February 5, 2002, under the guise that he would be cleared as a suspect, once and for all, and this would help him with his employer and negative media publicity. Unbeknownst to Mike, MCSO had already been in contact with his supervisor Wes Hardin, and made Hardin part of the plan against Mike.

4. On that same evening, a video camera was turned on to transmit images and sound to a monitor in another portion of the investigation unit, and this was watched by investigators there. The defense lawyers contended that two investigators, who were not trained as stenographers, made notes and "transcripts" from this monitor, and these "transcripts were relied upon heavily later."

5. According to the defense attorneys, at the end of the interview on February 5, Sergeant Weyler told Mike that if he had thoughts of suicide, he should write down where the bodies could be discovered and draw a map of the area.

6. According to the defense attorneys, as the interrogation ended, Investigator Barley handed Mike a phone for a prearranged call to his supervisor, Wes Hardin, who informed him that he was terminated from employment. Mike started crying, at which time, according to this account, Weyler again asked Mike to draw a map where the bodies could be found.

A very strange occurrence happened a couple days later in the form of a letter that was sent straight to Judge David Bottger from an anonymous writer.

The letter stated:

I am writing this letter to you concerning the Blagg case. I did not know this family. I am coming from the church arena.

Several weeks after the incident, I had a very vivid dream. I do not know if it is true. In the dream, I was like a "little bird on a balcony," just watching this situation. Michael entered the room and Jennifer and Abby were both dead. Jennifer had unmistakably committed suicide. I thought Abbey [*sic*] had died of cardiac arrest when she found her mom, but now realize perhaps she was smothered or something. Michael especially tried to check Abby. Then he got a blue plastic tarp and wrapped them in it. I saw him driving and then he hide [*sic*] the bodies in a tiny farm building. Then I woke up.

This dream has "bugged me" for months. Each time I have read the *Daily Sentinel* I keep feeling that the evidence of the police is lacking.

I feel Michael may be covering this up as a suicide for the following reasons: She was unhappy here and wanted to go home.

She had a hysterectomy and I am assuming she was on medication and could have no more children. To many in Christian faith, suicide means you do not go to heaven. Which is easier to tell her parents, "We can't find her, or she shot herself, in the head?"

Michael's protecting her reputation, might be the last gift that he could give her. I realize many men do hurt or abuse their wivies [*sic*], but I know many others who protect their wivies [*sic*] to the endth [*sic*] degree. Men usually do not do their dirty laundry in public.

Maybe at first, he was in denial, and wanted everyone to go and find them, just to bring his family back. But, I believe he was covering for her.

I have also talked to people who have had someone committ [*sic*] suicide in their family and the first thing they wanted to do, was clean up the mess. As for the watered down blood in the bedroom, if the hands and gun had dropped back across her face, maybe he was just washing the situation, so he could understand what happened better. If he had done this, he would not need to wash it, he would know.

Is Michael ever going to admit to this? I doubt it. In minutes, his life changed forever. And, he made the decisions he did to shield his family perhaps. I believe, if this was a suicide, he would rather take his secret to his own grave than to have people know. In the South, where he grew up, suicide carries heavier implications, than in the West.

When police ask him to tell the truth, and when he says, "I can't" it may well have nothing to do with him committing the crime and everything to do, with not wanting people to know this situation. He may not even want his own attorneys to know. Things like this can turn into 3 inch headlines in the *Daily Sentinel*.

Can he lie about this? Of course. To him it is a worthy cause. Much like shielding Jews from the Nazis. This is a lie he can live with, as he figures, "God knows the truth," and understands.

Would he be afraid for his future? I believe so. He understands the anger of the community but I believe he is sticking by his integrity to shield his family.

Was he planning to come back to her, when she was found? I understand he already had the ticket.

Did he steal from his employer? Did the *Daily Sentinel* say this was "left over from a yard sale"? Where I come from, junk like that is "no big deal," please take it and get out of here.

Obviously the police and lawyers have all the information here, so this may be very unappliable [*sic*]. But, their reasoning that he cried, or that he tried to committ [*sic*] suicide himself, was reason to believe he was guilty, jut blows me away. What happens in grief and exhaustion? People cry and despair, give up.

Is there anyway [*sic*] Michael could tell the truth, to both sets of lawyers, and to yourself, with everyone sworn to keep their mouth shut? I do not know law, but it seems circumstances put this man into an impossible situation. Is there any provision for someone to tell the truth in private—so, they do not have to trash the reputation of someone they love? Of course, both sets of lawyers, would have to agree, along with the evidence. I realize this would be difficult for you as a Judge, to stand against public opinion, and so many are emotionally involved in this case. But, surely someone can think of questions to ask, that would reveal, his beliefs. I believe he would have to be prepared to tell the truth. That he could feel "safe" for his family in this. I don't want to give him an "out" if he is guilty, but to see a man punished for trying to stand by his family, is too much. I know the police and many others have been inconvenienced, but no one has suffered as much as he has, if he is innocent.

I thank you for your consideration on this.

A concerned citizen.

Judge Bottger, of course, had to turn this letter over to the authorities, the DA's office, and defense lawyers. Just who the anonymous person was, was not revealed in later court documents, but a letter of a different sort was revealed—Michael Blagg's suicide note was printed in the *Daily Sentinel* on December 21, 2002. Also printed were various transcripts and files from the investigation, showing that Mike had been looked at as a suspect from very early on in the case. Several discrepancies about what Mike had told police, and what had actually happened, were damaging to his cause. For instance, he had told them that he hadn't accessed pornographic sites on his home computer for several months prior to November 13, which was not the case.

At a hearing that same December, investigators stated that they did not have any direct physical evidence that tied Michael Blagg to the crime scene—no murder weapon, no blood, and no absolute fingerprints. What they did have was a lot of circumstantial evidence including a note they say he planted in Jennifer's purse on November 13, 2001, and a near confession that he had made on February 5,

2002. There was also the fact that Jennifer's body had been discovered in the landfill near gauges, circuit boards, and documents from AMETEK Dixson. In fact, there were now sixty thousand pages of investigative materials that tended to link Mike Blagg to Jennifer's murder. Yet, even with all of these, it was not going to be a slam dunk for DA Frank Daniels and his deputy Bryan Flynn to convict Mike of the murder. Both Eisner and Singer were good lawyers, and it took twelve jurors to convict.

On the day of Christmas Eve, 2002, Mike was in court once again, at a hearing where Judge Bottger stated there was enough evidence for Mike to stand trial. Mike sat quietly, displaying no emotion when that was read. Then he smiled broadly as Judge Bottger cut Mike's $1,000,000 bail in half, opening the door to the fact that his family might be able to raise enough money to have him released from the Mesa County Jail. Mike had been in solitary confinement in the jail since he had been arrested in Georgia and brought back to Colorado in June 2002.

In part, the reduction of bail stemmed from defense attorney Eisner's argument that there was no direct physical evidence, and that the story about Mike visiting the escort service on several occasions was suspect at best, because Julie House's story kept changing. Eisner also attempted to cast doubt on Louella Cross's statements about Jennifer and Abby visiting the legal services office, shortly before they disappeared. Eisner pointed out that the mystery woman who came into the office had never given her name, and Cross could not say for certain that the woman was, in fact, Jennifer Blagg, nor that the girl was Abby Blagg.

On January 8, 2003, the day that Jennifer would have celebrated her thirty-sixth birthday, Mike Blagg pleaded not guilty at his arraignment in the Mesa County Court-house. He walked into the courtroom, sans shackles, after posting a $500,000 bond on the night before. Mike wore a navy blue suit and walked into court alongside his mother and sister, Clare. After his plea of not guilty, he stopped briefly in the hallway to be photographed by press photographers, and made one comment to journalists: "It feels good to be out."

Mike was surrounded by his defense attorneys, family members, and supporters from the church he and Jennifer had attended. His sister, Clare, said, "We are very happy to have him out, and we're looking forward to the opportunity to show he is innocent, in court."

David Eisner commented briefly, and said that Mike would be staying in Warner Robins, Georgia, with his mother until his hearing, which wasn't even scheduled until May. Of Mike's family, Eisner said, "They're relieved to be with him this morning."

As part of Mike's release, he was ordered to stay at his mother's home in Warner Robins, and he had to give up his passport and waive any future extraditions. He could not visit any other state besides Georgia, except Colorado. His family had met bail by posting a $50,000 cash bond, and had put up the titles to property in Georgia to secure the remainder of the bond.

On other subjects, besides the release of Mike, Eisner had been more talkative in court. He complained to Judge Bottger that prosecutors had not turned over certain items to him, including bedding from the bed where Jennifer's blood was found, fingerprint evidence, and the bullet recovered from Jennifer's skull. DA Daniels's answer to these concerns was that the CBI could hand the bedding and fingerprints over to Eisner soon, but the FBI wouldn't be testing the bullet for another two or three months.

Soon thereafter, Mike's attorneys sought to keep out of

court, when it came to trial, the pornographic Internet material that he'd been viewing. They said it was irrelevant to the case at hand, and violated his constitutional rights. Daniels, on the other hand, argued, "Mr. Blagg had an affair with his computer and used sex and the Bible to control his wife. He (Mike) and Jennifer had an argument over Blagg's involvement in pornography, and that provided a motive for her murder."

This disagreement went back and forth, Eisner stating that "such evidence is being offered for the primary role of portraying Mr. Blagg as a person of bad character." Not only that, it was argued that the methods used by police in seizing pornographic files from the computers "were completely unreliable and unworthy of consideration by a trier of fact." (In other words—the jury.)

On another front, Mike's attorneys stated that FBI agent Ron Walker was not qualified to be addressing a jury when it was empaneled. "The qualifications of Mr. Walker are inadequate to qualify him as an expert in crime scene analysis and any 'profile' generated in this case is not reasonably reliable."

One of the more interesting motions to exclude evidence was a revelation that after he tried committing suicide, Mike had spoken with a nurse and apparently had told her some things relating to the disappearance of Jennifer and Abby. Just what he told her was not documented in later court papers, and Mike's attorneys said any of this conversation was covered by doctor-client privilege.

If that wasn't enough, on March 10, 2003, the defense team came to court with a whole new theory—and it was a bombshell. They wanted DA Frank Daniels removed from the case, because they said that early on in the case, a man working within the Mesa County DA's Office had been considered a suspect by the investigators. According to them, this man had been stalking a neighbor of the

Blagg family, and the defense claimed that in a case of mistaken identity, the stalker had murdered Jennifer Blagg early on the morning of November 13, 2001, and probably murdered Abby when he discovered his mistake.

Chapter 8

Allegations

The latest revelation in the Blagg case was a stunner—and it would lead to rancorous debates between the defense lawyers, DA, and even the judge. Both sides of the aisle pointed fingers at the other, and accused each other of deception, grandstanding, and a lot worse. It was a hotly contested free-for-all, and it did not die down quickly or peacefully.

In March 2003, the defense attorneys for Michael Blagg claimed that police reports of November 2001 keyed in on a male prosecutor in the Mesa County DA's Office, who began stalking another deputy DA, Tammy Eret, when "his romantic overtures were rebuffed." Unfortunately for Jennifer Blagg, according to the defense attorneys, Tammy Eret lived right next door to the Blaggs' residence, and the stalker went into the wrong house in the early morning hours of November 13, 2001.

According to the defense attorneys, "The deputy DA (Tammy Eret) was being stalked at the same time leading [up] to the disappearances—and she felt seriously threatened. She was fearful enough that she carried a handgun to work with her in the heavily guarded Mesa County Courthouse."

The defense attorneys' theory proclaimed that Eret lived in a two-story house next to the Blaggs, and the woman also had a young child. According to them, in the early morning hours of November 13, the stalker broke into the Blagg house by mistake, saw Jennifer sleeping in bed, shot her by mistake, and then realizing his mistake, he murdered Abby. In a strange twist of fate, the deputy DA Tammy Eret, who was the intended target, drove right by Mike Blagg and all the police activity on November 13, 2001, at around 5:00 P.M., without even knowing there had been a murder at that house.

According to Mike's defense attorneys, "Investigators explored the possibility that the disappearance of Jennifer Blagg and her daughter, Abby, were attributable to the male deputy district attorney who may have either personally, or through another person, sought to harm the female deputy district attorney and went to the wrong house. The male deputy district attorney was the subject of a perfunctory internal investigation, involving the complaints made by the female district attorney, which led to the male deputy district attorney being assigned to another courtroom."

So here was a theory, within a theory—that possibly the male deputy DA who was doing the stalking hired a killer to murder the female deputy DA, but that person had gone into the wrong house and killed the wrong woman and the wrong girl. The defense even backed up this theory with the contention that a neighbor had heard strange male voices around the Blagg home very early on the morning of November 13, 2001.

All of this was laid out in black-and-white by the defense lawyers in another long-titled document, "Motion to Allow Defense Evidence of Alternative Suspect and

Motion to Disqualify District Attorney for the Twenty-First Judicial District from Further Prosecution in This Case."

The document stated that significant discovery in the case was devoted to law enforcement of a female deputy district attorney as a possible intended victim in the disappearance of Jennifer and Abby Blagg, and that the possible motive was revenge for being spurned. According to the defense attorneys, this man "meets the legal definition of stalking."

They added that even though the investigators didn't pursue this lead to the point of filing charges, the circumstantial evidence was sufficient to warrant a presentation by the defense of this person as an alternate suspect at trial. And they added that it would be improper for the district attorney's office to be involved in either the litigation concerning the admissibility of such evidence or, if it was admitted, to be on the case at all. Eisner and Singer further stated that despite the male deputy DA's stalking, he was only sent to work in a different court, rather than being terminated. The defense lawyers thought this was awfully lenient treatment for something so sinister.

There was another strange anecdote around this time. Someone named Michael Blagg was stopped by law enforcement officers in El Dorado County, California, on November 16, 2001, and they ran a background check on this particular Michael Blagg. It was not clear if they were referring to Michael Blagg, of Grand Junction, Colorado, or someone else, but the Mike Blagg, of Grand Junction, was clearly at AMETEK Dixson that day. The contention, by the defense attorneys, was that whoever had broken into the Blagg home had stolen some of Mike's credit cards and identification and had been looked for in California.

Because of all of this, Eisner and Singer wanted DA Frank Daniels removed from the case, because according to them, "he has a personal interest in this case." By this time, Tammy Eret was no longer with the DA's office, but rather a private criminal defense lawyer practicing in Grand Junction, and the unnamed male deputy DA was now serving in the army reserve.

To all of these new speculations, MCSO spokesperson Janet Prell told reporters, "We are very comfortable at this point saying that the deputy district attorney mentioned in the motion is not associated with the crime."

That was not going to assuage the matter in court, however. Within days, Frank Daniels was asking Judge Bottger to have defense lawyer David Eisner removed from the case, claiming that he had acted unethically when he accused a deputy DA working within his office as possibly being the one who had killed Jennifer Blagg. Daniels said of Eisner's motion, "This motion would be laughable if it were not for the fact that it is so blatantly mean-spirited, libelous, vindictive, unethical, and harmful to the reputation of a good man. The people object strenuously to this motion and object to the character assassination of a man, although not named, who is a good family man, a fine attorney, and an upstanding citizen." On top of all that, Daniels said, Eisner knew that the allegations were unfounded, and violated the Colorado Professional Rules of Conduct that governed legal behavior.

Daniels went on to say, "The public should be concerned about a state official, as David Eisner, behaving in such a manner and should be concerned about his ability to conduct this trial in a fair and ethical manner. Removing him and his office from the case is the only way to ensure continued public confidence in the system of state-funded defense counsel."

In addition to seeking Eisner's removal, Daniels wanted Judge Bottger to look into whether Mike Blagg was still eligible for a court-appointed lawyer. Daniels contended that Mike, who was now living with his mother in Warner

Robins, Georgia, had a part-time job and refused to work more hours so that he could qualify for a court-appointed lawyer. Then Daniels made reference to the question—how could Mike Blagg say he was indigent if he could somehow afford to post a $500,000 bond?

Daniels filed an eighteen-page document, blasting Eisner and his "alternate theory allegations." As to why Eisner was doing all of this, Daniels claimed that Eisner wanted a special prosecutor appointed to the case—a person who did not know as much about it, or care as much about it as Daniels did. Daniels stated, "While it is widely discussed that some members of society hold lawyers in less than completely favorable light, certainly it must violate accepted standards of legal ethics to falsely accuse an attorney of a murder solely to gain strategic advantage for a client or to generate publicity to help the client obtain a change of venue."

Daniels addressed more than just this one issue—he addressed the issue of Mike's pornography ultimately being seen by a jury, and called it, "The modern equivalent of an affair with one's secretary or neighbor. Viewing the evidence in this case as a whole makes it readily apparent that Michael Blagg's pornographic and sexual desires formed the motive for the fight and consequently the murder."

Another issue at stake was whether the jury would hear about Mike buying an expensive television, stereo, and computer equipment two weeks after he reported Jennifer and Abby missing. All of that was inconsistent with a grieving father and husband, Daniels contended. What also became a bone of contention was something Mike had supposedly told police about his computer room; he told them, "You might find my semen under the computer table."

Daniels lastly dealt with the mysterious Michael Blagg, of El Dorado County, California. He stated that "there is no evidence that someone had Michael Blagg's identification, nor is there any evidence that his identification was missing. The actual computer check was done on a 'Blagg, Mi,' with no date of birth. The scenario is very likely that an investigator in California heard about the crime in Colorado, remembered that they had a Michael Blagg in their system, and ran a criminal history check."

Still feeling outrage over the alternate defense theory, Daniels returned to it by concluding that what the defense was trying to say was that the deputy DA stalker had watched Michael Blagg go to work in his car, killed Jennifer, drove her body in the Blagg minivan, disposed of her body in the AMETEK Dixson Dumpster, kidnapped or killed Abby Blagg, and got back to court by 8:00 A.M. Daniels declared, "What is beyond belief really in this situation is that an attorney would file such a spurious and outrageous motion."

As if it weren't enough that both Daniels and Eisner were trying to take the other off the case—by April 2003, Eisner was trying to have Judge Bottger recuse himself. It stemmed in part from a motion that stated, "Defendant contends that recusal is required based on the order of March 19, 2003. This order denied defendant's demand for immediate discovery and production of all documents and information pertaining to Sanction for Ethical Breach—Removing Dave Eisner and the Colorado State Public Defender's Office from Defense."

Judge Bottger noted Section 16-6-201 of the Colorado Penal Code, which stated, "A defendant may seek recusal of a trial judge if the motion and required affidavits contain facts from which a reasonable person may infer that the judge has a bias or prejudice toward the defendant that will in all probability prevent him or her from dealing fairly with the defendant."

Bottger noted, however, "Defendant's real complaint centers on my 'unprecedented action' in not merely denying his motion, but ordering it and the supporting exhibits 'sealed as irrelevant, scandalous, and impertinent.'" (These were Eisner's statements concerning Judge Bottger.) Bottger added that his words had not been plucked from the air—and he gave exact definitions about what he meant by each word.

"'Irrelevant' means *not relevant—not applicable or pertinent*. 'Scandalous' means *disgraceful, improper, or immoral*. 'Impertinent' means *not pertinent, irrelevant*."

Bottger went on to say that defense counsel was wrong in calling those words, "gratuitous and inflammatory." As to the defense attorney asking to see sealed documents by the prosecutor, who had tried to get him kicked off the case for unethical behavior, Judge Bottger said that Eisner was not entitled to see them. Bottger had ruled at the time that Frank Daniels was not going to be removed, and that was that.

The last paragraph read, "For these reasons, IT IS ORDERED, that Defendant's Verified Motion to Disqualify and Recuse Judge David A. Bottger From Participating in This Case and for Expedited Hearing on This Motion . . . is denied."

As of April 2003, the CBI lab at Montrose was still running tests on certain items, including a sternum bone from Jennifer Blagg and hair standards from Michael Blagg. The list of potential witnesses grew and grew, until they reached more than 150. In fact, Judge Bottger said the defense was being "overbroad," when they wanted to call reporter Mike Wiggins, of the *Daily Sentinel*, all members of the New Hope Fellowship Church, all members of the Monument Baptist Church, all members of the Homeowners Association of South Carolina, and even Judge Bottger himself as witnesses.

Another hearing soon followed, focusing on FBI agent Bill Irwin, and whether his testimony was going to make it into trial or not. Present at the hearing was none other than Mike Blagg himself, along with his mother. Irwin testified that during the February 5, 2002, polygraph test that if Mike passed the test, investigators were willing to look elsewhere for the killer. But Mike did not pass the test, and the heat came down on him.

Irwin said that in the interrogation that followed, he used several techniques on Mike to try to make him confess, including rationalizing the killings, minimizing the seriousness of the crimes, and assigning blame to others. Irwin said that he and Sergeant Weyler tried sympathizing with Mike and talked about providing a decent burial for Jennifer and Abby.

Irwin told the court, "I confronted him in no uncertain terms. I believed he knew the location of Jennifer and Abby."

Sergeant Wayne Weyler was also questioned, and he stated that sometimes during the interrogation, Mike did not respond to questions at all, but just stared blankly. At other times, Mike avoided the question and gave an irrelevant answer. Finally near the end, it appeared to Weyler that Mike was about ready to confess and he said, "I can't," when asked to tell the truth about Jennifer and Abby. "I want to tell the truth, but I want a lawyer to tell me what the truth is going to mean."

Swirling around all the rest of these legal problems was the fact that Mike's defense attorneys continually asked for a change of venue, citing the huge coverage of the case in Grand Valley.

It seemed that almost no evidence that came before the court went uncontested by either side. The prosecution had to make an Offer of Proof in Response to Court Order concerning Louella Cross as a witness. The prosecution argued that "Ms. Cross would recount an incident that occurred, she estimated, two or three weeks prior to her first interview of November 16, 2001. Her testimony would be that Jennifer Blagg came with Abby Blagg to the office sometime in the late morning and Jennifer filled out an application to be represented by their office. The document went on to say that that office handled divorce cases where there was spousal abuse, and their definition of abuse included sexual abuse. While visiting the office, Louella Cross would state on the stand that Jennifer said, "'I can't handle it any more. I can't take any more of the abuse!'"

Getting this in was important to the prosecution. It was all a part of the framework of Mike's motive for killing Jennifer and probably Abby as well. Also part of the framework was having Jennifer's journal and other written material admitted for a jury to see and hear. One of these was Jennifer's writings about *The Keys to Peace,* and the notebook itself was described as "a small notebook found on top of a TV stand in the living room. There is no date on the final page; however, the page previous has a date of November 9, 2001. It is important to provide the jury with a full and complete understanding of the victim."

Two other items were a religious book, with notations in the margins by Jennifer about her fights with Mike, and a Bible with her handwriting about the lack of communication between herself and Mike.

The fight between Mike and Jennifer was a very big part of the prosecution's plan, and they told Judge Bottger, "The fight between Michael Blagg and Jennifer Blagg of November 9, 2001, was clearly of substantial importance to her [because] Jennifer phoned her close friend Edith Melson in South Carolina and told her that she was praying for her sex life and that she hoped that Melson would never experience the same feelings that she was."

Something new also came to light about Jennifer in the week before her death. Jennifer spoke with a friend named Glenda Bell at church about the rough times that she and Mike were having in their marriage. Glenda told Jennifer that she and her husband had separated, and Jennifer replied they now had more in common than just medical problems.

One of the areas still in contention was Mike's viewing of pornography at work and at home, and whether the jury would ever hear about it. As to this point, the prosecution wrote, "There are three areas of evidence the prosecution intends to use at trial that fall under the category of res gestae evidence—Michael Blagg's use of pornography, arguments between Michael Blagg and Jennifer Blagg, and Michael Blagg's suicide attempt."

Daniels told Judge Bottger that it was the prosecution's theory that Mike used pornography, such as images of men ejaculating on women's faces, as a large part of the problem between himself and Jennifer. This had spanned over a long period of time, and continued right up to the night of the murder. And then a bombshell: "Semen was found on the comforter of the bed on which a large pool of Jennifer Blagg's blood was discovered, and this semen was on top of the comforter." (This had been underlined by the prosecutor.) What that indicated was chilling, to say the least—a theory that Mike may have ejaculated on the comforter after killing Jennifer. And yet, this issue was not expanded upon at a later time.

The prosecution felt that it was important that the jury know the full extent of Mike's pornography usage so that they could assess the "extent of the damage it caused." They wanted the jury to know that he had been viewing porn sites on the Internet for approximately two and a half years, and that when pressed, he said he had Jennifer look at the sites at least a dozen times, though he admitted he looked at most of the 1,863 adult sites mainly by himself. Mike also admitted that he had a problem with porn, that it was an addiction for him, and that Jennifer had confronted him about it.

Mike had said that she caught him one evening about four months prior to her disappearance and confronted him about it, but he denied that he was on the Internet on the night of the disappearance/murder. When asked about specifics, Mike admitted to making collages of women performing oral sex acts on men, which were displayed on the computer, and that they were for his viewing pleasure. Most of the images were of men ejaculating upon the faces of women.

In a separate document, the prosecution noted, "Mr. Blagg wishes to sanitize his character and present himself to a jury as a pure man with no problems and no motive to commit these horrible acts so that the jury will not believe him capable of committing this crime. Fortunately, due to thorough investigation, we know otherwise."

As to the suicide attempt, the prosecution contended that it was relevant because it came within hours of Mike leaving the sheriff's office after his extensive interview of February 5, 2002. According to them, it was at this interview that Mike almost had confessed to the murder, and had wanted to know what might happen to him—"if he told the truth."

The defense suffered a serious setback when Judge Bottger denied their motion to throw out the ten-plus-hour interview of February 5, 2002, and the results of the lie detector test as well. Judge Bottger said that Michael Blagg had gone to the sheriff's office voluntarily and could have left at any time. Bottger added, "Mr. Blagg, with his military officer background, high intelligence, and prestigious education, doesn't strike me as the sort of person who'd be intimidated by a badge."

One route in the trial that the prosecution was going to take was answered by DA Frank Daniels in court on May 13, 2003. Daniels said, "That day (November 12, 2001), Jennifer tapes this to a mirror and she's killed." (He was referring to a note taped to the bathroom mirror.) "The note says that she would find peace and the will from Jesus to do it. What she was talking about was leaving Michael Blagg." It was this final threat by Jennifer that pushed Mike over the edge, according to the prosecution.

More bad news greeted the defense on June 3—Judge Bottger decided to admit Jennifer Blagg's writings that went back several years. Bottger's ruling stated that the reference to a fight on Novembre 9, 2001, was especially significant, because it showed that there had been problems in the marriage. Bottger noted, "The statement, 'Fought w/Mike on Fri' is relevant to the existence of marital discord immediately before the homicide and is therefore evidence of a material fact. As the last written words of the victim on the topic, it is more probative than any other evidence the people can produce."

The defense did score a victory with Judge Bottger when he denied testimony by two friends to whom Jennifer had spoken just prior to her murder. What she had told these two was not stated in court documents that were open to the public. Also out was a statement reputedly made by Abby to her Sunday-school teacher about a fight her parents had on November 9. The conversation with the friends was ruled to be hearsay, and Abby's comment to the Sunday-school teacher was out because the circumstances surrounding the six-year-old's statements and truthfulness of them were not clear.

Before the dust had even settled on these issues, the

team of Eisner and Singer were back with a whole new list of issues they wanted thrown out:

1. The defense attorneys said that Julie House's statements that Mike had used an escort service to try and obtain sex had always been vehemently denied by Mike, and that the police even questioned the validity of her statements.

2. There was a new contention by the defense—there had somehow been a rumor that Mike had been involved in an intentional gas leak at the family home in July 2001. The contention was that as early as that date, Mike had been trying to kill Jennifer and Abby—but Eisner and Singer said that there was no valid proof of this at all. Whether or not the prosecution was trying to get this admitted as evidence is not clear, but Eisner and Singer definitely wanted it ruled out. Just where the rumor came from was not addressed at the time.

3. The defense attorneys questioned whether it really was Jennifer Blagg and Abby who had shown up at Colorado Rural Legal Services in the weeks before they disappeared. The defense attorneys said that Jennifer would have no reason to go there, since she wasn't indigent, and that either she or her family had enough money to be able to deal with any marital problems without public assistance. They further said that Louella Cross's own words lent a lot of doubt. Cross had said about Abby, "I don't want to say for sure that it was absolutely her. . . . I want to make sure that you guys know that I kind of feel that that's the girl."

The defense attorneys poked numerous holes into Louella Cross's statements. Cross had told the investigator that the woman in question hadn't been in Grand Junction that long, whereas the Blaggs had been in Grand Junction for a year and a half by that point. The woman talking to Cross had said she didn't have any money—whereas Jennifer Blagg kept the family checkbook, had credit cards, and a blank check from her mother for emergencies. As for the South Carolina connection—Cross had said that the woman moved from South Carolina to California and then to Grand Junction. In fact, the Blaggs had moved from South Carolina to Grand Junction without any stopover in California.

The next portion did not show up in a police report released to the public—but it was contended by the defense attorneys: "The woman (Cross) said that she (Jennifer) was tired of her husband's lady friends and his girlfriend." Eisner and Singer pointed out that there was absolutely no evidence that Mike Blagg had either lady friends or a girlfriend.

Eisner and Singer stated, "The most compelling fact undercutting the trustworthiness of reliability of Ms. Cross's identification is the timing of the incident." Initially Louella Cross said that the incident had occurred two to three weeks before her interview with the investigator—which would have made it between October 26 and November 2, 2001. In a subsequent interview, she said that it was about a week before she was fired on November 9, 2001, which would have made it November 2, 2001. On two occasions, Cross said the woman and girl had come to the office during the morning hours, and Cross had supposedly told the woman she could get a restraining order the next morning at ten o'clock. Since the courthouse was not open on the weekend, the only days this could have happened would have been Monday through Thursday.

That was inconsistent with the Blagg schedule, and the hours of Colorado Rural Legal Services. The hours for CRLS were from 8:30 A.M. to noon, and 1:30 to 4:30 P.M. Abby Blagg had perfect attendance at the school during the period in question. The only days before the disappearance that she was not in school were on Friday, October 19, a teacher work-day, and Thursday and Friday, October 25 and 26, parent/teacher conference days—when the Blaggs were visiting with Jennifer's mother in Texas.

The list of potential witnesses kept growing by leaps and bounds—friends, family, law enforcement officers, and AMETEK Dixson employees. One of the most unusual potential witnesses was Mike's brother, John Blagg, of the American Embassy, La Paz, Bolivia. The defense served notice that they might be calling various scientific and medical experts, including one from Blue Ridge Services in Atascadero, California, one from Johnson-Laird Inc., of Portland, Oregon, one from Corning, New York, and one from Okemos, Michigan. Even a CBI agent would be tapped.

A big issue still remained for Judge Bottger to rule on—whether statements Mike Blagg made during his ten-hour interview would be heard by a jury. Mike had come very close to admitting guilt, or at least that was what some of his statements implied—especially the phrase "I want to tell the truth. I want a lawyer to tell me what the truth is going to mean."

On June 11, the defense won the victory they'd been looking for—the "truth" statement by Mike would not be heard by a jury. Judge David Bottger said that near the end of the interrogation "Mr. Blagg stated an unequivocal right to counsel," and his statement of "I want to tell the truth" came after his asking for a lawyer, and had to be suppressed.

A few more details of those later moments in the interrogation of February 5, 2002, came to light at this time as well. Mike had said, "May I have the opportunity to speak with a lawyer first?" Weyler responded, "It's up to you . . . you can have a lawyer."

Mike asked to pray for a bit and placed his face in his hands. During that episode, Weyler told him, "Now's the time. Let it out."

It was then that Mike had said, "I want to tell the truth. I want a lawyer to tell me what the truth is going to mean." That sentence alone meant that he had asked for counsel, and at that point the interview should have been terminated, according to the defense.

Even as late as August 2003, both sides of the aisle were asking for evidence to be admitted or excluded. Frank Daniels asked Judge Bottger to reconsider his decision not to allow into evidence Jennifer Blagg's note that she wrote shortly before being killed, stating that it "helps illuminate the motive for Michael Blagg to kill his wife." This was the *Key to Peace* note, one of the last things Jennifer had ever written.

Daniels added, "The people contend that this is an important piece of evidence and is part of a thread of proof the people seek to introduce to establish the defendant's motive in murdering Jennifer Blagg." Daniels contended that the note was one of a series of crucial events leading up to the murder. And Daniels let it be known about a new revelation—the sermon Jennifer had watched on television on Sunday, November 11, concerned, in part, sexual addiction. Within that sermon was the statement that sexual addiction was a "brand of thinking that will keep one from having peace." So this tied in very strongly to the note, *Key to Peace,* according to Daniels.

Daniels stated, "The videotaped sermon, plus notes Jennifer wrote about the fight and the note about peace, are all important links in the chain the people feel we need to properly argue the defendant's motive to commit murder."

Judge Bottger mulled over this new argument by the

prosecutor, and in a surprise reversal of his October ruling, he said that the note and the sermon were probative, and would be heard by a jury. In fact, the note had apparently been so important to Jennifer, she had taped it to the master bedroom mirror for Mike to see, along with an "Urgent Prayer Request Form."

There was still so much evidence for the defense lawyers to digest, that they told Judge Bottger they didn't think they could proceed to a trial until spring 2004. Eisner and Singer stated that the prosecution had not returned with results about tests that concerned the brake pedal of the minivan, a blue fiber found on a bullet recovered from Jennifer's skull, and various vacuumings and fingerprints from the Blagg home. Even Frank Daniels admitted that there was still some evidence that had not been tested.

Judge Bottger listened to all of this and said, "Based on the time required for the people's experts to complete their work, insufficient time remains for the defendant's experts to do theirs." So the trial would not commence until at least March 2004.

On November 13, 2003, the *Daily Sentinel* ran another article about the extent of time since the crime: "Two years later, girl's fate still a mystery." Written by Mike Wiggins, it stated, "By now, the gap in her mouth would have likely been filled with big girl teeth. Perhaps she would have let her blonde hair grow past her shoulders. Or perhaps she would have preferred it cropped just below the ears so that it framed her dimples and blue eyes. She liked to sing. Maybe she would have joined a children's choir. Nobody can say for sure. Nobody has seen Abby Blagg for two years."

David Loman, Jennifer's brother, told Wiggins, "Somebody, somewhere, knows something about Abby. All I want to do is put Abby with her momma." Connie Flukey, of the Abby and Jennifer Recovery Foundation, said, "We just believe somehow, some way, we're going to find her." Once a month, a group of eight to ten people still searched remote areas of the county, looking for any trace of Abby.

Strangely enough, some people in the Grand Junction area believed that Abby was still alive, perhaps sequestered somewhere with Mike's relatives or friends in Georgia or South Carolina or even in Mexico. But most in the area believed she was dead, and either buried in the landfill, out in the backcountry, or her body had washed down the Colorado River long ago in November 2001 when Mike placed it there.

The MCSO's thoughts were that Abby's body had been inadvertently pushed aside by bulldozers, away from Jennifer's body in the landfill. They had searched for seven more weeks in the landfill after Jennifer's body had been discovered, but to no avail. There were no plans by the authorities to search any further for Abby in the landfill or anywhere else. The landfill was so huge, it seemed to be an impossible task to try and find where Abby's small body might be. If Jennifer's body had been mangled and torn apart by a compactor and loader, it could only be imagined what might have happened to the body of a six-year-old girl.

Investigator Steven King believed that Abby's body would never be found and the focus for him and authorities now was to make sure that Mike Blagg was prosecuted to the full extent of the law. King said, "I think to some degree that is motivation for continuing to mount the effort to see this all the way through. You've got to deal with the circumstances, and we would be doing Abby and Jennifer a great disservice if we dwelled so much on the fact that we haven't found Abby that we lost focus on the task at hand."

* * *

As if the anonymous "bird on a balcony" letter wasn't enough, the court system received another anonymous letter simply entitled: "To the Justice Team in the Blagg Case: Bottger, Daniels, Eisner and Singer—From Master of Arts—Christian Counseling Psychology."

The writer or writers said that they had been following the accounts of the Blagg case, and that they did not know the Blagg family. Nonetheless, the writer said that he/she thought he/she understood "church thinking, theology and psychology." (For ease of further transcription, author has used the word "he" when speaking of the writer, since the writer did not identify himself as male or female.)

The writer surmised that the prosecution, defense, and judge were all debating the issues and trying to do a good job on the case. This person said, however, that there were a number of points that a secular court had missed. He then added that more evidence was known by those involved, and that he might be incorrect.

That being said, he wrote that Jennifer's note—"You will not take my peace"—sounded to him as if it was a reference to suicide by Jennifer. The writer related that when Mike Blagg came through the door of his residence, he suddenly had two deceased bodies on his hands. The writer then added that normally mothers who commit suicide "do not travel alone." He said he thought that Abby was killed by Jennifer in a less bloody manner by using pills.

Wondering why Mike Blagg had acted as he did, the writer noted in bold letters, **"a clash of theological beliefs."** The writer said that Jennifer came from a Baptist background, where the teaching was of "eternal security," which meant that as a Christian, no matter what the person did, Jesus would love him, and he would go to Heaven. The writer speculated that it explained Jennifer's writing, "Trust Him with the keys He's left me. Give them back and trust Him with them. I'll have peace, because He says I will." Since Mike Blagg grew up as a Catholic, he could still hear a priest say to him, "Suicide? That person is going straight to hell."

The writer then stated that Mike, in an "altered state of consciousness," reacted to the crime scene in his home by depersonalizing it and taking on "motivated forgetting." The scene Mike discovered was unsettling for him on Jennifer's part, and very threatening on Abby's part. The writer noted that Jennifer's situation was understood by Mike, but that Abby's situation was not. Mike had to have been wondering what she had been given to cause her death. Then the writer surmised that Mike's first thought would have been that he would be blamed by the authorities for something he didn't do. On top of that, Mike couldn't stand the thought that his wife was going to hell for her actions. The person wrote, "Then begins what we call in psychology, "reconstruction. He has to change the circumstances to fit his beliefs." By changing the circumstances, Jennifer could go to Heaven. "Mr. Blagg did not have to lie to the police, **he had to lie to himself.**"

The writer added that he believed the root cause of what pushed Jennifer over the edge was Mike's viewing of pornography. It was something he was responsible for, and still grappling with. Since Mike was from a "mixed culture—Mama going to church, and Daddy reading *Playboy*," he had received mixed signals about pornography as a child. Then the writer noted that he'd recently had a man in his office who at the age of six had been given pornography by his father. The man had never broken free from being addicted to pornography. As the writer put it, "It is like asking someone to renounce their mother tongue."

The writer then said that he understood Mike Blagg to be a "neat freak." Mike was so neat, in fact, that he had climbed into a bathtub so as not to make a mess when trying to commit suicide. Mike's way of thinking was not to make a mess that someone else had to clean up. That Mike was a manager only intensified this belief.

The writer said that Mike needed the element of "going home," but that a funeral for Jennifer and Abby had been denied him. Then the writer added a curious sentence, "Is there a possible way for all of you to step back, regroup and call off the dogs?" He said this was a classic case of disassociation and that it would take years for Mike to come to the reality of what really had occurred. Mike, according to the writer, was boxed into a situation where he couldn't tell authorities where Abby was, if it meant another change in the belief structure he had created. There was also no way of proving his innocence, even if he did.

The writer asked the prosecutor, defense lawyers, and judge to put themselves in Mike's shoes, and asked them what they would have done in a similar situation. The writer then said that the authorities could possibly come up with a way to let Mike "come clean," as he put it. He noted that Mike should be entering a "GAS stage" soon (general adaptation syndrome—alarm, resist, exhaustion). The number one issue for Mike, according to the writer, was the fear that Jennifer was going to hell. "As a husband, he is trying to save her."

Once again, the writer said that in Abby's case, they could "call off the dogs." At this point, Mike would be able to "tell the truth, apologize to the community and be healed. This fragmentation has hurt our town, but we can be healed and forgive this man."

It's doubtful that the author of this letter was the same person who wrote the anonymous "bird on a balcony" letter. For one thing, there is a knowledge of psychological terminology, and the sentence structure was different. Yet, even with this person, there were a couple of misspellings—as if the author did not spell-check the final draft. The writer misspelled Abby's name on all occasions, penning "Abbey," whether by mistake or on purpose to try and throw off the authorities. However, even though the person writing the letter claimed to not know the case or the family, he or she alluded to the fact of "this fragmentation has hurt our town"—in other words, Grand Junction. More than likely, the letter writer was from Grand Junction, or at least a nearby town.

The change of venue motion by the defense attorneys was still not a moot point; by autumn 2003, they got support for their point of view from fellow Mesa County attorney Edward Nugent. He stated that he hadn't seen this kind of publicity in the county since the Kenneth Botham case of many years before.

Nugent said that he'd actually heard people on the street say that they wanted to get on the jury so that they could convict Michael Blagg, and they were sorry that the death penalty was not being sought by the prosecutor. Nugent contended that not one person had come up to him and professed to believe that Mike was innocent.

By February 2004, there was a closed hearing by Judge Bottger, in a two-hour session between the lawyers—all outside the view of the public, especially the media. All of this took place in Judge Bottger's chambers. As the *Daily Sentinel* stated, "Pretrial conferences afford a judge and lawyers an opportunity to address a number of topics, including procedural questions, jury selection, stipulating facts about the case and resolving outstanding motions or evidentiary issues."

Still under discussion was whether Louella Cross was going to be able to be on the witness stand. One thing that was already set was the fact that Judge Bottger was going to allow one still "pool" camera and one film "pool" camera to be in court during Michael Blagg's trial. He said, "With my limited experience of expanded media coverage—it has been positive, and I've never had a problem with the media violating the law dictating that coverage."

One problem that cropped up was that Marilyn Conway, Harold Conway, David Loman, Jack Powell (Jennifer's uncle), Patricia Powell (Jennifer's aunt), Kendall Evans (Jennifer's cousin), and D'Anne Hobbs (Jennifer's cousin)—all signed a letter to Judge Bottger asking that they might be allowed to sit in the gallery during the trial.

The letter began: "We are the parents of Jennifer J. Blagg. It has come to our attention today, through a conversation regarding another issue, that family members may not be allowed in the courtroom during the trial, even though only Marilyn has been called to testify." It went on to say that a ruling had not yet been made, and that they did not understand why the DA's office hadn't petitioned or advocated a request on their part to attend the trial. The letter stated that they believed they had every right to witness the trial and hear testimony, and that this was the first time they had any inkling that they might not be able to do so.

"Special arrangements have been made by us to be absent from work, arrange for transportation and lodging, as well as other issues pertinent to being in Grand Junction for the duration of the trial."

David Loman also wrote a letter to Judge Bottger about the same issue, and ended with, "I have deemed this the final chapter in a horrible life event and have put my focus into hearing what is to be said. I had anticipated being in the courtroom from opening statements until the verdict is read. I feel being able to hear what is said in open court is something that will ultimately help me live with the horrible thing that happened to my sister, Jennifer. Please allow me to witness this trial from start to finish."

The fact that Frank Daniels hadn't addressed this was probably an oversight on his part, since he had been very supportive of Jennifer's family and friends. Daniels soon wrote out a document, "Motion to Afford Crime Victim's Rights," and it covered several different points.

Daniels contended that at a pretrial conference held on February 12, 2004, his office had requested that Marilyn Conway be able to remain in the courtroom during the trial. The defense had objected at that time, and Judge Bottger declined to rule on it until the trial had actually started.

Daniels also pointed out a discrepancy between the Conway letter and actuality—not only was Marilyn Conway going to be called as a witness by the prosecution, but so were Harold Conway, David Loman, and Patty Powell. Daniels said that Marilyn Conway and David Loman had constitutional victims rights pursuant to C.R.S. 24-4.1—"the right to be informed of and present for all critical stages of the criminal justice process." He went on to point out about the others, "The statute goes on to say, 'If the victim is present, the court, at the victim's request, may permit the presence of an individual to provide support to the victim.'"

Obviously, Jennifer Blagg would not be present, but Daniels contended that Marilyn Conway, as the victim's mother, had serious health problems, "and needs the support of her husband and sister in the courtroom."

By February 23, 2004, the jury selection process got under way, with more than two hundred men and women reporting to the Mesa County Courthouse and filling out questionnaires on what they already knew about the high-profile case. Interestingly enough, the prospective jurors were joined by Mike Blagg in the juror orientation room, where he was introduced to them by Judge Bottger. Bottger also introduced the primary investigators and lawyers on both sides, followed by a reading of the state's disqualification rules.

After that, Judge Bottger, Mike Blagg, the lawyers, and investigators left the room so that the prospective jurors could answer a multitude of questions and personal information, as well as how much they had learned about the case through newspapers and television. Finally on March 1, 2004, the jury selection began by both prosecutor and defense attorneys weeding out those who they thought would not be fair-minded to their arguments, while keeping others to be impaneled.

As a mark of how much publicity the case already had garnered, twenty-one of the first twenty-four prospective jurors were excused for knowing an abundance of information about the case and having already formed an opinion about Mike's guilt or innocence. At the afternoon session, eight out of eleven prospective jurors were excused. For those who made it to voir dire, eighteen out of twenty-one said that they had formed strong opinions, and only one said she had not learned anything in the media about the case. Of those who were excused, many said that they had a negative reaction to learning about Mike's supposed addiction to Internet porn.

The first three people not to be excused stated that they did have strong opinions about Mike's guilt or innocence, but they insisted they could put these opinions aside and determine guilt or innocence solely based upon facts that were introduced into court.

By the next day, six more potential jurors had been saved for impaneling as Mike Blagg sat near his lawyers and jotted down notes on a notepad. One young man who was kept stated that his idea that Mike was guilty wasn't very strong. One man who certainly didn't make it onto the jury was an individual who wrote, "Hang him high!"

in answer to the question "Do you think Michael Blagg is guilty?"

One of the few things that the prosecution and defense eventually did agree on was "the Blagg jury will be impartial," and there would be enough people to insure that. David Eisner told the *Daily Sentinel*, "We're going to have enough to seat a jury. In fact, we thought it would be much harder than this."

One of the more intriguing persons to be called for jury duty was a man who called former Mesa County sheriff Riecke Claussen's sister, his "life partner." He even acknowledged he'd thought about what Sheriff Claussen might think if he ended up on the jury. Eisner wanted to dismiss the man, but Daniels objected and asked the man, "Can you assure us that your relationship with the former sheriff will not interfere with your ability to be fair and impartial?"

"Yes, I can," the man responded, prompting Judge Bottger to keep him in the jury pool.

Another person of interest to reporters was a woman whose ex-husband had been killed in a Denver area shooting spree in 1995, along with two others. And yet another was a relative of the screenwriter and novelist Dalton Trumbo.

While the jury selection was ongoing, reporter Mike Wiggins, of the *Daily Sentinel,* spoke with individuals close to the case about how they were feeling, knowing that the actual trial was nearly at hand. David Loman, Jennifer's brother, said that he had saved all his money so that he could afford to "relive the horror that has robbed me of my sister." He hadn't taken a vacation all year so that he could sit in the courtroom for possibly six weeks to attend the trial every day. He'd waited more than two years for something to be resolved—at least now part of it would be, even if Abby remained missing.

The jury selection was just about winding down by the end of the first week of March. Among people excused by Daniels was a man with a criminal history, a college professor, and a woman who had once worked for a criminal defense firm. Eisner excused the man who had been involved with the sheriff's sister, a woman who worked at AMETEK Dixson, and a woman who attended law school for two years and had once thought of becoming a prosecutor.

Eisner focused on asking potential jurors if various allegations would cloud their judgment, especially in the realm of pornography. He also wanted to know if they felt an obligation to Mesa County law enforcement, the community, and the victim's family, to deliver a guilty verdict. One woman said, "I don't answer to the family, I answer to the system."

Daniels, on the other hand, asked potential jurors if they were easily fooled, and were they good judges of credibility. He also drove home the point that the prosecution had lots of circumstantial evidence, but no direct evidence that Mike Blagg had murdered his wife.

Even Judge Bottger had his say. He addressed the potential jurors by saying, "You may find yourself thinking Mr. Blagg may be guilty, or even that he is probably guilty, but unless you are convinced beyond a reasonable doubt that Mr. Blagg is guilty, your sworn duty is to return a verdict of not guilty."

Mike Blagg and his supporters were also gearing up for the trial. Mike told one newsman, "Two years ago, I had everything. I had a good job, wonderful family, incredible wife and daughter. Everything was going perfect for me." Mike's mother, Betsy Blagg, agreed and said, "In every letter, Jennifer would tell me how much she loved Michael. Everything was marvelous. They couldn't be more happy, and he was absolutely in love with her."

Mike's sister, Clare Rochester, told a reporter, "He did

not kill his wife. He did not do anything to harm or take his daughter. It did not happen."

Since Mike was out on bail, he started each morning before the trial commenced by going to church, and then took a trip to his lawyers' office to confer with them about his defense. Other than that, he did not go out into Grand Junction very often. Except for a handful of supporters from his church, Mike had very few friends around town by spring 2004.

Mike still had some supporters within the New Hope Fellowship Church who made statements about the fact that they did not think the man they knew could have harmed his wife and daughter. But the defense team of Eisner and Singer were not going to have to convince Betsy Blagg and some of Mike's fellow parishioners of his innocence; they were going to have to convince twelve men and women who were his peers in the community that he had not murdered Jennifer in cold blood on November 13, 2001. They had to convince them that a stranger had shot her in the head and had taken her body to a place where it eventually would be picked up and taken out to the Mesa County Landfill. Eisner and Singer were going to have to convince the jurors that Mike Blagg was not a cold-blooded killer, but rather a victim as well.

Chapter 9

Revelations

The trial got off to a rocky start, right from the beginning, and Judge David Bottger was furious. In an unprecedented move, the *Daily Sentinel* depicted a graphic of sixteen chairs in a jurors' box, twelve jurors and four alternates, and in each chair there was a short description of the person who sat there and their background. What made Bottger so angry was the fact that some of the information shown on the front page of the newspaper was fairly specific as to the location that person worked, thus making them fairly identifiable:

"Profile of Blagg Jury"

Top row:

Woman—Was attending Colorado State University at time of murder.

Woman—State employee.

Man—No information available.

Man—Asked to be removed from jury so he could go back to work.

Woman—Works for Coldwell Banker.

Woman—Retiree who moved to Mesa County around the time of the murder.

Woman—Works at Wal-Mart.

Man—Lived in Salt Lake City when Elizabeth Smart was kidnapped.

Bottom row:

Man—Works for cable advertising company.

Man—Retiree who served in the navy for two weeks in the 1940s.

Woman—Owns Fish and Birds Etc.

Man—Grandparents own McLean Funeral Home.

Woman—Described herself as a sensitive person.

Woman—Owns a ranch.

Woman—Limited knowledge of case.

Woman—Works at St. Mary's Hospital.

Even before any opening statements by the prosecution and defense, Judge Bottger announced to a packed courtroom, which included numerous journalists for regional and national newspapers, plus a camera team for CBS's *48 Hours,* "I am appalled by this!" Bottger gave the *Daily Sentinel* a tongue-lashing and said that one of the jurors had taken "great exception" to what had been printed. Bottger declared that he didn't blame her for being angry.

Judge Bottger announced to the crowded courtroom, "I consider this extraordinarily irresponsible. I've never had this problem before, and I'm angry that I have it today. Apparently, this particular newspaper is more interested in selling newspapers than in making sure there will be a fair trial, and you people (the jury) will be able to do your jobs." Bottger put all the media on notice that there would not be any more of this kind of behavior in his courtroom.

Finally it was time for opening statements, and Frank Daniels began by describing the summer of 2001 in the Grand Junction area. He said it had been a typical hot summer, and the Blaggs' first summer in the area. Michael Blagg had a good job for AMETEK Dixson and the family attended two churches in the area, the New Hope Fellowship Church and Monument Baptist Church. Jennifer volunteered at her daughter's school and attended Bible-study classes. It seemed like a happy, devoted upper-middle-class family living the American Dream in their comfortable home out in the Redlands.

Jennifer had no real friends, however, Daniels contended, and she was almost a prisoner in her own home. Mike made her keep the blinds shut all day long, and constantly phoned her to see where she was and what she was doing. Some neighbors didn't even know that a family lived in their home. Next-door neighbor Tammy Eret thought the house was vacant. Jennifer had health problems, which included a thyroid problem, chronic fatigue, dizziness, a low libido, and painful reactions whenever she did have sex with Mike. As time went on, these symptoms seemed to increase, and she spoke of a growing sense of depression.

On July 13, 2001, Jennifer had gone to a doctor about her sex problems and low libido. Daniels contended that Mike was irritated at this point by Jennifer and her lack of interest in sex the way he wanted it. At about that same time, Mike increasingly went on the Internet and downloaded various photos of women giving men oral sex. He even made a collage of these images, with men ejaculating onto women's faces. All the women in these images were subservient and accommodating to the men.

Around this same time, Mike was having emotional problems of his own, and he went to a psychiatrist because of insomnia, depression, and a constantly twitching leg. By October 2001, Mike was viewing huge amounts of Internet porn—such things as XXX "Fantastic Facial Cum Shots."

That autumn, Jennifer had a lot of weakness, and lost fifteen pounds. In October, Abby was excited by the prospect of Halloween, but by then, Mike and Jennifer were fighting a lot about sex and other issues, and there was constant turmoil in the household. Jennifer's notations in her journal were becoming more accusatory and hopeless. Almost in despair, she wrote at the end of October, "Love God with all your might!" God seemed to be her only salvation now from a bad marriage.

According to Daniels, there was a big fight between Jennifer and Mike on Friday, November 9, 2001, about his continual viewing of Internet porn. Jennifer did not go to church with Mike on Sunday, November 11, but rather watched a religious television program. The sermon, in part, concerned how people lost power to control events in their own lives and featured a segment about addiction to porn. "Why We Lose Our Peace" was its title.

On Monday, November 12, Jennifer took Abby to school and obtained a Prayer Request Form, which was, in fact, a severe-crisis form. She wrote down on a piece of paper, "Get transcript," which concerned the television sermon of the previous Sunday.

Whether there was another fight between Mike and Jennifer on that Monday night will never be known, but Frank Daniels alleged that Mike Blagg was incensed at Jennifer that night and took a pistol out of its storage space. While Jennifer was sleeping, he placed a pillow over her head and shot her through her left eye at close range. The bullet passed through her eye socket and pulverized her brain.

The bullet did not exit her skull, but it did carry a small blue fiber into her brain.

Daniels even conjectured that Abby was "taken care of first." Mike smothered his daughter with a pillow so that she would not hear the gunshot. Afterward, Daniels said, Mike Blagg took a black-and-red tent and carried his two victims to the garage, where he loaded them into the van. Daniels conjectured he did all of this between 3:00 and 5:00 A.M., on November 13, 2001—cleaning up the house as best he could. He also allegedly jimmied the back door to make it look like it had been broken into, and scattered contents of Jennifer's purse on the master bedroom floor, trying to make it look like a burglary that had turned into a murder. After he had the two dead bodies in the minivan, he transported them to the AMETEK Dixson Dumpster, where he put them inside. It was a large container, and he was able to hide the bodies, within the tent, under other piles of trash.

Other employees noticed that Mike kept going to the loading dock that day, and seemed excessively nervous. He also took his own trash to the Dumpster, something he did not ordinarily do. Daniels stated that Mike must have been trying to set up an alibi by calling home so many times on November 13 to try and talk to Jennifer, even though he knew she was already dead. Mike phoned at 6:59 and 7:00 A.M., and at 12:30, 3:19, and 4:00 P.M.

Even when Mike got home, his actions did not jibe with what he claimed. He was supposedly bringing a present into the house to hide in a closet, yet he said that he called out, "I'm home!" And when he saw the blood in the master bedroom, he never went upstairs to check on Abby, until Abby was mentioned by the dispatcher. Only then did Mike show concern for Abby. Then there was the clear liquid added to the bed area around the blood. It was conjectured that Mike might have intended to clean it up, but there was just too much blood, so he gave up on this project.

A police canine team that was brought in to try and follow the scent of Jennifer and Abby couldn't do it past the garage area, so it seemed they had been driven out, already dead, in the minivan. That a burglar/killer would take dead bodies away in the victims' own minivan, and then return the same minivan to the garage, was too hard to swallow. CBI agents searched the van and found trace evidence of blood—some of it appeared to have been wiped. DNA analysis proved that it was Jennifer's blood. Daniels contended there would not have been any blood from Abby if she had been smothered to death.

There were plenty of Mike's fingerprints on and within the van, as might be expected, but the CBI agents could not find prints of any "burglar/killer." Some landscape workers, who had been in the area that same day, were fingerprinted, but none of their prints were found on the van or within the home.

There was also Mike's unusual behavior after the disappearance of Jennifer and Abby. Instead of acting like a grieving husband, he took money from an insurance settlement over the robbery and bought more than $5,000 worth of electronic goods at Circuit City. Mike's claims on the jewelry alone came to $24,000. Some of the equipment Mike bought was computer related—and he logged on to Internet porno sites after the disappearance.

Even more strangely, investigators who were watching Mike followed him to AMETEK Dixson, where he started loading office furniture and a paper shredder into a pickup. Mike took these items back to his apartment, and was soon thereafter asked to come down to the MCSO for a polygraph test. His failure of the test led to a ten-hour interrogation, where he often didn't answer questions, or gave answers that had nothing to do with the question that was being asked.

Mike also tried denying things that were obvious, such as stealing the items from his workplace. When confronted with the evidence, he finally admitted, "Yes, I should not have done that." He also denied looking at porn very much, when the investigators had proof that he'd looked at more than eighteen hundred porn sites.

Perhaps the most glaring bit of evidence against Mike was his near admission of guilt when he said that he wanted to tell the truth, but he wanted to know what the truth might mean. (The prosecution was allowed to get some of this testimony in, as far as the jury was concerned.)

After the admission, he told the investigators that they could come by his apartment the next day and pick up some of the stolen items. Daniels contended that Mike waited until the investigators showed up, and then feigned a suicide attempt, knowing that they would find him before he died.

Daniels spoke of the huge searches done by the MCSO and other agencies, as well as twenty-two hundred volunteers, who found no evidence of Jennifer or Abby in the backcountry. Mike stuck around Grand Junction during all this time, but it was when authorities began to focus on the landfill, he suddenly left the area and moved back to Georgia. This despite the fact that he had once told authorities that they'd have to dynamite him out of the Grand Junction area to get him to move anywhere else.

Daniels pointed out that Jennifer's almost mummified body was found buried alongside trash from AMETEK Dixson, and newspapers that were close in date to November 13, 2001. A fairly small-caliber bullet was found in her brain, and it was pointed out that while in the navy, Mike was familiar with a 9mm weapon, and that he had even owned one while living in Texas. Daniels said that the shameful way in which Mike treated Jennifer's corpse was beyond belief and spoke of Mike's narcissistic nature.

From that point, Daniels began to show the jury slides of the Blagg home at the time of the 911 call, the jewelry and purse contents dumped on the floor of the master bedroom, and the bloody bed. He showed slides of Abby's room, Jennifer's notes, especially the one taped to the bathroom mirror, and photos of the minivan. In all, Daniels showed more than fifty slides of the crime scene, and also slides of the Dumpster and area where Jennifer's body was recovered at the landfill.

Daniels left the jury with the mental picture: "That night, as Jennifer lay in bed in the most intimate part of the house, Michael got his gun, loaded a round into the chamber, and shot her in the face. She bled a lot. More than Michael expected she would. The blood kept flowing out of the hole in her head as her heart kept pumping. Michael retrieved a tent and tarp out of the garage, carefully wrapped Jennifer's body in it so as not to leave a trail of blood, placed it in the family van, and drove to the manufacturing plant where he worked. Once there, he placed the body in a trash bin."

Daniels left the jury with the image of Michael Blagg as a selfish, cold-blooded killer, who murdered his wife and daughter so that he could start over again with a clean slate.

Ken Singer, for the defense, painted a dramatically different picture of Michael and Jennifer Blagg. He told the jurors, "The evidence will show that the prosecution's case is based on inferences, assumptions, and speculation. You will find that is based, everywhere you go, on suspicion vision."

Singer said that not long before Jennifer's disappearance, Jennifer's mother had told a friend that the marriage between her daughter and Mike was a good one, and she didn't see any problems. Mike and Jennifer and Abby had gone to visit Marilyn Conway in Texas in November of 2001, so Marilyn was able to see them up close and personal. Of this visit, Marilyn said, "It was normal. Jennifer was happy and smiling. Jennifer was deeply in love with Michael, God, and Abby."

Singer showed the jury a photo of the Blagg family together—Mike, Jennifer, and Abby—as they all hugged each other, and Singer said, "This is the photo of a loving family. It was a marriage where love, affection, and devotion was rampant. The prosecution's argument is based on suspicion, suspicion, suspicion."

Singer then asked the jurors to follow him back through the hours of November 13, 2001. "Picture six A.M. and it's dark out. Across the street is the house of a neighbor, and that neighbor took the dogs out and went through a gate. Then the neighbor stopped. Why? Because she hears the voices of strangers, two or three males, near the backyard of the Blagg home. The voices made her stop and go back inside her house."

Singer pointed out that a CBI investigator found scuff marks on the back fence of the Blaggs' home, and tire marks in the vegetation on the street side, as if a vehicle had stopped there. Singer noted that the batteries were dead on the back door's alarm, and the door was easily popped open with a tool. It could be popped open even by the simple use of a credit card.

As if he were the burglar, Singer told the jurors to follow him now down the hallway to the master bedroom. In the bedroom is a dresser on the right, and a closet, but it is still dark in the room. And on the bed, the burglar was suddenly surprised by a woman lying there. "What else was found on that bed?" he rhetorically asked. His answer was that some human hairs were found on the bed, and they did not belong to Jennifer or Mike. "They were a stranger's hairs!" Singer declared.

Even more strange, when the investigators discovered the bloodstains, they found some DNA mixed up with the blood on the comforter, and the DNA did not belong to Jennifer, Mike, or Abby. Whose DNA it was, was not determined, according to Singer, and he said very loudly, "Someone else was there!"

"Now follow me back out the door, down the hallway, through the laundry room, to the garage. Open the door, look down on the step, and there is a bloodstain—DNA that does not belong to Jennifer, Mike, or Abby. It's that of a stranger. Someone else was there.

"Now let's go back to the bedroom and the jewelry box. The fingerprints on the jewelry box are unknown. There is a fingerprint on the mirror of the jewelry box. It does not belong to Michael Blagg. (Very loud) His fingerprints are not on the jewelry box!"

Singer pointed out that there was an unknown palm print on the back door's knob. And he also pointed out that any fingerprints of Mike in the minivan would be natural. After all, he had driven it on occasion as well.

Moving to the front entryway, Singer noted, the investigators took shoe impressions, and two of them were of a man's shoes and did not belong to the officers' shoes or those that belonged to Mike. Who did those shoes belong to? Singer rhetorically asked. He answered his own question by saying they were the shoes of strangers.

Singer said that investigators looked for signs of blood smears or droplets in the house all through November 14 and 15, but they couldn't find any. Singer then pointed to a blank screen on the wall, and said, "If there was blood on that screen—luminol would find it." He pointed out that the investigators used a lot of luminol in the Blagg home and did not find blood that had been wiped up or cleaned in any way. "They luminoled the garage. No blood, no smears, no wipes. There were only very small droplets of blood on the molding of the van that came from some indeterminate time. They luminoled the whole interior of the van and found no more blood than that."

As for the bullet in Jennifer's brain, Singer noted that an FBI agent said that lots of guns could have fired that bullet. Even if it had been fired by a 9mm handgun, like Mike had once owned, Singer said that there were at least 5 million 9mm handguns in the United States. Singer stated that Mike had owned a 9mm handgun in the 1990s, in Corpus Christi, Texas, but there was no evidence he had ever owned one in Grand Junction, Colorado.

Then Singer proclaimed, "Let's move away from the house. It's five-thirty A.M. and Michael is number one in charge at AMETEK Dixson that day." Singer noted that there were two important projects happening at the manufacturing plant on November 13—there was the transfer of an entire production line to Mexico, and an upcoming changeover of the computer system. "It's a big deal, and it's Mike's position to save money. He had to check everything. He was at the loading dock that day because it was important to make sure things were going smoothly for the move."

Singer pointed out that Mike was seen by fellow employees many times on the loading dock, but not one of them saw him near the Dumpster. Not only that, but there apparently was no blood found in the AMETEK Dixson Dumpster later by investigators. Singer asked, "Where did the blood go if Jennifer was in the Dumptser?" He said that CBI luminoled the Dumpster at five different spots, and all five came up negative for blood.

Moving on to the AMETEK Dixson yard sale, Singer said that there was a lot of old furniture and equipment at the yard sale, and Mike was in charge of it. "Before the public was invited, employees got to cherry-pick the items." Singer pointed out that Mike never did move back into the home on Pine Terrace Court after the disappearance of Jennifer and Abby, so he needed furniture and equipment. There was no crime here, Singer stated; other employees were getting items from the yard sale as well. Singer also noted that Mike took the items in broad daylight; he didn't sneak in at night to try and take them. According to Singer, Mike didn't steal anything.

Singer moved on to the landfill investigation, and even showed a video of the process. He said that on November 13, 14, 15, and 16, 2001, two thousand tons of trash were deposited there, in an area three times the area of the courtroom everyone was now sitting in. It was in an area 150 feet long by two hundred feet wide by twenty-five feet high. Then Singer noted that no AMETEK Dixson trash was found in the bucket that brought Jennifer's body to the surface. The only thing close to the time frame was a newspaper dated November 17, 2001. The closest point that any trash from AMETEK Dixson was found was twenty-five feet away in a different depth level. In fact, AMETEK Dixson trash was spread out all over the place, along with items from Office Depot and other sources.

Singer cited Neal Bolton, an expert in landfills. Bolton said there was no way to judge if Jennifer's body came from a strata that contained only AMETEK Dixson trash. When the trash was off-loaded at the landfill, and spread around, massive amounts of trash were spread in three directions. Singer noted that when the BFI hauler on November 14, 2001, dumped the AMETEK Dixson load, he spread it all out in a line only two feet high and many yards long. It was the truck driver's job to walk the line and look for large "foreign" objects, and he didn't report anything out of the ordinary that day. The operator even remembered that particular day, and said that he'd only had "two roll offs that day."

As for Investigator Steven King, Singer said that Mike

had looked upon him as his advocate and friend in the disappearance of Jennifer and Abby. "They talked about all sorts of things." On November 13, 2001, Mike had a five-hour talk with King. Then on February 5, 2002, according to Singer, Mike had no idea that King and the other investigators were now looking at him as a suspect. There was also FBI agent Irwin, who was in and out of the room. "Of a ten-hour interview, the FBI only wrote a five-page report," Singer announced. And it was at that point that Irwin and the others kept going over the same topics, over and over again, trying to confuse Mike, according to Singer.

Singer said that the circular technique of the investigators wore down and ultimately confused Mike, to a point where he would admit to almost anything. One instance was his fight with Jennifer on November 9, 2001, when Mike said they were arguing about a possible job move. It was only after continued "bullying" by the investigators that Mike said that the fight might have been over porn, but even then he didn't really admit to it, rather he said it was "possible," so that "they would get off his back."

Singer even said that the investigators "screwed up" while using EnCase [a forensic program for computers that "mirrored" the files on a hard drive, so that all the files could be seen without having to start the computer and risk having files deleted], and the porn Mike was supposedly looking at on the Internet on the evening of November 12 could have been on another night altogether. Mike freely admitted to authorities that Jennifer had vulvar vestibulitis and that's why they would look at porn together to try and find a different technique from missionary sex. Also, Singer countered the notion that Mike was constantly on his computer looking at pornographic images. Singer noted that in actuality it was proven that out of 451 days, during 2000 and 2001, Mike had looked at porn sites on fifty of those days. That was hardly a daily habit. Singer also showed a chart that in October and November 2001, Mike's viewing of porn actually decreased, instead of increased.

Then Singer quoted Mike's suicide note—stating that in it he did not once admit to harming Jennifer and Abby in any way, but that he planned to see them in Heaven after he was dead. As to the allegation that the suicide attempt was fake, Singer showed the jury a photo of Mike in a bathtub filled with bloody water with an open Bible and family photo on the edge of the tub. Singer quoted an investigator who had said, "Mike, you're dying," and after saying that, he tried to get a confession out of him.

At that point, Mike supposedly opened his eyes and said, "I did not kill my family. I do not know where they are."

Singer claimed that the prosecution's contention about the note that Jennifer had posted on the bathroom mirror was overblown. She had notes on religious themes pasted all over the house, and the note in question could have meant anything, not an ultimatum that she was leaving Mike and taking Abby with her.

Singer showed the jury a note that Mike had at AMETEK Dixson, reminding him about his upcoming anniversary on November 16. Singer showed another note from Jennifer, which said, "Mike, I love you, and enjoy spending time with you. I truly wouldn't want to be with anyone else."

In a similar note, she had written, "I desire to always be there for you. . . . All my love, Jennifer, your bride."

On November 8, 2001, Jennifer spoke with her mother in Texas for forty-four minutes, and not once did she bring up the subject of any discord in the home.

Singer spoke of the supposed fight on November 9 between Mike and Jennifer. The very next day, Jennifer got together with Diana Shirley, her best friend in Grand Junction. Not once did she mention to Diana about a fight or any other problems with Mike. Around that same time, Diana saw Mike drop Abby off for rehearsals on an upcoming Christmas pageant. Diana Shirley said that she didn't see anything out of the ordinary in Mike or in the Blagg family.

Jennifer phoned her mother on November 10, and according to Singer, there was not one word about any fights with Mike, nor was there anything out of the ordinary in her nine-minute call to Marilyn Conway on November 11.

Diana Shirley phoned Jennifer on the evening of November 11, 2001, and they talked about not going bike riding together because it was too cold. There was nothing that caught Diana's attention. On Monday, November 12, Jennifer picked up Abby from school and Diana saw her there. Once again, there was no tip-off about anything wrong in the family.

Even at 8:30 P.M., November 12, Jennifer phoned her mom and talked for forty-four minutes. Marilyn Conway didn't detect anything that was upsetting her daughter. Even a little later that evening, a neighbor phoned Jennifer and they talked for a while. The neighbor didn't notice anything different in Jennifer's tone of voice.

At the end of his opening argument, Singer projected a photo of Mike and Jennifer Blagg smiling at each other. They definitely appeared to be a happy, loving couple. Singer said, "Michael Blagg did not commit this crime, and what each and every one of you will know from this evidence is that Michael Blagg did not have an affair with a neighbor, with a coworker, and never had an affair with his computer. He most assuredly did have an affair—he had a love affair with Jennifer."

Mike had sat expressionless throughout most of the long presentation. The only time he seemed to flinch was when images of Jennifer's mummified body had been projected onto the screen by Frank Daniels.

* * *

Now began a long parade of witnesses for the prosecution, starting with the playing of the 911 phone call by Mike on November 13, 2001. There was absolute quiet in the courtroom as Mike's emotional voice emerged from the speakers of a tape machine. Every so often, his crying could be heard between his own words and those of the dispatcher. The only time his voice seemed to change was when he was discussing Jennifer's various medical conditions. At those times, his tone seemed flat and analytical.

The first actual witness was sheriff's patrol deputy Tim Moore, who recalled receiving a call from the dispatcher and being routed toward the Blagg home on Pine Terrace Court in the Redlands. Moore recalled meeting Mike on the front porch of the house, and making sure that he was okay. Then Moore obtained the keys from Mike and got permission to go into the house. It was 4:37 P.M., and Deputy Doty arrived about the same time. Moore said, "We put on latex gloves."

Moore spoke of going through the kitchen and noticing that the back door was open, and when they went down the hallway, they saw bloodstains on the bed and carpet, along with a jewelry box with some of its contents spilled on the floor. Moore said that he had been at numerous other burglary scenes during his career, and "this one didn't feel like other burglary scenes that I had been to." He noticed that nothing in the rest of the house seemed to be out of order or rifled through.

On cross-examination, there was a long exchange between Moore and Eisner:

EISNER: What do you generally do first? See if someone needs help in the house, or a quick sweep?

MOORE: A quick sweep.

EISNER: You talked with Michael Blagg?

MOORE: Yes. I asked, "Are you okay?"

EISNER: How long did it take you to go through the house?

MOORE: It was pretty quick through the front rooms. Longer in the master bedroom. I saw blood on the side of the bed.

EISNER: Did you see bloodstains of different sizes?

MOORE: Yes.

EISNER: How long do you think they (the bloodstains) were in there?

MOORE: Four or five hours, based on my judgment.

EISNER: You've seen bloodstains of different sizes in your work?

MOORE: Yes.

This matter of how long Moore thought the bloodstains had been there helped Mike in his cause. If they'd only been there for four or five hours by 4:30 P.M., then he couldn't have done the crime. Everyone had seen him at AMETEK Dixson from at least 6:00 A.M. on.

Deputy Jeff Doty had been patrolling in Clifton, and arrived at the crime scene not long after Deputy Moore. He noticed mail piled up around the Blaggs' front door and a package in the hallway. Doty didn't make an estimate about how long he thought the blood was in the bedroom.

There was a moment of levity in the courtroom when the topic arose of what kind of boots Doty wore that day. The deputy said they were the same kind he was wearing to court today, and a question came up about the pattern on the bottom of his boots. Doty stood up on one leg and lifted his other leg and boot off the floor. It was quite a balancing act, and Frank Daniels quipped, "Kind of like DUI stuff." (An obvious allusion to making a driver, suspected of being under the influence while driving, stand on one leg and see if they would tip over.) Officer Doty laughed, and so did the jurors.

Eisner, on cross, started grilling Doty about a puddle of water he noticed near the front door of the Blagg home. Doty said that neither he nor Moore tracked water into the house. Eisner wanted to know how it got there, and brought up the possibility that some stranger could have tracked in the puddle of water.

Sergeant John Coleman testified that he'd arrived at the Blagg home not long after Moore and Doty. He spoke briefly with Mike out on the porch, and said, "He didn't look well. He was nervous, excited, and shaking." At that point, Coleman had the ambulance crew take a look at Mike.

Sergeant Coleman became the officer in charge at the scene, and he told Moore to go outside and not let anyone else into the house. Coleman went into the master bedroom and his impression of the bloodstains was that "they were there more than three or four hours, and less than twenty-four hours. The blood patterns on the bed were on the right-hand side. They then dripped onto the floor. None of the rest of the house was rifled."

The cross by Eisner had the following comments:

EISNER: You didn't observe puddles of water in the foyer?

COLEMAN: No.

EISNER: Did you make a note of unusualness of the bloodstains in your report?

COLEMAN: No.

MCSO investigator Glade Johnson recounted the long evening of November 13, 2001, as he and fellow investigator

Barley suited up with protective gear and videotaped the entire Blagg home. It was a thorough and intensive videotaping, and the jurors grew restless after viewing the scene for a while, as the camera shots seemed almost to be in slow motion, as they went on and on. One of the more chilling scenes was of Abby's room, with the bed unmade, the covers pulled down, a doll on her bed, and the fact that Abby had never been found.

During a break, Mike Blagg rose, stretched, and seemed calm. He folded his hands behind his back and took a short look into the gallery. After the break, there was video footage of investigators searching around the Colorado River, and discussion about the police dogs that had followed the Blagg's scent to the riverbanks. It was a known factor that the Blagg family did take walks down there on occasion. Lieutenant Quarles, of the Grand Junction Fire Department, spoke of floats down the river and searching for the bodies of Abby and Jennifer. Quarles had been in the U.S. Coast Guard and knew all about river searches and retrieving drowned bodies. Mike was very attentive and watched the video of the river search with keen interest.

An aerial photo of the Colorado River was shown on a screen, and Quarles pointed to the area searched from the Blue Heron to the Connected Lakes area. Other photos showed the search on BLM (Bureau of Land Management) land near Blake Park, where all that was discovered was the carcass of a buried dog.

Eisner wanted to know if he saw the butt of a gun in the closet, which would lead to that search. The agent admitted that he hadn't:

EISNER: Did you see a bag of money?

AGENT: I didn't see it.

EISNER: Didn't you sign a log?

AGENT: I don't remember.

EISNER: It wasn't until you'd been through the entire house that you noticed water in the foyer?

AGENT: Yes.

Eisner kept going back to these mysterious water spots, and even showed a photo of the five-inch by one-and-a-half-inch wet area. He kept contending that an intruder could have left the wet spot there as he either entered or exited the house.

The testimony went back to the search dogs, and one of their handlers, Geraldine Earthman, of the GJPD, told of arriving at Pine Terrace Court at 5:40 P.M. on November 13, 2001. She brought her dog to see if Jennifer and Abby had left the residence on foot. The dog Zara went as far as the front porch, and in another area went as far as the garage door. Zara gave no "alerts" past those areas that Jennifer and Abby might have walked away from the residence. This seemed to point to the fact that their bodies had been driven away, and not that they'd walked away on their own power.

On cross, Eisner picked up on the wind factor of November 13, and wanted to know if it was possible that Jennifer and Abby had been driven out in a vehicle from the garage area. The answer he received was "Yes." He also drew an admission that anyone could have driven that minivan.

The next witness was Matt Saluto, of the CBI lab. Saluto arrived at the Pine Terrace home on November 13, 2001, began to process the scene, and his first impression had been that the overall scene was "clean"—in other words, the whole house hadn't been tossed looking for valuable items. Saluto took numerous photographs and collected some items. The photographs ranged from those of the entryway, to the back door. Each of these photos was entered into evidence, and they numbered nearly 150 in all. It was a lot for the jury to see and take in as they were brought into evidence, one by one.

One of Saluto's more interesting comments concerned the blood pool on the bed. He said, "The pool seemed to be watered down . . . and the (blood) left a pattern on the fitted sheets of someone lying on it."

Further photos of the outside of the Blagg home were entered into evidence, and they included the fence in the back of the property to scenes along the street in front of the house. Investigator Scott Ehlers introduced these MCSO photos, one by one, including photos of the entryway to the house, which depicted some kind of clear liquid near the front door. There were photos of the minivan in the garage and the garage area as well.

One set of photos depicted Jennifer Blagg's note that was written on an Urgent Request Form. On the section where she wrote, "He's (Jesus) left me some keys also, health key, marriage key, material key, and my will as to what I do with these keys"—she circled the word "will."

Most of the photographs and videos were entered into evidence with no objections from the defense, but that was not the case with People's #239. This appeared to be a still image from a Maxell DVD of the inside of the Pine Terrace home—perhaps the closet near the stairwell. Singer was allowed to approach Judge Bottger over this image, and there was a short discussion not overheard by the jury or the gallery. The judge appeared to smile at one point, and said that #239 would not be entered at present.

Questions about the missing jewelry came up, and Investigator Ehlers admitted that the local pawnshops had been checked in the weeks after the disappearance, and none of the missing jewelry showed up at any of them. On December 13, 2001, the list of missing jewelry was even sent to pawnshops in neighboring states. On cross, however, Eisner got Ehlers to admit that forty other states weren't checked at all.

A few of the more interesting photos concerned an extra-large orange T-shirt and blue Tommy Hilfiger boxer shorts. These were items that Mike had said he had been wearing on November 13 early in the morning. Apparently, there was no blood found on these particular items. Nor was suspicious evidence found in a Dirt Devil vacuum cleaner bag, found in the closet near the entryway. Eisner contended that Mike did not use a vacuum cleaner to try and get rid of evidence.

Eisner zeroed in on the Blaggs' finances:

EISNER: Initially you were looking for financial problems?

EHLERS: Yes.

EISNER: No problems?

EHLERS: Correct.

Eisner also got Ehlers to admit that it was easy to get into the back door of the Blaggs' home, just by using a credit card to slip the lock open. As far as footprint marks on the outside of the back fence, Ehlers said he checked and didn't see any. He had also checked the vegetation in that area to see if it had been trampled down. It didn't appear to be so to him. He even checked the roof of the Blagg home, and hadn't seen any signs of anything unusual up there.

In some ways, the talk about finances was a good opening for Daniels. He didn't use it to see if there were financial problems between Mike and Jennifer; rather, on redirect, he asked if Jennifer or anyone else had used her credit cards after she went missing.

DANIELS: Why look for financial records?

EHLERS: To see about credit card use or big withdrawals.

DANIELS: To see if she made reservations on airlines?

EHLERS: Yes.

Friday's testimony began with CBI agent Darren Jewkes talking about fingerprints. Twenty-two of twenty-nine usable prints came from Mike. Seven other usable prints were typed to being from a woman or small child. The prosecution pointed out that Mike's fingerprints were found in key crime scene areas. Eight prints from Mike were found inside the minivan—Jennifer's minivan.

To check on the yard workers, who had been in the area on November 13, Jewkes ran their prints to see if they showed up anywhere in the Blagg home. They did not.

One macabre factor was discussed by Jewkes—the fact that after Jennifer Blagg's body reached the CBI lab in Montrose, her hands were cut off to try and get useful fingerprints. Her hands were so badly decomposed, however, that only four fingerprints were of any use.

On March 12, 2004, the prosecution displayed Mike's extensive viewing of porn sites. MCSO investigator Michael Piechota told of finding that Mike had downloaded 668 pornographic photos, had visited 1,876 porno Web sites, and had 119 pornographic text files on his computers. A battle ensued over whether the jury would see the actual photos. In a partial victory, the prosecution was allowed to show the jury redacted photos of men ejaculating onto women's faces, with the most egregious parts covered over. It was still very graphic evidence, however.

The defense meanwhile zeroed in on the porn issue, by saying that the supposed final fight between Mike and Jennifer, on November 12, 2001, over his viewing porn on the computer, never occurred. Eisner said that Piechota was wrong about this date, and an FBI analysis had shown that the last time Mike downloaded porn on his computer was on October 16, 2001.

Eisner said to Piechota, "You're saying you have the expertise to say the Blaggs' home computer accessed pornography on November 12, 2001, at eight-fifty P.M., but you don't have the expertise to explain why that's a mistake? Is that what you're saying?" Piechota had to agree that there had been a mistake about the November 12 date and the viewing of pornography at that time.

Eisner also pointed out that many of the pornographic Web sites noted by authorities were actually unsolicited pop-up ads, which depicted other Web sites. Mike had never viewed these pop-up Web sites.

On redirect, Daniels noted that there were hundreds of pornographic Web sites that Mike had visited, while only accessing five religious sites, ninety-eight real estate sites, and 140 employment and health sites.

One of the more bizarre aspects of all this talk and showing of porn was the fact that thirty-five students from Fruita's Monument High School were in the gallery at the time. It's doubtful their teacher knew what they were in store for in their quest to see the court system in action. They may have gotten more than they bargained for with testimony describing Internet porn and "CumShots.com."

At the end of the court session that day, a reporter asked Mike Blagg how he thought the trial was going. Normally instructed to say nothing, Mike turned and answered, "I think our guys (the defense lawyers) are doing great. I have all the faith in the world in them."

* * *

On Tuesday, March 16, Edith Melson, Jennifer's best friend from her South Carolina days, took the stand. She said that Mike had been "controlling and sometimes wouldn't let me go to see Jennifer at home, or even talk to her on the phone. She couldn't go out without telling Michael where she was going. Even when she was sick, and I brought food over to the house, he wouldn't allow me to see her."

The very negative picture of Mike that Edith was portraying brought several reactions from Mike's sister and mother, who were in the gallery. Clare, Mike's sister, shook her head so vigorously at times that a bailiff went over and told her to stop doing it.

Some of the most damaging testimony came when Edith stated that a few days before Jennifer disappeared, Jennifer had phoned her and spoke of coming out to see her, with only Abby traveling along. Edith said, "I was very much surprised about Jennifer discussing a trip that didn't include her husband. She never traveled without Mike. She asked me to pray for her for something 'like you've never prayed before.' I didn't know specifically what I was supposed to be praying for, because she didn't tell me at the time. What she said was, 'I have something to tell you. I pray that I will get the courage to tell you.'"

Edith said that she and Jennifer would talk on the telephone three or four times a week, but always during the daytime, when Mike was at work. Often when Edith tried calling when Mike was home, he would say that Jennifer wasn't feeling good or was asleep. Edith said, "He was very controlling."

Edith also declared that she had seen a red-and-black tent in the Blaggs' garage (supposedly while they lived in Simpsonville, South Carolina). When Jennifer's body was discovered in the landfill in Mesa County, it was wrapped in a red-and-black tent.

On cross, Eisner tried to hang Edith Melson with her own words. Edie had told FBI agent Newton in February 2002 that she was unaware of any marital problems between Jennifer and Mike. She had also told a Greenville, South Carolina, newspaper, back in late November 2001, that she thought the Blagg family was "wonderful and close-knit." Even as late as November 2002, Edie still told the media that she was unaware of any marital problems between Mike and Jennifer.

Daniels had neighbors of the Blaggs, who lived on or near Pine Terrace Court, testify about the family. One of the neighbors testified that she had been awakened by a noise about 1:30 A.M., on November 13, 2001, coming from the direction of the Blagg home. And two other neighbors said that their dogs had started barking in the middle of the night on November 13. Daniels contended that the noise was Mike Blagg shooting Jennifer in the head. Dogs, in particular, would start barking at such a sound.

The prosecution built its case, brick by brick, with circumstantial evidence. They didn't have a smoking gun—in fact, they didn't have a gun at all. What they did have was Mike Blagg's unusual behavior after the disappearance of Jennifer and Abby. One of these circumstances concerned Mike spending more than $5,000 on a home entertainment system on New Year's Eve, 2001. He bought a big-screen projection television, a DVD player, a receiver, a subwoofer, speakers, cables, and an extended warranty. A Circuit City employee, Devon Tilly, said that at the time, "He (Mike) tried to wheel and deal," trying to get the best price he could for the equipment.

Daniels asked Tilly if Mike had said anything when he bought all the merchandise. Tilly answered, "He said, 'Man, this country is great. You can buy a bunch of stuff and walk away not paying anything,'" referring to a no interest promotion the store was offering at the time.

Tilly said that Mike had been wearing a pin with Jennifer and Abby's photos inside of it. Tilly didn't know who they were at the time, or who Mike was, until other employees clued him in. Daniels wondered aloud if these actions were the actions of a grieving husband and father. In fact, two weeks later, on January 14, 2002, Mike went back to Circuit City and bought a $1,200 computer and modem. A computer that, Daniels said, Mike used to view more porn.

Eisner, on cross, stated that on Mike's first visit to Circuit City, Jennifer's stepdad, Harold Conway, had accompanied Mike there. Eisner explained that Mike's actions in buying all the equipment was a way of coping with all the stresses of his missing wife and daughter. He needed to escape by watching movies and listening to music.

The Blaggs' neighbor Tammy Eret took the stand, and she recalled Mike in his vehicle traveling very slowly around the cul-de-sac before parking in front of the house on November 13, 2001. She said, "It caught my eye, obviously. I didn't think it was normal."

Not one word about Tammy Eret's supposed stalker was brought up before the jury. Judge Bottger was adamant that none of that kind of testimony was going to be allowed.

Other neighbors of the Blaggs told of a secluded family, who stayed inside and drew their blinds, even in the daytime. The man who rented the house to the Blaggs, Chris Durham, invited them over to his house a few times. When he got no response, he gave up. Durham told his wife, "Well, I guess they just don't want to be our friends."

Ashley Parko, who babysat Abby between May and August 2001, said that Mike had initially been friendly, but became more distant and cold as time went on. She said, "He was extremely protective of Jennifer and Abby. He would call home and check in on Jennifer." Eisner did get Parko to admit that Jennifer thought it was "cute" that he did check up on her, and that she didn't complain about the issue.

Diana Shirley painted a very different picture of Mike and Jennifer than Parko had. She stated that he was a "devoted and loving husband and father, and that neither he nor Jennifer ever confided anything negative about their marriage." Pastor Art Blankenship said generally the same thing, and added about Mike on the afternoon of November 13, "He (Mike) was almost absolutely quiet. The only comment he made (after the disappearance) was 'Art, have you ever been involved in anything like this in your life?'" Art admitted that he hadn't.

Eisner had Blankenship state for the record that while staying with him, Mike broke down on several occasions and cried. Even though Mike was generally a reserved man, he became very emotional when talking about Jennifer and Abby.

Kevin King, a former Orlando, Florida, police officer, whose wife attended Bible study with Jennifer, was with Mike one day when the search was just beginning, and he said that Mike bent over and appeared to break down. "But I didn't see any tears," King testified. "He was also passionless when he appeared on television. I would have reacted a whole lot different."

Eisner jumped up on cross and told King emphatically that he was in no position to judge how Mike Blagg should or shouldn't react. Eisner said that King obviously had not had a wife and daughter disappear from his home, with a pool of blood left inside the house. King was still defiant, however, and said that he would have done anything, including being arrested, to go and search if his own wife and daughter were missing. Eisner shot back that Mike believed he had "the Lord who would help him through difficult times," and that, in essence, it was in God's hands.

Linda Gardner, a worker at AMETEK Dixson, spoke of Mike being at the plant on the night of January 11, 2002. Soon thereafter she noticed that a paper shredder and workbench were missing. Later, it was discovered that Mike had taken these items to the place where he lived. On cross, she did admit that he may have been acting strangely because of stress and that he might not have thought in his mind that he was stealing.

Eisner tried to have Judge Bottger sever the theft count that related to AMETEK Dixson property, saying they had no bearing on the murder charges. Bottger, however, stated that "all the counts are inextricably intertwined," and he refused to dismiss the charges.

AMETEK Dixson coworker Shawn Wallace testified that Blagg normally had been outgoing and motivational, up to about two months before the disappearance. Around that time, Mike seemed to become more withdrawn and lethargic. Wallace also said that sometime on November 13 he saw Mike pushing a cart at the facility with two large boxes, and offered to help him. Mike had turned to him and sternly said, "No, just get away!"

On cross, Eisner attempted to discredit Wallace by questioning him on his dabbling in metaphysics. When Wallace had gone into Mike's office on November 14, 2001, he had placed his hands on the pictures of Jennifer and Abby to see if he could get a sign about what had happened to them.

Joan Cordova spoke of arriving at AMETEK Dixson on November 13, to find Mike already there and he seemed to be dazed. She asked him about the open security doors, and he told her, "I'll get back to you about that." According to Cordova, Mike seemed to be emptying a lot more trash than usual that day.

Eisner questioned why Cordova had not gone to the authorities about any of this for several months. She said that she had been worried about losing her job if she said anything negative about Mike.

With AMETEK Dixson witness Teri Lloyd, Eisner elicited, "He appeared to be the same Mr. Blagg that day. Business as usual."

There were, of course, breaks between trial sessions on the weekends, and *Denver Post* reporter Nancy Lofholm spoke with Jennifer and Abby's family members about how they were holding up and what they were doing when not in the courtroom. In fact, it was a tough time for them because Abby would have been turning nine years old that March. Lofholm wrote, "By now, she most likely would have outgrown her favorite doll, Claire. Claire was left lying on Abby's pillow the day she vanished two years and four months ago. By this milestone, Abby would probably know all the lyrics to 'Amazing Grace,' rather than singing 'la, la, la, la' after the first verse. She most assuredly would be stuffing more birthday money into the Mickey Mouse piggy bank she kept tucked away in [her] bureau drawer. It held $25 when she disappeared."

Lofholm noted that if Abby's favorite ice cream was still cookies and cream, she would have been treated to that by her extended family in Grand Junction on her birthday. Instead, her uncle Dave Loman and some of his friends were going to spend Abby's birthday looking for a bit of disintegrating nightgown or a depression that could be a grave in the hills beyond the Redlands.

Interestingly enough, Lofholm had asked Mike Blagg that same question about searching for Abby a week before, and he had responded that "I look for Abby every day." Then he admitted that he didn't look for her in a physical sense, but rather in a spiritual one.

Loman, however, was searching in a very physical sense for any sign, no matter how small, of where Abby's body might be found. And he was angry at Mike and Mike's side of the family. Loman said, "Not a single one of them has lifted a finger to do a gol-darned thing. We have not even had a call. They have not given any information or help to the foundation (the Abby and Jennifer Recovery Foundation)."

Loman went on to say that there didn't seem to be a rock in Mesa County that he and the other searchers didn't have a name for, or more than eight trees they hadn't become acquainted with. He and the others kept on looking in the hills and canyons, despite the fact that the authorities now believed that Abby's body had been dumped in the landfill, along with Jennifer's body, and pushed to some other location under tons of trash. Yet Dave Loman persisted, and said, "I'd have a hard time looking my own children in the face if I didn't do everything in my power to find Abby."

One of the more damaging witnesses against Mike took the stand on March 22, 2004. Rita Mayhew had been a production supervisor at AMETEK Dixson and she took Mike, her daughter, and coworker Linda Gardiner to dinner at the Orchard Mesa restaurant one night in January 2002. While at dinner, according to Mayhew, Mike made a comment about "how lucky he was to be a single guy out for drinks with three beautiful women." This was only two months after Jennifer and Abby disappeared, and they were still viewed as missing persons rather than deceased. It made Mayhew feel very uncomfortable.

DA Frank Daniels asked, "Do you know how he would have known that he was a single guy at that point?"

Mayhew answered, "No. We felt it was a really odd statement."

Eisner tried to lessen the damage by stating that the comment made by Mike was innocent. He had Mayhew admit that Mike wasn't trying to pick her up, and perhaps he was just trying to be friendly. She still felt that it was an odd comment, however.

Clayton Yancy, AMETEK Dixson's technical publications manager, testified that on the morning of November 13, 2001, Mike had come into his office and asked him to scan a photo of himself, Jennifer, and Abby for a Christmas card. Yancy then said that Mike had never done anything like that before. Later in his testimony, Yancy brought up about a computer that had been stolen from work in June 2001. He said that security in that part of the plant had to be increased after the theft, and Yancy implied that Mike had stolen it.

After the lunch break, Eisner jumped on this and asked Judge Bottger for a mistrial. Eisner said that the prosecution's hints that Mike had been the thief of that computer were "inflammatory and prejudicial," with no evidence to back them up.

Bottger did not go so far as to declare a mistrial, but instructed the jury to consider Yancy's testimony about the computer only as "evidence that the managers increased security at the plant after the theft and that Mike Blagg was aware of the new security features."

Jim Boden, AMETEK Dixson's maintenance director, testified about the trash compactor and Dumpster in which, the prosecution said, Mike had placed the body of Jennifer and possibly Abby as well. But the defense made telling marks by saying that there was too much light near the Dumpster for Mike to dispose of a body without being detected. Nighttime photos of the compactor/Dumpster area were then shown to the jurors, which showed a well-lit area.

On March 23, the jurors got to see Mike on the evening of November 13, 2001—thanks to a video of the five-hour session he had at the MCSO. Seated in a chair at a table, across from Investigator Steven King, Mike seemed to be almost emotionless as he discussed the disappearance of

Jennifer and Abby. In some ways, Mike's own words were coming back to haunt him. He told King at the interview that he had *left* for work at around 6:00 A.M., but an AMETEK Dixson security camera showed him to be at the plant at 5:56 A.M.

The video interviews portrayed a recitation of the facts as Mike presented them to investigators on November 13. He was so unemotional during the interview that the *Daily Sentinel* headlined this portion of the trial: STONE-FACED BLAGG DESCRIBED DAY OF DISAPPEARANCE IN INTERVIEW.

Mike talked evenly and calmly to King during the interview, and he didn't cry. When he was left alone for ten minutes, the tape kept rolling, and he sat at the table with his head in his hands. At one point, he pulled his hands away and looked at them. Then he bowed his head and either began talking to himself, or praying.

Steven King commented to Mike at the time, "I have to tell you that I have this strange feeling . . . that you are handling this extremely well. I'm not sure if my child and wife were gone and I came home and saw the things you saw, if I wouldn't be at St. Mary's Hospital right now being medicated."

Mike answered that it was his Christian faith that was keeping him together. He said, "It is only through the strength of the Holy Spirit that I am able to be sitting here in front of you now. Every fiber, every core member of my body, wants to scream out and shout and grab something by the neck and say, 'You did it,' and tear 'em limb from limb! And my number one concern is getting to the point where you guys say, 'All right, let's go find the person who did this.'"

Sergeant Weyler came in during the interview and asked Mike how he could explain the blood on the master bedroom bed, but no blood elsewhere in the house. Mike answered, "I haven't got a clue how it wouldn't trail someplace. I don't know how that would happen."

Asked why, if he was so concerned at work after several unanswered phone calls to Jennifer, he didn't return home, Mike answered, "I was concerned, but I wasn't thinking like this. I would never think like this. Even in my most unbelievable nightmares, I don't think like this. That stuff happens to other people. That doesn't happen to us."

At one point, Weyler asked Mike, point-blank, "Did you take them somewhere?"

Mike said, "No, I did not, and I would never do that."

On March 25, jurors heard about Mike reading a newspaper in December 2001, and becoming angry that the investigators still considered him a suspect. He contacted them and expressed his frustration and anger that he was "still under their microscope." It was during one of those interviews, before he was arrested for the thefts from AMETEK Dixson, that he told investigators he would never leave Grand Junction until he knew what happened to Jennifer and Abby. Of course, two days after the search began at the landfill, Mike left Grand Junction for Georgia.

One of the interesting revelations by Investigator King concerned when Mike was first allowed back into the house on Pine Terrace Court. "Mike was shaking and placed his hands over his mouth. He seemed afraid to look into the master bedroom where Jennifer's blood was found. He walked into the kitchen, sat down at a table, and started crying."

Mike showed emotion, again that same day, when he was looking through a closet, and one of Abby's coats fell to the floor. Mike picked it up, held it to his face, and began crying. He then went to the living room, sat down on a couch, and buried his face in the coat.

In a December 10, 2001, interview with investigators, Mike told authorities, "I think I'm getting to the point where my sorrow is getting to the frustration and anger stage. If there's nothing to link me, and I know there's not, because I had nothing to do with this, why aren't we able to say, 'They're not suspects.'" In saying this, he was alluding to a comment King had made earlier that Jennifer might have been responsible for killing Abby and then herself.

On January 25, 2001, Mike brought up this same issue of suspects by saying, "All I need from you guys is that you guys don't think I'm a suspect, that you've moved on, and at that point, I'm cool." Then once again he swore that he would stay in Grand Junction until Jennifer and Abby, or their bodies, were found. He said, "I'm not leaving here. I'm not leaving here unless someone dynamites me out of here."

It was now time to confront whether Mike's suicide attempt of February 6, 2002, was real or feigned, and the prosecution and defense took very different views on the matter. Steven King had ridden to the hospital in an ambulance with Mike, and he noticed that when an attendant tried to put a tube down Mike's throat, he raised up and gagged. King thought that this was visual proof that Mike was not in as serious condition as he was trying to portray. King stated that during other suicide attempts, he had not seen a similar kind of reaction in other people. King said that Mike had seven stitches in his wrists, and there were several hesitation cuts in evidence, but he thought the whole suicide attempt was staged by Mike, possibly to try and get sympathy from the community.

Eisner was all over King on the issue of the suicide attempt. He point-blank asked if King viewed the suicide attempt as being faked. King answered, "I'm sure if he had stayed there long enough, he would have expired. But when we arrived, I didn't think it was a life-threatening situation. I felt that there was a certain amount of staging there."

King described the scene as Mike in a bathtub of bloody water, with an open Bible and photo of his family lying on the edge of the tub. "Mike still had color in his face and appeared semiconscious." Then King stated that he thought Mike had slit his wrists when he knew the investigators would be coming into his apartment. "My belief was that he was faking it. My belief was that he was attempting to get sympathy from the community."

Eisner came back with the fact that Mike had just gone through a ten-hour interview where investigators repeatedly told him that Jennifer and Abby were dead, and they thought he was responsible. About that interview, King said, "Blagg was an interviewer's dream, and an investigator's nightmare." He explained that this was because he perceived Mike as being well-educated and well-spoken—able to be manipulative and cagey. King declared, "When Mr. Blagg came into this interview, I looked at him as a victim. When he left this interview, I looked at him as a person of interest."

Getting back to the suicide attempt, Eisner pointed out that a paramedic performed a mental evaluation of Mike, and Eisner asked King, "Would it surprise you if he got the lowest possible score?"

"Was he trying?" King shot back, meaning Mike Blagg sought that result.

This drew a response from Judge Bottger, who told King that he couldn't ask a question of a lawyer. He was there to answer questions and not to ask them.

If things had been pretty contentious and rocky during the testimony about the validity of Mike's suicide attempt, the trial ran into further difficulties when construction workers in the vicinity of the courthouse were installing new sewer lines and hit a power line that knocked out electricity, forcing an evacuation of the courthouse for several hours. Then on Friday, March 26, workers broke a water main and Judge Bottger adjourned court early because there was no water in the bathrooms or air-conditioning in the courtroom.

On Monday, March 29, FBI agent Bill Irwin took the stand and said he was the first investigator to confront Mike Blagg as being a suspect, not a victim. Before him, the other investigators had been "friendly." Irwin delcared, "I told him he knew where his wife and daughter were and he could take us to them. Then I told him the investigation was like a jigsaw puzzle and we were nearly finished with it. There were only a few pieces left to solve the puzzle."

Asked by Daniels how Mike reacted to that, Irwin said, "He had no response."

Mike's answers to several key questions differed as the interrogation went on that day. To the question of what the November 9 fight between him and Jennifer was about, he answered twice that he couldn't remember, once that it was about a possible job move, and finally admitted it was about him viewing porn on the Internet. Even this had variable answers from Mike. At first he claimed that he and Jennifer had viewed the porn to find creative ways to have sex—later he said he was addicted to Internet porn.

Agent Irwin continued that near the end of the ten-hour interview on February 5, 2002, Mike was close to a confession. Irwin said that Mike had his head on Sergeant Wayne Weyler's shoulder and was crying. It was at that point, prodded to tell where Jennifer and Abby were, Mike said, "I can't." That could be interpreted two different ways: "Either, I can't tell you because it will harm me, or I can't tell you because I don't know."

It was when the investigators talked about the different degrees of murder that Mike asked about what might happen if "different scenarios occurred."

The defense hammered in on Irwin, stating that of a ten-hour interview with Mike, the FBI had produced exactly six pages of a written report. The MCSO investigators didn't do much better, Eisner claimed—they had produced only thirty-one written pages. Irwin, however, said that even when investigators weren't in the room with Mike, they were in an adjoining room, where they could hear his voice and see his expressions.

Eisner touched on the counseling Mike had received while in South Carolina and noted that not even Investigator Hebenstreit was sure if Mike had seen a psychiatrist or psychologist there. Hebenstreit had written down in his notebook: "Irwin—psychiatrist?" Eisner said the whole counseling session in South Carolina had been because Mike was trying to improve his communication with Jennifer. Apparently, these sessions had happened at the Palmetto Health Ministry and Church Relations.

Eisner also read back verbatim what had occurred when Agent Irwin had first confronted Mike about thinking he was responsible for killing Jennifer and Abby. "'Michael, the results clearly show you know where your wife and daughter are right now,' and he started to protest, and you held up your hand. 'We know what happened.'" Eisner said, "From that point, you talked about physical evidence in the case, which led to the puzzles. And Mike responded, 'I've been very patient. I didn't plan anything.' That's after a great deal of conversation. And after a while, you asked, 'Did you plan it?' And he answered, 'I didn't plan anything.'"

At one point, Eisner even got Irwin to admit that two pieces of the interrogation were based on inaccurate information. One of these was the original investigators' contention that the thing that sparked Mike to murder Jennifer was that she caught him viewing Internet porn on the night of November 12, 2001. They had originally said he had been viewing CumShots.com. Apparently, Mike had not logged on to his home computer at all that night, and Eisner said, "At the interview, the officers wanted you to pound him on that and they pounded him on that. In fact, it turned out to be wrong. Now they (the officers) come into court and say in front of this jury, 'Small detail.' Even though you spent a lot of time going over it and going over it, stressing on Mr. Blagg that that was the precipitating moment. 'Now that we find out they're wrong—now we'll come into court and say, 'Gee, it didn't affect our questioning.' Is that what you're now saying?"

To this, Agent Irwin replied, "No, I said it did. And I would have preferred that we'd not had that problem. But it wasn't a major issue."

Eisner came back with, "It's all important, right? The fact that they're claiming that he wrote this note at work after an argument and that he's making it up to justify the fact that he's killed her, according to the prosecution's theory. He comes home, comes back from work—"

Suddenly there was an objection from Daniels, who said, "That's never been the prosecution's theory!"

Judge Bottger agreed and said, "The objection is sustained. The jury will disregard that comment."

Another inaccurate piece of information, according to Eisner, was the investigators' dismissal of the fact that Mike had ever talked to a recruiter from Longmont. According to Eisner, this had been a cold call, so that was why Mike could not remember the recruiter's name or whom he worked for. Mike had not called him, this person had called Mike.

Another thing that Eisner pointed out was that Mike had volunteered to go on the searches for his missing wife and daughter. He had even told police, "Let me be the first volunteer to search for Jennifer and Abby." He was not allowed by investigators to do so on any search.

Eisner asked Agent Irwin about what had transpired between Mike and the investigators near the end of the interview of February 5, 2002. Agent Irwin said, "Investigator Barley asked Mr. Blagg, 'What are you scared of? Going to jail?' And Mr. Blagg answered that he was and that there were plenty of things he was scared of. Going to jail was high on the list. There was a short break as some food and water were brought in at that stage, and then Mr. Blagg asked the investigators, why don't you tell me what the scenarios are, at which point Investigator Barley talked about the different ranges of punishment for different degrees of crime. According to Barley, it could be looked at as coldly calculated or something that happened in the heat of passion and spur of the moment in an unplanned fashion. At the very close of the interview, Mike asked about a lack of understanding between heat of passion and premeditated. Investigator Barley attempted to clarify that for him."

To this testimony by Irwin, Eisner said, "Would it be normal for a person if they felt they were being wrongfully accused to fear going to prison or jail for something they didn't do?"

Agent Irwin agreed that might be the case.

Eisner then said, "So Mr. Blagg is telling you he's afraid to go to jail. That in itself doesn't mean admitting to you that he killed his wife and is responsible for his daughter's disappearance, did it?"

Irwin responded, "Certainly not by itself, no."

Eisner added, "And this discussion about the degrees of homicide—it was the officers who first broached that subject. Mike didn't come in and say, 'Yeah, while I'm here, I'd kinda like to hear about what some of my options are.' He didn't start that conversation?"

Agent Irwin answered, "No."

Agent Ron Walker, on direct, said that he had studied the crime scene at Pine Terrace Court and concluded, "The emptied-out jewelry box and scattered purse contents were staged. The fact that only Jennifer's insured possessions were missing led me to believe that someone with a proprietary interest staged the crime scene." Of course, the main person with proprietary interest—who did file insurance claims—was Mike Blagg.

Walker went on to say that what was not taken from the Blaggs' home was also of significance. There were high-value items left there, including firearms, a laptop computer, and even money. Walker noted that it would have taken quite a while to stage the crime scene, wrap up and remove Jennifer's body from the bed, get rid of Abby's body, and clean up any spilled blood, which led from the master bedroom to the garage. The time factor stressed that only someone who felt comfortable in those surroundings would have spent that much time in the home. Walker contended that Mike Blagg, more than anyone else, would have been comfortable in the house for that period of time.

Walker said that he believed Jennifer's body was removed from the bed to destroy physical evidence and make it more difficult to pin down the time of her murder. He also believed that her body was taken to the van in the garage, driven away to a dump site, and then the van was returned to the garage. Jennifer's minivan keys were even placed back beneath her purse in the master bedroom. That was not something a stranger would do, according to Walker.

On cross, Eisner attempted to chip away at Walker's credibility by continually referring to Walker's work as "indefinite assessment." He claimed Walker already had made up his mind about Mike's guilt as a suspect, long before he knew all the facts in the case. Therefore, according to Eisner, Walker made the facts try and fit his assessment theories as to who the perpetrator was. It was a kind of wish-fulfilling scenario, as far as Eisner was concerned.

* * *

Perhaps one of the most critical areas Eisner zeroed in on was when, near the end of the interview of February 5, 2002, it seemed as if Mike might confess. Eisner reiterated the conversations as they occurred, verbatim, trying to prove that Mike Blagg had never said that he had murdered Jennifer and Abby, and had taken their bodies somewhere:

BLAGG: I believe the truth. The truth will set you free. (He then laid his head on Sergeant Weyler's shoulder.)

WEYLER: Tell me the truth.

BLAGG: (Crying) I can't.

WEYLER: You can.

BLAGG: I can't.

WEYLER: Tell me the truth. Just tell me. You can't carry it any longer.

BARLEY: You're so close. You can do this. You're a man.

BLAGG: (Head down and silent)

Weyler again encouraged Mike to tell the truth, and Mike put his hand to his forehead. Weyler said, "What happened?" To which Mike replied, "I can't."

WEYLER: You've already said it by your actions. Don't you want to help these people?

BLAGG: Of course I do.

WEYLER: Then why won't you tell me?

BARLEY: Do you want to take us to the bodies?

BLAGG: I don't know where.

WEYLER: You said you can't, but you can.

BLAGG: I love them.

WEYLER: This is about love for yourself and Jennifer and Abby. God knows.

BLAGG: There's no way on earth to get away from God.

WEYLER: Tell me the truth. What happened?

BLAGG: I can't.

WEYLER: Why? Can you at least take us to the bodies? Please! Please! These people deserve that.

BLAGG: You've got to understand. I don't know where the bodies are!

WEYLER: Why?

BLAGG: I didn't put them anywhere.

WEYLER: Who did?

BLAGG: I don't know who did.

WEYLER: How did they get to where they are?

BLAGG: I don't know.

WEYLER: Did you harm Jennifer?

BLAGG: No.

BARLEY: Do you know who did?

BLAGG: No.

The last day of March found Eisner pounding away at the initial search of the Blagg home, and he kept Sergeant Wayne Weyler on the stand for more than three hours answering questions. He got Weyler to admit that he hadn't collected samples of the clear liquid found on the bed or on the bloodstain. What Weyler had reported was that the clear liquid appeared to him to have been added to the bloodstain. Weyler also admitted that he didn't see evidence anywhere that blood had been wiped or mopped up in the house.

Next, Eisner jumped on the questioning during the ten-hour interrogation of February 5, 2002, as far as Investigator Hebenstreit was concerned. Jim Hebenstreit, who used a laptop computer to record the conversation, initially had tried to take down every word. However, he now admitted that after a while, "there was a lot of summarizing."

April brought the jurors a videotaped version of the meticulous and grueling search of the landfill, from May 13, 2002, to June 5, 2002. As the *Daily Sentinel* noted, "The search went like this—an excavator operator extended the arm of the excavator into the pit, scooped out a bucket of trash and spread it out on a deck. Investigators used rakes to sift through the garbage, looking for evidence, before a bulldozer pushed the trash away. Operating in this fashion, officials created a search area 250 feet wide, 150 feet long, and seventeen feet deep."

MCSO lieutenant Dick Dillon told the jurors, "Sometimes we'd get into heavy deposits of AMETEK Dixson trash, and other times there would just be fragments." It was on the morning of June 4, 2002, that Investigator Stoffel noticed a human leg dangling from the lip of the bucket. When the body was found, it was wrapped in a black-and-red tent and identified as Jennifer Blagg. On finding the body, Dillon said, "The feelings amongst the investigators soared off the chart that we had found what we believed to be Jennifer Blagg."

Jurors watched in rapt attention as the camera operator zoomed in on the bucket containing Jennifer Blagg's leg. Mike, meanwhile, sat with his head lowered and eyes closed during part of that segment. Then he opened his eyes and appeared to crane his neck to view photos of

Jennifer's body. He occasionally seemed to shake as he viewed the photos. During a break, right after the photos were shown, Mike appeared to have trouble standing, and he was quickly surrounded by his pastor and the pastor's wife.

MCSO investigator Henry Stoffel spoke of a "large wedge-shaped plume" of AMETEK Dixson trash that came from the same strata of trash as Jennifer's mummified body. There were newspapers dated from the week of her disappearance and some gauges and circuit boards from AMETEK Dixson.

By the time the investigators finally quit searching in the landfill, they had moved more than forty-six hundred tons of trash in fifty-one days of heat, gusty winds, and the wafting stench of rotting debris.

Eisner's take on all of this: even though the prosecution said that Jennifer's body was found in a vein of AMETEK Dixson trash, on closer inspection it was impossible to tell. Dillon, on cross, admitted that investigators observed, but did not collect, a lot of AMETEK Dixson trash. He also said that officials kept "minimal" records of where the AMETEK Dixson trash was found, and "other than the areas identified from six global positioning system readings, I can't positively say where anything was found."

Another point that helped the defense was that CBI forensic scientist Alex Rugh testified that a blue substance on the tent, in which Jennifer's body had been wrapped, was not consistent with blue paint from the AMETEK Dixson Dumpster. The source of that blue substance could not be determined.

Even more helpful for the defense was the fact that lab agent Sherri Murphy identified forty hairs recovered from bedding of the master bedroom bed. Of these forty, sixteen hairs did not belong to Mike or Jennifer.

The prosecution zeroed in on all the phone calls Mike

had made to his home on November 13, 2001, as a means of setting up an alibi. In one call, he said, "Hello, my beautiful bride. I hope you're out and about doing all kinds of cool and nifty things." In a later call, Mike said, "Man, where are you guys? It's three twenty-two P.M., and I haven't talked to you all day long. I love you, sweetie. I hope everything is going well for you." The prosecution contended that Mike made sure to get the time on that message to show his feigned concern. Then they asked, if Mike was so concerned about Jennifer, why didn't he phone Abby's school, where she volunteered?

The minivan also became a point of contention between the prosecution and defense. Sergeant Rusty Callow testified that there were between forty-six and fifty miles on the minivan's odometer that Mike could not account for. It was surmised that Mike had used the van to deposit Jennifer's body in the AMETEK Dixson Dumpster, and to possibly get rid of Abby's body someplace else.

The MCSO chief deputy coroner, Dr. Dean Havlik, testified about how he presumed Jennifer had been killed in her bed at Pine Terrace Court. He said that her killer had held a gun within two feet of her head and fired into her left eye. "Jennifer Blagg would have been unresponsive immediately and would have died within minutes of being shot."

Monday, April 5, brought an incredible revelation to the courtroom—it was pronounced by Frank Daniels that CBI agent Janel Smith, who originally had ruled out Mike for a mystery bloodstain in the master bedroom of the Pine Terrace Court home, was now going to testify that he could not be ruled out. This small droplet of blood was on a comforter, and Janel Smith said, "It could have been there since the last time the comforter was laundered." Eisner and Singer were up in arms, and contended that the prosecution had perpetrated a discovery violation with this new information, and they asked for a continuance so they could look at the new evidence. Eisner told Judge Bottger, "Our whole theory has been this bloodstain is clear evidence of a stranger, and lo and behold, at the eleventh hour, we get this!"

Why this was so important was—Smith was going to testify originally that the small bloodstain came from an unknown person, adding validity to the defense's argument that a stranger had killed Jennifer. Now Smith was going to contend that Mike could not be ruled out as contributing to the bloodstain. Eisner hadn't even learned about this change of events until lunch break on Monday, April 5, when Smith left a phone message for him on defense investigator Pam Sharp's phone answering machine.

Eisner told Judge Bottger, "She (Smith) had the information for years, and for her to suddenly change her information puts us at a disadvantage. Our whole theory has been that this is clear evidence of a stranger." Then Eisner added that he might try to find a DNA expert to refute Smith's new testimony.

In the end, Judge Bottger ruled that he didn't think this reversal was a discovery violation, since Smith had not performed any additional tests to come to her new conclusion. At least Singer did get Smith to admit, when she testified, that she saw no signs that Mike had tried cleaning up the crime scene, such as wipe marks and the like.

This was nothing compared to the next prosecutorial revelations, which occurred on April 6. At that point, Marilyn Conway, Jennifer's mother, was on the stand, and she had some very interesting things to say. It started out innocently enough, with Conway talking about Mike asking her certain questions about the ongoing investigation during 2001 and 2002, and his seeming concern about Little Park Road. Mike wanted to know why that was important, and how the detectives had come up with a theory that Jennifer's minivan had traveled forty-five miles since it had last been filled with gasoline.

Marilyn Conway spoke of the last time she phoned the Blagg residence on the evening of November 12, 2001, just before the disappearance of Jennifer and Abby. Marilyn recalled that Mike had told her that Jennifer was taking a shower. This seemed to be fairly common during fall 2001—Conway would try to contact Jennifer, but rather Mike would pick up the phone and tell her Jennifer wasn't available. Conway said, "It happened more than once. I would call Jennifer during the day, and say, 'Jennifer, did you not feel well last night? I called, and Michael said you were already in bed.' And she would say, 'Well, he didn't tell me you called.'

"Jennifer was not happy in Grand Junction," Marilyn said, "because I was ill and that played a part in her wanting to move to Texas. There was a dissatisfaction of wanting to move closer to me because I was ill. A child wanting to be closer to their parent."

From there, Conway spoke of Mike's ease around handguns, and that when Mike was on cruises in the navy, there was always a loaded handgun in the nightstand near Jennifer. Marilyn had witnessed this in the Blaggs' residence in San Diego. She added, "Jennifer had a little thirty-two when she lived in La Jolla, when he went on a cruise. She always had one there."

Years later, in South Carolina when Mike was out of the navy, Marilyn was aware of a handgun in the Blaggs' master bedroom closet. She said of this gun, "It was handsome, had a wooden handle, and I held it and I told Mike I didn't think I could handle a gun like that anymore. I previously had been able to handle a pistol. It was heavy. I don't know whether it was a three fifty-seven or not, I cannot swear to the type of gun that it was. But it was about like the police carry. I recall that gun as being nickel-colored—the silver-type color."

One incident particularly stuck in Marilyn's mind about Mike's seeming dependency on guns. She said, "We had gone to the mountains, and Jennifer and I were going to sit on a park bench, and my husband and Michael were going to go walking. Michael didn't want to leave Jennifer and myself without a gun. He said what if a snake, what if a bobcat or badger, was around, and he patted his hip and said, 'I'm the one with the gun.' Jennifer told him that [we] would be fine, there wouldn't be any problem. So they went on, but they didn't go very far. I think he watched us so no one would bother us."

As the testimony went on, the topic came up as to whether Mike could have carried a heavy weight, such as Jennifer's body, out of the bedroom, without having to drag it. As evidence, Marilyn testified that she had seen Mike pick up Jennifer on various occasions when they were just fooling around, or as she put it, "Playing around at my house or his house. One time, he picked me off the ground. It was raining outside and Jennifer and Abby wanted to go play in the rain, which they did, and I was still in my night-clothes. I didn't particularly want to go out in the front yard, so I went from the front door around to the garage. And Mike lifted me off the pavement, two or three times, and onto the sidewalk, while they played in the rain. I believe this was during their last visit in October 2001."

When the topic of the supposedly stolen jewelry came up, Marilyn Conway introduced some stunning new evidence. Marilyn spoke of a sapphire ring that belonged to Jennifer, and Mike had claimed it as stolen on his insurance form. It was a ring that Mike had given to Jennifer years before. Marilyn said of that ring, "We were packing things in the Pine Terrace Court house, after Mike was let back in, and I didn't go in the house for several days after it was released to Michael. His mother and Clare had already gone home, so it was after Thanksgiving and I was in the house then. I was going through the drawers and I found that sapphire ring in a dresser drawer.

"It was in a little plastic . . . I call them a jewelry Baggie. They're very small. The ring itself, the mounting, was not in there that I recall, but the sapphire and some loose diamonds were, and I called Michael's attention to it. And I carried it around in my purse for several days. We were going to eat, and I was going through my purse, as women do, and I found it and I gave it to Michael and said, 'Here, you'll want to keep this.' And he walked back into the garage before we had let the garage door down and deposited it in the jewelry box that we found under the bed. The one with the inlaid rose on top of it, and he put it in there. I asked him if he was going to leave it in there. Wouldn't somebody bother it? And he said nobody would bother it. I haven't seen it since then."

This was particularly damaging, because, in essence, Marilyn was saying that Mike had lied about jewelry that was supposedly stolen, and he illegally had collected insurance money on items that were never stolen. This not only made him look like a thief, where the insurance money was concerned, it punched holes in the defense's theory of a burglar who had invaded the Blaggs' home and killed Jennifer in the process.

Eisner, on cross, had some serious damage control to do, as far as the rings were concerned. Before he had gone very far, however, Marilyn Conway sprang something else on him that no one saw coming. Eisner was speaking about credit cards that Jennifer had access to, and also the fact that in the event that something drastic happened to the Conways, Marilyn Conway and her husband, Harold, had set Jennifer up as a cosigner on both their checking accounts, so that she could have access to these as the executor. Along with this, Marilyn had given Jennifer a couple of blank checks in case of an emergency.

It was at this point that Marilyn said of those blank checks, "Yes, Michael hurt her in Corpus Christi in 1991, and I gave her two checks and told him to take her to the airport if he ever wanted to get rid of her. She could always come home."

In stunned surprise, Eisner asked, "He hurt her in Corpus?"

To which Marilyn replied, "Yes, he did."

Regaining his composure, Eisner asked, "Did you ever tell (Investigator) Lisa Norcross about that?"

Marilyn answered, "I'm sure at some point I did. I understood it was too long ago to come into play."

Pressed on this issue, Marilyn admitted she might not have told any investigator about this incident. "I probably didn't, because I forgot about it for a long time. It came to mind just now because you were asking about the checks and that's why I gave her the checks."

Of these checks, Eisner was very dubious about Marilyn's current reasoning for them. He told her that on a previous occasion she had mentioned the blank checks to Norcross, and he said, "You explained the circumstances where you were actually helping Michael move out of the house on Pine Terrace and there was some disagreement whether he actually saw any checks."

Marilyn answered, "Yes. Yes. Michael was very upset and he gave me a very hard look, like, 'Well, I didn't know she had any money or access to money.' And I said, 'Well, she's had them for years.'"

Eisner countered, "Is that what you told Investigator Norcross back in 2001, or early 2002? According to those reports, you never told Norcross it was because he hurt her in Corpus."

"No, I did not tell her."

"In fact," Eisner said, "you told a *Denver Post* reporter on December 9, 2001, that the Blagg family—Michael, Jennifer, and Abby—was the kind of a family that people envied for their old-fashioned, loving closeness."

Marilyn answered yes.

Eisner would not let go of this supposed abuse of Jennifer by Mike. He pointed out that Investigator Norcross had asked Marilyn if she had ever seen any signs of abuse against Jennifer or Abby, by Mike. Marilyn had not only told Norcross that she had seen no signs of abuse, but she knew the signs to watch out for because she had witnessed abuse as a child.

Eisner also brought up the subject that Marilyn Conway had been worried about Mike's state of mind in late 2001 and early 2002, and this led into the topic about his suicide attempt. Marilyn admitted, "I asked Lee McElfrish not to leave Mike alone. [Lee McElfrish was a friend of Mike's from church.] I told him I didn't think it would be wise to leave him alone."

Later, before the suicide attempt of February 6, 2002, Marilyn had told Investigator Norcross, "Somebody should watch him because I think he might be suicidal."

Getting back to the topic of the rings that had been on the insurance list of missing jewelry, and supposedly discovered by Marilyn in the master bedroom, Eisner asked, "As you described it, the sapphire ring had been taken apart somehow?"

"Yes, dismantled, whatever you want to call it. It had been taken out of the original mounting."

"Was the sapphire still there?"

"Yes, the blue sapphire was there and some diamonds were there."

"And you testified today that you were aware that this was an item that he apparently had declared on his insurance form and that you had personal knowledge that he actually had it in his possession after the events of November thirteenth."

"Yes, sir."

"When's the first time you reported that fact to anybody, other than testifying about it today?"

"Uh, the day that insurance man was here."

"That was when he testified last week?"

"Yes, sir. I was here and I mentioned it to Teri (who worked for the DA's office) if that would be something I needed to bring up when I heard that Michael had turned it in on the insurance. And I just left it at that."

"So you told the district attorney's office about this last week?"

"Yes, I told Teri."

"So you're saying you told the DA's office about this for the first time last week when you heard about it. You've had several conversations over the years with Lisa Norcross and other people in the DA's office about jewelry of different kinds. And during those conversations you didn't say anything about the sapphire ring?"

"No, sir. I forgot about it."

Eisner also attempted damage control about the guns that Marilyn Conway said she had seen in various residences in which the Blagg family had lived. Eisner questioned whether the investigators' theories had influenced Conway. He said, "About a week after Jennifer's remains were discovered, Investigator Barley and Detective (inaudible) called you because they obviously at that point in time knew that Jennifer had died by means of a firearm. And they wanted to know anything you knew about it and you told Investigator Barley, you'd heard about a gun, but you'd never actually seen a gun. Do you remember telling him that?"

"I was aware that they (Mike and Jennifer) had a nine millimeter in a discussion with them, but I don't believe I ever saw the nine millimeter."

"The investigators were trying to see if you could help them put a nine millimeter into the bedroom in the drawers next to the bed, weren't they? And you told them first, 'Well, I'd heard something about a nine-millimeter gun, but I've never seen it.' Didn't know anything about it. Didn't know the make or model. And then I believe it was two months later, on August 27, 2002, you got a call from Investigator Martinez, of the DA's office. And he was following up on this nine millimeter. And at that time you said, 'I've actually seen this nine millimeter on two occasions. Once in Arizona and once in South Carolina.' Remember telling him that?"

"Well, probably. I don't remember telling him that."

"In fact, you commented on how handsome the gun was, but you didn't know the caliber."

"That was the gun I remarked about earlier that I saw in the bedroom in South Carolina."

"And that was clearly not a nine millimeter?"

"That's what I was saying. Yes."

As soon as Frank Daniels got on redirect, he began to ask Marilyn about the alleged abuse that Mike had inflicted upon Jennifer in Corpus Christi, Texas, in 1991. He asked her, "How did you know that she was somehow injured by Michael?"

Marilyn answered, "She told me that she was, and Michael got on the telephone and he said he'd never hurt her again. And I said, 'All you have to do is take her to the airport and I'll see that she gets home. I'll come and get her right now.' And he said, 'I love Jennifer and she loves me and I'll never hurt her again.' And I said,

'Michael, don't ever do anything to hurt her. I will be down to get her.' And he said, 'No, we'll be fine.'"

Daniels asked, "Did you ever know Michael to talk about having a separation?"

Eisner spoke up and said, "Judge, I'm going to object to the inference that there had been such a discussion. There are no facts in evidence to support that."

Judge Bottger replied, "Well, ladies and gentlemen of the jury will understand that the lawyers' questions are questions. The questions are not evidence. If a question, any question, implies something which is not part of the evidence, in other words, not supported by what a witness says or what an exhibit says, then you need to disregard that inference because the evidence comes from the witnesses and exhibits, and not from the attorneys."

Daniels also touched upon what Marilyn Conway knew about Mike's viewing of pornography. He asked her, "You talked by telephone with Michael Blagg when he got out of the hospital. And did you confront him with the issue of Jennifer being involved with pornography?"

"Yes, I did. I told him that there was no way that I would ever believe that Jennifer brought pornography into the house. It wasn't Jennifer. And he said, 'Yes, ma'am, I know that.'"

As to the 9mm, Marilyn replied to a question about it: "It was in the home that I live in now, in the living room. There were my son, David, Jennifer, Michael, and myself. I walked into the living room, and David and Michael and Jennifer were sitting there together. My son, David, had a woman friend that he worked with that had a nine millimeter and they were discussing Michael and Jennifer's nine millimeter. And I asked what they were talking about, and they told me."

Eisner was definitely back for a recross-examination,

and he asked Marilyn, "Since 1991, did Jennifer ever complain to you again about him hurting her?"

Marilyn answered, "No, sir."

"Did you ever get any specifics on how she was hurt? I mean, did she go see a doctor? Did she need to be treated?"

"I understood that he cornered her in the corner and was trying to choke her and he was drunk, and obviously she thought that he didn't know what he was trying to do."

"He did admit to you, as a navy pilot, that he was kind of a wild young guy. He would drink and do things like that, right? And early on in the relationship, she encouraged him to drop those pilot ways. Stop drinking. He didn't drink around you, did he?"

"We might have a glass of wine or something. I never saw Michael drunk."

When Mike's mother, Elizabeth Blagg, took the stand, she also testified about a 9mm pistol that had been in her home. When asked by Eisner if she was hiding the murder weapon in her house, she said, "No, I am not." The pistol in question, according to Elizabeth, had belonged to her husband years before. And according to Elizabeth, Mike was never in possession of this handgun. He had seen it in the house in Georgia, but he had never owned it himself.

On April 7, Judge Bottger ruled about the possibility that Frank Daniels might have committed a discovery violation concerning the ring that Marilyn Conway had mentioned— the ring that she said she'd alerted Teri in the DA's office about. Bottger said that he would grant the defense a short continuance, if he asked for one in writing, but he would not declare a mistrial. Judge Bottger did give Daniels a mild reprimand, and pronounced, "This trial, every trial, is about a search for the truth, not a game of hide-and-seek. I think it would have been preferable in the interests of fairness, in the broad sense, if this information had been disclosed."

As the trial moved on, arguments shifted to unidentified shoe prints and palm prints found in the Blagg home. A CBI agent, Wayne Bryant, told of three unknown shoe prints found in the entryway of the Blagg home and twelve unknown palm prints found in the home and in the van. The prosecution claimed that Mike, Jennifer, and Abby could not be ruled out for the palm prints, and the defense argued just as strenuously that the palm prints had been left by a stranger—the same stranger who had murdered Jennifer.

Bryant also testified about the bullet recovered from Jennifer's brain, and said it was probably fired by a 9mm gun. Insurance forms from years past showed that Mike had owned a 9mm handgun. On cross, however, Bryant admitted that 5 million 9mm handguns had been produced in the twenty years before Jennifer was murdered.

Investigator George Barley testified about the comprehensive and exhaustive investigation that was the totality of the Blagg case. By the time they'd gone to trial, investigators had produced more than twenty-two thousand pages of reports on the case. Eisner didn't zero in on the reports, but he did zero in on the landfill search. He got Barley to admit that Jennifer's body was found in a "swath" of trash that contained debris from AMETEK Dixson. [Eisner contended that the investigators could not be more specific as to where the body was found other than that it had been discovered in a "swath" of trash]. Barley could not be any more specific than that.

One of the more elusive, and potentially helpful, items in the reports, as far as Mike and the defense were concerned, was the fact that a small amount of DNA was found mixed with Jennifer's blood on a comforter. CBI agent Janel Smith was finally on the stand and testified that she had originally excluded Mike as the contributor of that particular DNA. Smith had tested seven bloodstains on the comforter, and six of them came from Jennifer. The seventh contained a mixture of DNA—part of it from Jennifer, and another from an unknown source. The unknown source, she now said, could have come from Mike Blagg.

Ken Singer asked Smith, "Could the DNA have been deposited on the early morning hours of November 13, 2001?"

Smith answered, "Yes."

The implication was, according to Singer, that the DNA had been deposited there by a stranger who had murdered Jennifer Blagg.

Another mystery bloodstain was discovered on the garage steps. Both Mike and Jennifer were excluded from being major contributors to that bloodstain, although Jennifer could have been a minor contributor.

All of this, of course, seemed to lend credence to a stranger who had entered the home on November 13, 2001, and killed Jennifer and Abby. On the other hand, the prosecution was helped by the fact that no blood spatters, bloodstains, or drag marks led from the master bedroom to the van. Daniels alleged that this was because Mike had shot Jennifer and then carefully wrapped her body in a tarp and tent, so that blood would not spatter upon the floor of the house.

Finally, on Thursday afternoon, April 8, Daniels called his ninety-sixth and final witness, Frank Kochevar, who worked at the Mesa County Landfill. It had been long, thorough, and exhausting—but it wasn't over yet. The defense team of Eisner and Singer were just warming up.

Chapter 10

Judgment Day

The defense was not going to call nearly as many witnesses as the prosecution had, and Eisner started out by calling AMETEK Dixson employees who had a different story to tell about Mike than the prosecution witnesses had told. Homer Frasure described Mike as "very, very courteous." He described the family dynamics in the Blagg family as "very loving and close."

Coworker Kim Willis testified that on November 13, 2001, she had asked Mike to empty a recycling bin. This was in contrast to others who had said that Mike had gone around asking if he could empty trash cans, something he had not done before. Even Willis agreed about this detail, however, saying she had not seen him emptying trash cans before November 13 into the Dumpster.

Eisner attempted to poke holes in the prosecution's contention that Jennifer Blagg's body was found amidst AMETEK Dixson trash. He called Neal Bolton to the stand, a man who specialized in landfill operations and had written a book on the subject. *Denver Post* reporter

Nancy Lofholm referred to Bolton as a "dumpologist" and wrote, "The man literally wrote the book on landfill operations. Author of the *Handbook of Landfill Operations,* he said there was no way to conclude the body [went] to the landfill in trash from the AMETEK Dixson manufacturing plant. 'In the evidence I've seen, there's no way to tell it came from that load. And there's no way to say that it didn't.'"

Bolton noted that the segment in which Jennifer's body had been found was spread throughout a three-thousand-square-foot area and had no pattern to it. Bolton declared, "From what I've seen, you absolutely can't say it was part of any specific load. One load of waste does not get put in one small area. One load of waste gets pushed, spread, and moved in a lot of directions." Bolton went on to say that a compactor would take at least three pushes to place the trash in the location it was found, and that AMETEK Dixson trash was mixed in with other material that did not come from the facility.

Bolton showed the jury videos and diagrams, and even used a toy compactor to explain how landfill operations were done. The jury seemed to be very intent as he showed how the compactor would spread out the trash in three sweeps over a three-thousand-square-foot area.

On cross, Daniel contended that Bolton was in no position to judge the vein of trash in which Jennifer's body was found, because he had only looked at photos of the site. Bolton had not been at the landfill firsthand to view the recovery project, and Daniels implied that Bolton was inclined to help the defense, since he was being paid a fee that could go as high as $20,000 for his study of the Mesa County Landfill.

Perhaps even better than Bolton, from the defense standpoint, was the actual BFI operator, Bill Scott, who had dumped the trash on November 13, 2001. Scott said that as always he got out of his vehicle and looked at the swath of trash he had just dumped, and nothing caught his eye that day. He did not see a black-and-red tent, in which Jennifer's body was supposedly stashed. At the time, he wasn't looking at a pile twenty feet high—it was only two feet high. Scott, however, admitted to Daniels on cross that "I just kind of looked it over (the pile), real quick."

MCSO investigator Lisa Norcross testified that Jennifer's mother, Marilyn Conway, had told her at one point that "Mike and Jennifer are so much in love," and that she was unaware of any domestic violence. This was in contrast to Conway's statements that Mike had hit Jennifer in 1991. Norcross knew of no such incident.

Mike's sister, Clare Rochester, took the stand to refute some testimony given by Marilyn Conway, and Rochester testified that she boxed up items from the Blaggs' master bedroom after Mike was allowed back into the house. She also spoke of the master bedroom and about items she saw in there, and that she had not found any loose sapphire from a ring:

EISNER: Did you have an occasion to look under the bed in the master bedroom?

ROCHESTER: Yes, sir, I did.

EISNER: And why did you do that?

ROCHESTER: Well, this was a pretty emotional time for everybody and I didn't want to leave anything in the master bedroom, bath, or Abby's room. I didn't want to leave anything in there that would make it difficult for either Marilyn or Mike. So one of the things I did was look under the bed, and there was like a little dust ruffle on the bed, so I lifted that up and there were a lot of things under the bed.

EISNER: Can you describe the kind of things you saw?

ROCHESTER: Well, it was actually pretty interesting. Some of the things were under the bed because . . . Well, one of the things under the bed was a notebook. I opened it up and read a little bit of it, and it was like an emergency-preparedness notebook. It was pretty clear that it had been done in the event that something happened to Michael, so that Jennifer and Abby would be well-taken care of. They would have all of the phone numbers that were important. They would know what all the account numbers were. They would know what to do in the event that Mike was gone—who to call, what steps to take. I asked my brother about it and it related to 9/11, just in case something catastrophic happened, they would be prepared.

EISNER: Just generally, can you tell us what kind of stuff was in there that you saw?

ROCHESTER: There was a lot of paper debris under the bed. A lot of religious information and books. I couldn't name any of them, but they were all religious. There was also a lot of information related to Jennifer's medical conditions, which I read through briefly. There was a jewelry box where . . . Well, I had to get down on my stomach under the bed and reach to be able to pull it out.

EISNER: Which side of the bed was it under?

ROCHESTER: It was far enough from the center to be considered, I guess, on Jennifer's side, but it wasn't dramatically on Jennifer's side. It was toward the middle of the bed, but slightly closer to her side. There's a certain respect that you want to have in that room because, um, because while I had no idea what happened to her, I mean, there was still, even though a big piece of bedspread had been cut out, there was still blood on Jennifer's side of the bed. There was a place on the carpet, too, that had been cut out. The box wasn't that far over that I couldn't reach it, so I squished down on my stomach and got under the bed and pulled towards me and then pulled it out from the side that is Mike's side of the bed.

EISNER: I'd like to show you what's been admitted as Defendant's Exhibit LL, which is a photograph that Scott Ehlers took of the items under the bed. Why don't you take a look at that picture for a second? Do those items appear to be any of the things that you saw when you were taking things out from under the bed?

ROCHESTER: I remember some papers. Some of the things that I remember as being under the bed are not necessarily things that are here.

EISNER: There is what appears to be a colored box . . .

ROCHESTER: Yeah, there's a box, and without it being a bigger picture, I couldn't tell you for sure if that is the box. I know what the box looks like, but this picture is not clear enough to tell about that box. (Eisner showed her a section of the photo that he was interested in, depicting a squarish looking jewelry box.)

EISNER: I'm going to hand you what's been marked as HHHH, and ask if that's the picture of the jewelry box that you remember in the bedroom.

ROCHESTER: This is definitely the jewelry box that I took from under the bed.

EISNER: Do you have a similar jewelry box to that?

ROCHESTER: I do. When Mike was in the navy, one of his assignments was to Japan, and he brought me home as a Christmas present this jewelry box, or one similar to it in style. Some sort of medallion that I guess is jade. When I pulled that box out from under the bed, I thought to myself, "Jennifer had a design on it." Inside the box there were lots of little pouches. Little silk pouches. My dad also traveled overseas and so I'm used to those pouches as being for jewelry that you would buy overseas. They're pretty little drawstring silk pouches and inside the pouches there were lots of pearls and also this little necklace. I don't know if it's garnet or what, but it's a red-stone necklace. This necklace was there and those other items were there.

By saying this, both Clare Rochester and Eisner were attempting to point out that Mike would have declared these things missing if he had lied about the other items of jewelry. A thief, however, would not have known about the little jewelry box or the pearls under the bed.

EISNER: Did you have occasion to examine the boxes that were under the stairs?

ROCHESTER: Yes, sir. I wasn't really thinking of it as examining them, I was just there to look for anything that was loose. So I was looking at the boxes to see if there was anything that I needed to do to help get them ready so that when the movers came in, it would just be an easy job. One of the things I noticed that they had under the stairs were boxes marked silver, crystal, things like that. They appeared to be sealed and I thought to myself, you know, "These would be some of the first things that I would open up and have out in my house when I settle into a new house."

EISNER: When you came in, were there other boxes in the living room or the hallway area that it appeared to you the police or the sheriff's department had obviously gone through?

ROCHESTER: Yes, sir. I do believe there were. I don't remember if they were in the living room, but if I'm not mistaken, they were in the hallway near that closet, and they were boxes that had clearly been opened.

EISNER: Had they been resealed?

ROCHESTER: I think they were still open.

EISNER: What was your purpose (of being in the house)?

ROCHESTER: Well, I had two main purposes. One was an overwhelming desire to do something to be useful. To be able to pack up the house. I was going to have to go back home and the majority of the packing was going to be done after I left. But more than anything, it was just to extend a loving gesture to both Marilyn and Mike that those would not be areas that they would want to pack, because it would be so emotional, and so that was an area that I could go in and do the most good.

EISNER: Did you make a point of getting everything you could out of the dressers, the nightstands, or did you leave things?

ROCHESTER: I did not leave anything. Not one thing.

EISNER: If you would have seen a jewelry Baggie—a clear jewelry Baggie or some type of plastic container that contained any kind of jewelry in it—would you have collected it?

ROCHESTER: Absolutely!

EISNER: Did you see anything in the dresser drawers that was consistent with being jewelry?

ROCHESTER: No, sir. The only thing that was in there that had anything to do with jewelry was that I did find empty satin pouches, just like had been with the pearls. There were some empty ones and absolutely nothing in them. I opened them up because I thought they were great pouches.

EISNER: Did you pack those up with the other things?

ROCHESTER: I did.

EISNER: So to the best of your memory, when you finished emptying out the dresser in the master bedroom, was there anything left in it?

ROCHESTER: Not one thing in the dresser or any other furniture there.

Once again, according to Clare Rochester, there was no loose sapphire from a ring in a drawer in the master bedroom, nor any loose diamonds. These were items that Mike had declared had been stolen. By this testimony, Eisner attempted to show that Marilyn Conway was now making things up on the stand, trying to make Mike look like a liar and a thief.

Eisner asked Clare if she was involved in the decision making about Mike moving from the house on Pine Terrace to the town house on North Club Court, because there had been some contention that he had moved there for his own selfish reasons. She answered that a lot of people had been involved in giving him advice about moving somewhere else. She said, "A lot of people were giving Mike suggestions of this house might be available or that house might be available, and I went on numerous occasions to go look at houses, and frankly they were very depressing. Very sad-looking dwellings, in my opinion. Not the kind of place you would want to bring the girls back to after they were rescued from whatever traumatic event had taken place. We didn't know what happened to them, so we were looking for a place that would be safe, and so I went out looking for apartments for him and came across what was going to be a gated community. The town house was directly next door to the one Mike ultimately rented. I went through it and it was beautiful. It was clean, it was new. I felt like this was a place that he could bring the girls home to that they would feel safe and secure. It might not be big enough, with a yard and swing set for Abby, but it would be the kind of place they could come and reground themselves as a family."

Then Clare told a story about how Mike viewed Abby and how lenient he was when it came to disciplining her. According to her, he was nothing like the controlling ogre that the prosecution was trying to make the jurors believe. Clare said, "Jennifer was at a conference related to something for her or her mother's illness. I was very interested in Michael being able to come over to Warner Robins so that my kids would be able to meet Abby for the first time. And Abby was very little at that point—maybe three years old. I was really excited that he was going to come and bring her, and we'd get our kids togther for the first time because we'd shared lots of information, and lots of pictures through my mom.

"As far as I was concerned, I knew Abby. I knew their family and what a beautiful, loving family they were, but I'd never gotten to actually see her myself. I was really excited and I had about a nine-hour journey to get there from Louisiana with two relatively young children. Mike had a little bit shorter journey.

"My mother called me when I already had left and was on my way, and she said, 'Clare, if you're coming just to see Mike and Abby, you might as well turn around. They're not going to be able to come.' And I said, 'What do you mean they're not going to be able to come? Is everybody okay? Is anybody sick?'

"And she said, 'Well, no, Abby's just crying and she doesn't want to get in the car seat and she doesn't want to come.' And I said, 'Well, you tell Mike to put her in the car seat and buckle her up and make her come.'

"Anyway, my mother said, 'Well, he's not going to do that.' So I got the phone number and I dialed Michael and I said, 'Michael, what's going on here?'

"He said, 'Well, sis, Jen and I, we went on a trip to the beach and Abby cried the whole way there and the whole way back, and it was really traumatic for her.' When he put her in that car seat, it was really traumatic for her, and he didn't want her crying all the way to Warner Robins.

"I said, 'You're going to let that baby decide that you're not going to come to Warner Robins?'

"And he said, 'Well, I'm making a dad decision, and I'm not going to make her do it. She's sitting in her room. And when she calms down, I'm going to go in there and talk to her and explain that her aunt Clare and her cousins are going to be disappointed that she's not going to be able to come, but I'm not going to make her do it. I'm not going to make her cry.'"

From Clare's emotional time on the stand, the testimony went back to the more mundane stolen items from AMETEK Dixson. A coworker said that Mike had receipts for the workbench and table that investigators said he stole. This coworker contended that Mike had bought those items, and had not stolen them.

Lee McElfrish, a man who attended the same church that the Blaggs did, testified that he had developed a close relationship with Mike after the disappearance of Jennifer and Abby. McElfrish said, "He (Mike) treated Jennifer like she was a gift that God had given him. The guy was just an immaculate representation of what a husband should be." McElfrish added that he was envious of the marriage that Mike and Jennifer had. He stressed that when the searches by volunteers were beginning, Mike put his head in his hands and started to cry.

McElfrish also stated that he saw a receipt that Mike had for the items that were supposedly stolen from AMETEK Dixson. He did not believe Mike was the kind of guy who would steal anything, especially furniture and other items from a place where he worked.

On cross, Daniels suggested that McElfrish only knew "one side of Michael Blagg," and McElfrish agreed that he didn't know Mike and Jennifer well outside of church. One thing McElfrish did say, however, was that his opinion of Mike hadn't changed, even when he heard about the allegations of his viewing lots of pornographic Web sites, or the suicide attempt. According to McElfrish, Mike was still the same man he had always known.

There was one more very important witness who had an opportunity to take the stand—Mike Blagg. Asked by Judge Bottger if he wished to do so, Mike quietly answered, "I will not be testifying."

The parade of witnesses was over. Nearly 120 of them had been called to the stand for often grueling or tedious questioning. Jennifer's family and friends quietly left the courtroom, while Mike's family and friends huddled around and exchanged hugs and handshakes. Clare Rochester told a reporter, "I have faith in the judicial system and the jury's ability to sort through all the evidence and discern the truth that Mike is innocent."

Outside the courthouse, Marilyn Conway told reporters that she was extremely pleased that the testimony was finally over. Asked how she felt about Clare Rochester's statement that there was no sapphire ring at the Blagg home, Conway said, "I can't change the fact that I handed Mike the sapphire, and I'm not going to change that now. I told the truth. I can't change the truth."

April 14 witnessed Frank Daniels and David Eisner locked in a battle of closing arguments over Michael Blagg's guilt or innocence, and reporter Nancy Lofholm noted, "In closing arguments that aimed barbed and sometimes personal insults in both directions, the case began wrapping up. The courtroom was packed as Mesa County District Attorney Frank Daniels began the summation of a two and a half year investigation."

The courtroom was indeed just as packed as it had been on the first day of trial, as closing arguments got under way. Daniels told the jury that Jennifer's murder was precipitated by her failing health, sexual problems, and Mike's increasing obsession with Internet pornography. Daniels contended that Jennifer's health problems did not begin until she met Mike, and they were consistent with a woman who was being abused emotionally and possibly physically.

Daniels stated that Mike had tried to say that both he and Jennifer had viewed the pornographic Web sites to learn alternative methods of sex. Daniels said, however, that it was Mike who was obsessed with the pornographic Web sites, and he even made a collage of men ejaculating on women's faces. "It was a form of sexual abuse on his wife," Daniels declared.

Daniels said that on the morning of November 13, 2001, "there were no screams, no shouts, no alarms, no strangers. The evil was done in the dark of night." As for the crime scene in the master bedroom, Daniels declared that Mike had staged the scene after murdering Jennifer. Everything there, he contended, was inconsistent with a crime scene caused by an intruder. Many valuable items that were in plain sight had not even been touched. The bodies were removed from the house in the Blaggs' own minivan, which was then returned to the garage. Daniels asked, "Who else would have motive to conceal the time of death? Michael Blagg didn't want the investigators to have that information. That's why Mike got rid of the bodies. Who else would care?"

Daniels stated that when Mike returned home on the afternoon of November 13, 2001, and called 911, it took four minutes, and prompting by the dispatcher, for Mike to even go and look in Abby's room. Daniels said that Mike hadn't looked before, because he knew she was already dead. He had killed her.

After Jennifer and Abby had disappeared, Daniels declared, Mike had displayed behavior that was odd and inconsistent with a grieving husband. He bought nearly $7,000 worth of computer and entertainment equipment. He went with some women coworkers to dinner and told them how beautiful they were. Daniels said, "Michael Blagg's behavior does not exhibit behavior consistent with a true victim."

As far as the landfill operation went, Daniels praised the investigators' thoroughness in their fifty-one day search, and said that a surveyor's measurements proved that Jennifer's body was found in the middle of a "vein of AMETEK Dixson trash." As far as the defense's contention that no trash from AMETEK Dixson was found near Jennifer's body, Daniels declared, "None of what they said is true. Their so-called truth is as changeable as a spring day, as permanent as an ice cube on a hot summer's day."

In his closing argument, Eisner was just as forceful and told the jurors that the prosecution had "failed miserably" in their attempt to prove their case. He stated they had gone after Mike because they couldn't find anyone else on which to pin the murder. Taking a rhyming theme, right out of Johnny Cochran's O.J. defense style, Eisner proclaimed, "Suspicion vision has driven this case from its inception." Several times, he would repeat the phrase "suspicion vision."

Eisner said that investigators kept pounding at Mike in the ten-hour interview of February 5, 2002, with some information that later proved to be false. Eisner also claimed that investigators twisted facts that didn't fit into the theory of their case—bending them just enough to make them fit. Eisner claimed that friends and family members gave no indication of trouble in the marriage, and that Mike loved both Jennifer and Abby. The message that Jennifer had taped to the mirror, a day before her disappearance, had been a big part of the prosecution's case, but Eisner had a very different take on it. Rather than a proclamation by Jennifer that she was leaving Mike, and taking Abby with her, Eisner said that the note was a reference to tools she could use for growing spiritually. In fact, Eisner pointed out that Jennifer had notes pinned at different locations all over the house concerning various spiritual matters.

"Who's fooling who in this case?" he rhetorically asked the jurors. "Is the defense fooling you? Or is the prosecution fooling you? After six weeks in this case, it should be painfully obvious the one trying to do the fooling is the prosecution."

Eisner stated that investigators had whipped local sentiment into a frenzy during the search, and they needed a scapegoat when they couldn't find anyone else to pin the blame on. Their scapegoat, according to Eisner, became Mike Blagg. Eisner pointed out that family, friends, and coworkers spoke positively about Mike in the days after the disappearance, and only began to turn on him after his suicide attempt. Eisner said they began to turn because of the seeds of mistrust the investigators had planted and then began to nourish. Long before the trial, Eisner claimed, Mike Blagg had been looked at as guilty by much of the media.

Eisner noted that crime scene tech Janel Smith had found no "wipe marks" that might have shown that Mike had tried to clean up a murder scene. And Eisner contended that the spots of blood from Jennifer in the minivan might have been deposited when the stranger put her body in there, but then changed his mind and removed it. Or these blood spots could have come from Jennifer at any time before she disappeared on November 13, 2001.

Turning to the landfill search, Eisner said that investigators made major mistakes and couldn't for a fact pinpoint in what strata of garbage Jennifer's body had been placed. He said it was impossible to draw a straight line from Jennifer's body at the landfill back to the AMETEK Dixson Dumpster. "This sand castle must go the way of other sand castles," he declared, "reduced to nothingness."

Eisner accused Jennifer's mother of lying on the stand, especially in the matter of the sapphire ring, which she supposedly had found in a master bedroom dresser drawer after Mike was allowed to return to the house on Pine Terrace Court. He noted that Clare Rochester had gone through all those drawers and never saw any sapphire ring. Eisner also stated that until the trial, Conway had never mentioned the story about Mike trying to choke Jennifer in 1991, after he had been drinking. As to why Jennifer's mother would suddenly say these things in court, when she had not told them to investigators before, Eisner said, "Maybe she felt like things weren't going well, and she needed to give the prosecution a boost."

Eisner concluded his presentation by showing a large exhibit of a prayer request that Jennifer had written, in which she stated her love for Mike. He also displayed a large photograph of the Blagg family on vacation, three months before the disappearances. It portrayed a happy Mike, Jennifer, and Abby.

"Michael Blagg began this trial as an innocent man, and nothing has been presented in this case to change that," Eisner declared. "He is still an innocent man."

Daniels had one last turn in rebuttal, to sway the jurors toward his line of thinking. He told them about the large photo they had just viewed, and said, "That's the way it could have been, that's the way it should have been. It wasn't, however." Daniels told jurors to use their common sense when looking at and discussing all the evidence that had been presented. Daniels claimed, "The defense's notion that a stranger murdered Jennifer Blagg is just ridiculous! They're serving you a plate of speculation and asking you to call it reasonable doubt."

Then Daniels attempted to reassure the jurors about Marilyn Conway's credibility, along with that of county surveyor Frank Kochevar, who had documented where AMETEK Dixson trash had been found in the landfill. Daniels reiterated retired FBI agent Ron Walker's contention that the crime scene had been staged. Daniels said, "Justice for Marilyn Conway, and justice for the law enforcement officers is justice for Michael Blagg and Michael Blagg's family. It's time for you to bring justice to this situation, and you must convict Michael Blagg to bring justice to the situation."

After 113 witnesses, more than three hundred exhibits and twenty-five days of testimony, the jury of eight women and four men began deliberating a verdict at 11:40 A.M., on April 15, 2004. After the jurors went into the deliberation room, Judge Bottger shook hands with defense lawyers

David Eisner and Ken Singer, as well as prosecutors Frank Daniels and Bryan Flynn. Jennifer's family and supporters quietly left the courtroom, while those backing Mike stayed and shared hugs with the defense lawyers.

Daniels told a reporter, "This is a case that I've been close to. It's been an incredible amount of work, and an incredible amount of emotional attachment." Then he added to another reporter, "I think it will take some time for the jury. I've never seen anything as voluminous as this case. I've never done one this long."

Eisner also spoke of the length of time he had spent on the case. He said, "My last twenty-two months of carrying Michael Blagg's fate on my shoulders will be over." And then he spoke of the weight of that burden and how it had consumed his life.

Outside the courthouse, Marilyn Conway told reporters, "We're just glad to be at this point. We'll see what happens. I have all the confidence in the jury."

On April 16, 2004, the jurors had reached a decision after ten hours of deliberaton—and the Mesa County Courthouse was packed with family members, the media, and the merely curious. As Michael Blagg sat at the defense table, in a suit and tie, he bowed his head and seemed to be praying quietly. Prayer had been a big part of the Blagg trial and Jennifer's family seated in the gallery seemed to be praying as well.

As Mike prayed, the decision was read, and undoubtedly, his prayers did not have the result he sought. He was found guilty of first-degree murder, which carried a life sentence without the possibility of parole. He also was found guilty of abusing his wife's corpse, stealing items from AMETEK Dixson, and defrauding his insurance company over allegedly stolen jewelry.

Asked by Judge Bottger if he had anything to say before sentence was pronounced, Mike simply answered, "I am innocent of these charges, and I have nothing more to say."

Mike was hurriedly escorted from the courtroom in handcuffs as his mother yelled to him, "I love you, sweetheart!"

Mike turned and mouthed back to her, "I love you."

Then the courtroom door closed and he was gone from view.

Mike's family quickly left the courthouse with only one short statement uttered by Elizabeth Blagg—she still believed in her son's innocence. There was a rush of media people taking interviews of the prosecutors, defense lawyers, jurors, and Jennifer's family members. DA Frank Daniels said, "Michael Blagg is guilty of these crimes. As far as I'm concerned, he's a narcissistic pig!"

Investigator Steven King told reporters, "The flaw in Blagg's planning was that he didn't have any experience in knowing what a true kidnap/burglary scene should look like. On an individual basis, maybe he was smarter than I am, but he wasn't smarter than all of us together. Investigators followed many leads, but over time, Mike offered misinformation and statements that just didn't fit. This led us back to him as the prime suspect."

King said that he was surprised that the jurors went through all the mountain of evidence so quickly, and came to a decision of guilty on all counts. Then he added, "I think Grand Junction is a safer place without Michael Blagg, and Heaven is a better place with Jennifer and Abby."

David Eisner, surprisingly, came over and shook hands with King after the decision. Eisner told reporters, "A little bit of me is hurt, and I'll always carry it with me."

Elizabeth Blagg had left the courthouse with only one brief statement, but Marilyn Conway was more talkative, and very magnanimous in her remarks. She said, "God has been with us through the trial, and I hope He has been with the Blagg family, too. We've lost a daughter, but we've lost a son-in-law, too. For years, Michael Blagg was a son-in-law to me. I loved him. My daughter loved him, and Abby dearly loved her father. It's over with now, and it's a relief. It was an earthly justification that the Lord gave us. We will take it, and we will live with it. There is no cheer or joy about what took place in that courtroom. Relief? Yes. But no joy."

Connie Flukey, spokeswoman for the Jennifer and Abby Recovery Foundation, was less forgiving of Mike. She said, "If that guy's a man, he'll tell us where he put Abby. Not what he did with her, but where he put her."

Four of the twelve jurors also spoke to reporters at a news conference. Three of them were women, and one was a man named Todd Hoyt. Hoyt said that even though the deliberations lasted less than two days, "it felt like a week to us." He added that before beginning, they had prayed, and some members of the jury cried.

Juror Andrea Taylor said, "We dug through things they didn't even notice." Taylor said, "Being a Christian woman, I don't believe he was a Christian. I felt his sincerity was tested as soon as I made eye contact with him. He tried too hard to come on as sincere, and he did not."

The two other female jurors at the news conference also picked up on this theme. Mary Gonzales said that she turned away when Mike made eye contact with her. She thought he tried too hard to express despair and regret. Gonzales said Mike would smile at her whenever she came into the courtroom. It made her uncomfortable, and she would quickly look away from him.

Nineteen-year-old Melissa Lopez, the youngest member

of the jury, said, "Looking at him, it was hard to believe him. He tried too hard to come across as a sincere man. The last week, he looked at us with despair, pleading that he was hurting." She also spoke of Mike's controlling nature, and recounted one tale that he would follow his wife to the beauty shop and keep an eye on her there for two hours while she had her hair fixed. At church socials, he would watch her so closely that several people took note of it.

Todd Hoyt agreed that Mike Blagg had made eye contact with the women jurors, but not the men, in his bid for trying to express his despair and innocence. Hoyt thought that it was a sham. What Hoyt did say, as to what the jurors found compelling in the evidence, was interesting, and not what many expected. The jurors tended to discount the pornographic Internet material as being a prime factor; instead, they concentrated on the fact that the Blagg family only had two sets of keys to the minivan, which was used to transport Jennifer's body from the house to the landfill. One set was found under her purse, and Mike had the other set on his key ring. If the minivan had been used by an intruder, then why would the intruder put the second key back in Jennifer's purse? That just didn't make sense to the jurors.

Another key factor for the jurors was a small piece of blue fiber found on the bullet that lodged in Jennifer's brain. They deduced that Mike had placed a blue towel or blue pillow over the gun before shooting her in the head at close range. It was this piece of evidence that convinced them that Mike had preplanned the act of murder, instead of doing it on the spur of the moment, which might have garnered a second-degree murder charge. But for that small bit of blue fiber, Mike might have received a lesser sentence, with the possibility of parole.

One more situation made them believe that Mike, and

not an intruder, killed Jennifer. Hoyt noted that the crime scene looked staged, and "it was just that her items were disturbed, and not his." Also, evidence from Jennifer's South Carolina friend Edie Melson made Hoyt believe, "She (Jennifer) was about to leave him."

One of the things that did not sway them was the prosecution's contention that Jennifer's body had been found in a "swath" of trash that contained material from AMETEK Dixson, even though they commended investigators for their laborious search through the landfill. And they took into account the fact that in one instance Mike had backed into the confined space by the AMETEK Dixson Dumpster at night, when there was surveillance on him, and he didn't have any trouble backing in there in the dark, as if he had done it before.

Taylor said, "Jennifer Blagg's journals and notes in the margins of her religious books persuaded many that Mike was controlling and narcissistic. We all thought she was about to leave him. Her books, her journals, her notations, they were all telling the story of her life." Referring to the pornography on the Internet, she said it was evidence about Mike's character, but not evidence directly leading to the murder.

Mary Gonzales agreed that Jennifer's journal was a powerful statement about Mike, and did give evidence of a marriage in trouble. She told reporters, "If you were able to read all her writings, the relationship was clear. The crime scene was staged. There were unsigned credit cards in her purse, and a robber would have taken them."

Taylor and Hoyt said that they both wanted Mike to testify, but they doubted that whatever he had to say would have changed their verdict. Interestingly enough, they did believe Marilyn Conway when she suddenly announced on the stand that Mike had choked Jennifer in 1991. They didn't think this statement was said by Marilyn on the spur of the moment, just to influence them. They accepted Marilyn Conway as a credible witness.

Asked by one reporter if they agreed with DA Frank Daniels's statement that Mike was a "narcissistic pig," they smiled, and Lopez answered, "We never said 'pig.' But we all said 'narcissistic.'"

They also agreed that both the prosecution and the defense had done a good job. Hoyt said, "Daniels knows when to purr and when to grrr. And Eisner was very professional."

On a final note, one reporter asked what they thought had happened to Abby Blagg. Hoyt answered that they all had talked about that after rendering a decision about Mike's guilt or innocence. Hoyt said, "There's about twelve different versions."

Jennifer's brother, David Loman, spoke to reporters about the whole ordeal that began on November 13, 2001. Loman, who had been so strong throughout the proceedings, nearly collapsed into Connie Flukey's arms after the verdict, crying, "I couldn't fix this. I could only live it. My tears today were to let go and go on with the life I'm supposed to lead."

Loman later told reporter Mike Wiggins that before he returned home to Oklahoma, he and his family were going out to a small cross that he had stuck in the ground at the landfill near where Jennifer's body was discovered. They had done this on March 21, 2004, the day that Abby would have turned nine years old. Loman said he would place some flowers there and talk to his own girls about Jennifer and Abby. Then he added, "I'm going to put a nail in that cross, because we've put a nail in this. This is the end."

It was not the end for Michael Blagg, however, and on April 20, he and sheriff's deputies flew from Grand Junction to the Denver Reception and Diagnostic Center for the state prisons. The center was a reception center for incoming inmates who were destined for maximum-security prisons. While there, officials drew blood for DNA purposes from Mike, photographed and fingerprinted him, and sent the information to the CBI.

Mike was also interviewed as to his educational, vocational, medical, substance abuse, mental, and social backgrounds. The data was used to set up his inmate classification and determine to which prison he would be sent. A couple other determinates in Mike's case were the high profile of his case, and the fact that he had no prior arrests. Alison Morgan [a spokesperson for the Colorado Department of Prisons] said that Mike would not be sent to anything lower than a Level III facility, where medium-security inmates were housed, surrounded by double fences and guard towers. Mike was originally assigned to Limon Correctional Facility, but later transferred to the Centennial Correctional Facility in Colorado because he had been assaulted by other inmates at Limon.

After the trial, Investigator Steven King spoke with CBS's *48 Hours Mystery.* King told them about various aspects of the case and then said, "The bottom line is that Michael Blagg is gonna have a long, hard life in prison. And then he's gonna have to face God. And Jennifer and Abby will be sitting on God's lap that day, and that's when justice will be served."